An Enquiry into the Hermeneutical Understanding of Yogi-Pratyakṣa in Jain Philosophy

An Enquiry into the Hermeneutical Understanding of Yogi-Pratyakṣa in Jain Philosophy

Dr. Jibin Paul

MLBD PUBLICATIONS

Motilal Banarsidass Publications

MOTILAL BANARSIDASS
PUBLICATIONS
4741/23, Ansari Road, Daryaganj, New Delhi - 110002 (India)
Email: mlbd@mlbd.com | sales@mlbd.com | exports@mlbd.com
Website: www.mlbd.com

An Enquiry into the Hermeneutical Understanding of Yogi-Pratyakṣa in Jain Philosophy
by
Dr. Jibin Paul

First Edition Published in 2025

Published in India by Motilal Banarsidass Publications

ISBN : 978-81-979177-7-6 (PB)

Printed and bound in India

Dedicated to the Almighty God,

the source of all Truth, Wisdom, and Bliss

Acknowledgments

This book, the culmination of my doctoral research, represents a significant milestone in my academic journey. I am deeply grateful to Almighty God for His boundless wisdom and guidance and this work is a testament to His grace.

My heartfelt thanks to Banaras Hindu University, Varanasi, and the Department of Philosophy and Religion for providing me with the academic foundation and support necessary to complete my Masters and PhD. I extend my sincere gratitude to Prof. Mukul Raj Mehta, my research guide, whose mentorship has been invaluable and whose kind gesture of writing the foreword for this book is deeply appreciated. I am particularly thankful to the Indian Council of Philosophical Research (ICPR) for their generous scholarship, which has significantly contributed to this endeavour.

Special thanks are also due to Mar. Andrews Thazhath, Mar. Tony Neelankavil, and the Archdiocese of Thrissur for their unwavering support and encouragement. I owe a debt of gratitude to Marymatha Institute of Philosophy for their role in my academic journey. My family's love and encouragement have been my strength throughout, and I am particularly grateful to the Arora Family and my cherished friends, especially Dr. Shalini Arora, for their constant support. A special acknowledgment is due to Motilal Banarasidas Publications for their willingness to publish this book. Finally,

I would like to express my deepest appreciation to you, the reader, for engaging with this work. Your interest and support are what make all the effort worthwhile.

Dr. Jibin Paul
Marymatha Institute of Philosophy, Thrissur

FOREWORD

In a landscape where philosophical inquiry often seems ensconced in its own historical and disciplinary silos, Jibin Paul's *An Enquiry into the Hermeneutical Understanding of Yogi- Pratyakṣa in Jain Philosophy* emerges as a clarion call for interdisciplinary engagement and nuanced interpretation. This work is not only a significant scholarly contribution but also the culmination of Paul's rigorous PhD research project.

The book embarks on a profound exploration of the concept of *yogi-pratyakṣa* (generic term for Extrasensory perception), a term rooted deeply in Indian thought, is shedding new light on its epistemological and soteriological dimensions. At the heart of this work is an ambitious project: to unravel how the mystical and introspective aspect of *yogi-pratyakṣa* — the direct perception experienced by a yogi—intersects with broader philosophical paradigms and practices. Paul's study is not merely an academic exercise but a hermeneutical venture into the very essence of Jain thought, which contends with the nature of knowledge and the path to spiritual liberation.

The book is grounded in two central hypotheses: first, that *yogi-pratyakṣa* functions as an interdisciplinary subject with significant epistemological and soteriological implications, and second, that Jain philosophy provides a unique perspective on this interaction. Jainism integrates interdisciplinary aspects, offering a distinctive framework through which to examine *yogi-pratyakṣa*. This inquiry is meticulously designed to address the contextual nuances of Jain philosophical texts, bringing forward a hermeneutic approach that resonates with the contemporary relevance of these ancient doctrines. By engaging with the contextual understanding and interpretation of *yogi-pratyakṣa*, the book aims to resolve the epistemological questions surrounding it and reveal its implications for modern philosophical and soteriological discussions.

The research is notable for its rigorous analytical framework and its ability to bridge the gap between traditional Jain thought and contemporary philosophical discourse. Paul's findings not only clarify the epistemological and soteriological underpinnings of *yogi-pratyakṣa* but also illuminate its broader implications in today's context. As you delve into this work, you will encounter a rich tapestry of philosophical insight and interpretive depth. Jibin Paul's dedication to elucidating the complex interplay between *yogi-pratyakṣa* and Jain philosophy stands as a testament to his scholarly rigor and commitment to advancing our understanding of these profound ideas.

This book is not just a scholarly contribution but an invitation to reconsider the boundaries of philosophical inquiry and to appreciate the intricate connections between ancient wisdom and contemporary thought. It is my hope that readers will find in these pages both intellectual stimulation and a deeper appreciation for the nuanced and integrative nature of Jain philosophical inquiry.

Prof. Mukul Raj Mehta
Department of Philosophy and Religion
Banaras Hindu University, Varanasi

Table of Contents

Chapter 3: The Psychological and Epistemological Backup of Yogi-Pratyakṣa: Pramāna-Pratyakṣa-Yogi-Pratyakṣa

Chapter 4: Yogi-Pratyakṣa in Jain Philosophy

Chapter 5: Kevalajñāna: The Paramount of Yogi-Pratyakṣa

Preface

Extrasensory perception and experience have become one of the most conventional and controversial phenomena across the universe. In addition to the subliminal perceptual experiences, certain experiences have also occurred even in the absence of sensory mediation. Anecdotal evidences and firsthand experiences vindicate the occurrence of these kinds of experiences. These occurrences are commonly referred to as Extrasensory Perception (ESP) or Parapsychological experiences (Psi). It is a developing field in psychology and holds a revered place in spiritual circles. Despite its growing interest, the scientific investigation of extrasensory perception is often fraught with ambiguous interpretations and inconclusive results. Similarly, spiritual movements can sometimes exploit and politicize these experiences. This dichotomy often results in a claustrophobic situation for the general public, who may find it difficult to navigate between conflicting claims and interpretations. Thus, this research is an investigation into the understanding and interpretation of the nature and function of extrasensory perception and its implication in the contemporary context.

Indian philosophy offers valuable insights into extrasensory phenomena, thanks to its rich array of terminologies and concepts that provide a robust philosophical foundation for understanding such experiences. One key term within this framework is *yogi-pratyakṣa*, which broadly refers to extrasensory perception. Considering the interpretive dimension of the present research, *yogi-pratyakṣa* represents a generic term for the extrasensory phenomenon. This research aims to explore and interpret *yogi-pratyakṣa* as a distinct phenomenon, emphasizing the importance of a hermeneutical approach. Hermeneutical understanding demands a contextual understanding and interpretation (*subtilitas applicandi*) of *yogi-pratyakṣa*. It reckons the relevance and contemporaneity of the research. Hence, the objective of the research is to find answers to context-related queries. The inquiry concerns the soteriological implications and epistemological validity of *yogi-pratyakṣa*. The focus is to examine the soteriological and epistemological dimensions of *yogi-pratyakṣa* and how it fits into the broader landscape of Indian philosophy. The study operates on two main hypotheses: first, that *yogi-pratyakṣa* represents an interdisciplinary field; and second, that it is deeply rooted in both soteriology and epistemology. Notably, Jainism offers a unique perspective by aligning *yogi-pratyakṣa* with these philosophical domains more explicitly than other Indian traditions. In Jain philosophy, *yogi-pratyakṣa* is the perception (*pratyakṣa*) of the self (*yogi*) without the assistance of sense organs and mind. Thus, the research problem revolves around elucidating the nature and function of *yogi-pratyakṣa* within Jain thought and assessing how this interpretive framework addresses context-specific questions.

The interpretive, reflective, and comparative dimension of the research suggests the hermeneutical methodology as the proper research approach of the study. With the aid of interpretive and investigative tools of Indian philosophy, the research understands and interprets the thesis within the framework of the Gadamerian hermeneutical methodology. The procedure of the research begins with analyzing the pre-understanding of the concept ('fusion of horizon') and framing out the rationale of the research. Ensued from the interpretive-comparative encounter ('the logic of questions and answers'), the subsequent chapters unfold different hermeneutic spirals ('hermeneutical circle') of understanding and interpretation. It results in the application and implication of the *yogi-pratyakṣa* in the contemporary context. This application is the conclusion and findings of the research.

Having delineated the research subject, methodology, and procedure in the preface, the first chapter sets the descriptive analysis of the research topic. It begins with an overview of the fundamentals of the hermeneutical approach to research. Through a review of relevant observations and literature, the chapter establishes the rationale for the study. Observations are known as the hermeneutical situations in the hermeneutical approach. There are three hermeneutic situations: the understandings of indian philosophical systems, the development of western parapsychology, and the emergence of new-age movements. Each hermeneutic situation raises pertinent questions about the epistemological validity and soteriological implications of extrasensory perception. The chapter then investigates these questions by analyzing Jain source texts and recent literature, thus clarifying the scope and significance of the research. Incidentally, this chapter places *yogi-pratyakṣa* in the horizons of context and text.

The second chapter discusses 'the Metaphysical Credentials of *Yogi-Pratyakṣa* (extrasensory perception)' in Jainism. *Jīva* or soul is the nexus of Jaina metaphysics, epistemology, and soteriology. This chapter delves into the nature of the soul in Jain philosophy, focusing on its essential qualities, consciousness (*Upayoga*), and its impediment, *Karma*. It triggers the examination of the relationship of *dravya-guṇa-paryāya*, which determines the nature and relationship of soul-consciousness-cognition. It examines the relationship between *dravya-guṇa-paryāya*, which defines the nature and interactions of the soul, consciousness, and cognition. Additionally, the chapter elaborates on the theory of karma and its impact on the triadic relationship of soul, consciousness, and cognition. The primary objective of this chapter is to interpret the functional interplay between the soul, consciousness, and cognition and to investigate the metaphysical underpinnings of cognitive processes that facilitate the occurrence of *yogi-pratyakṣa*.

The third chapter discusses 'the Epistemological and Psychological Underpinnings of *Yogi-Pratyakṣa*' in Jainism. It is an attempt to understand and interpret *Pramāṇa* in Jainism with special reference to the concepts of *Pratyakṣa* and *Yogi-Pratyakṣa*. The central concern of this chapter is to analyze cognition as *pramāṇa*, especially when it occurs independently of sensory mediation, and to explore the psychology underlying *yogi-pratyakṣa*. In addition to discussing the common definition of *pratyakṣa* across Indian philosophical systems, the chapter defines, enumerates, and logically examines the distinctive and unique aspects of the Jaina definition of *pratyakṣa*. It also scrutinizes the constitution and meaning of the sense organ and the mind in Jain tradition. The impeccable presentation of *prama*, *pramāṇa*, and *pratyakṣa* helps to interpret the epistemology and psychology of *yogi-pratyakṣa*. The chapter emphasizes the epistemological role of the soul as both the subject and instrument of extrasensory perception, independent of the senses and mind. Simultaneously, it highlights the pivotal role of the self-conscious and self-luminous soul in the psychology of *yogi-pratyakṣa*.

The fourth chapter, titled "The Conceptual Analysis of Yogi-Pratyakṣa," explores the role of *yogi-pratyakṣa* within Indian philosophical traditions, with a particular focus on Indian realistic systems such as Nyāya-Vaiśeṣika, Sāṁkhya-Yoga, and Jainism. The chapter clarifies the unique conceptual meaning of *yogi-pratyakṣa* and examines the varying degrees of this perception in Jainism compared to other philosophical systems. In Jainism, *yogi-pratyakṣa* refers to advanced levels of perception that arise due to the suppression and elimination of karmic limitations affecting the pristine nature of the self. These higher degrees of perception are independent of the senses and are attributed to the self-illuminative nature of the self. Jainism identifies several types of extrasensory perception, including clairvoyance (*Avadhi*), telepathy or mind-reading (*Manaḥaparyāya*), and omniscience (*Kevalajñāna*). This chapter specifically investigates the nature and characteristics of *Avadhi* and *Manaḥaparyāya* as intermediary stages leading to *Kevalajñāna*, the ultimate realization of *yogi-pratyakṣa*.

The fifth chapter provides a logical examination of the pinnacle of *yogi-pratyakṣa*, namely *Kevalajñāna* (omniscience). This chapter investigates the nature of omniscience as the ultimate cognitive reality and the culmination of *yogi-pratyakṣa*. It represents the highest point on the epistemic ladder. By analyzing and substantiating the nature and existence of omniscience, Jainism addresses and counters critiques regarding the logic of *yogi-pratyakṣa*. The chapter strengthens Jaina perspectives by responding to criticisms with well-founded logical arguments. Furthermore, the chapter argues that cognitive actuality is equivalent to liberation, through a detailed examination of *guṇasthāna* (stages of spiritual progress), *arihantahood* (the state of a perfected soul), and *siddhahood* (the state of complete liberation). It provides a comprehensive explanation of the intertwined nature of epistemology, psychology, and soteriology within Jainism.

The sixth chapter presents a collection of proofs for the existence of *yogi-pratyakṣa*. Drawing from traditional Jain texts, the chapter addresses criticisms and provides a robust defense of *yogi-pratyakṣa*. It introduces three positive proofs and three negative proofs. The positive proofs offer constructive arguments that support the progressive development of cognition, ultimately leading to omniscience. The negative proofs demonstrate the absence of valid counterarguments from critics, highlighting the shortcomings of their positions. These proofs collectively contribute to establishing both the epistemological validity and soteriological implications of *yogi-pratyakṣa*.

At the conclusion of the research, the book summarizes the key findings and examines their implications in the contemporary context. This study does not aim to provide a conclusive working theory of extrasensory perception (*yogi-pratyakṣa*). Instead, it explores the potential for scientific and logical understandings of extrasensory perception as a form of human cognitive activity, while also recognizing its transcendental aspects. By systematically and comprehensively examining the epistemological and soteriological foundations of *yogi-pratyakṣa*, the study addresses relevant contextual questions. Additionaly, the research highlights the distinctiveness and significance of classical indian thought within the domain of cognitive psychology. Significantly, the study's implications offer a clear invitation for further exploration into the profound aspects of Indian cognitive psychology.

Abbreviations

Āpta-Mīmāṃsā	— AM
Bhāṣa Pariccheda	— BP
Dravya Sangraha	— DS
Nyāyasūtra	— NS
Mīmāṁsasūtra	— MS
Nyāyaviniścayavivaraṇa	— NVV
Padārthadharmasaṅgraha	— PDS
Pramāṇamīmāṁsā	— PM
Pramāṇa-Naya-Tattvālokalaṃkāra	— PNT
Pravacanasāra	— PS
Premeyakamalamārtaṇḍa	— PKM
Samayasāra	— SS
Sāṁkhya Kārikā	— SK
Tattvacintamani	— TC
Tattvārtha Sūtra	— TS
Vedānta Paribhāsha	— VP
Yoga Sūtra	— YS

CHAPTER 1

Introduction

The introductory chapter outlines the observations and rationale behind the research. It frames the research hypothesis and problem through an investigation of these observations, which are categorized as hermeneutical situations. This chapter introduces the research scope and objectives, and underscores the significance of the research problem. To begin, the chapter explores the principles of hermeneutical research, followed by an analysis of the context—referred to as hermeneutical situations—and a thorough review of relevant literature (text). This progression helps to refine the study's focus and establish its significance. The chapter concludes with a clear summary of the research rationale and offers a descriptive analysis of the research topic, encapsulating the study's objectives and relevance.

1.1 Hermeneutical Study of Concepts

The word "Hermeneutics" initially refers to text interpretation, especially in the fields of philology, biblical exegesis, and jurisprudence. On the threshold of the new phase of hermeneutics, there is a paradigm shift from the interpretation of sacred texts to the interpretation of human activities. These human activities encompass verbal and non-verbal communications.[1] Thus, the human experience

1 Felice Addeo, in his article, "Hermeneutic as a Research Method:

and phenomenon are also termed the 'text' in the realm of hermeneutical study and are subjected to interpretations. These hermeneutical interpretations are procuring meaningful and useful results in a particular context. It widens and augments the scope of the hermeneutic study. Henceforth, the interpretive encounter of the hermeneutic approach becomes the reliable as well as the relevant method of investigation in the social and human science research.

Hermeneutics is defined commonly as the art of interpretation or the art of understanding. In "*The Task of Hermeneutics,*" the hermeneutic philosopher Paul Ricoeur states, "Hermeneutics is the theory of the operation of understanding of texts."[2] Hans-Georg Gadamer, one of the prominent exponents of hermeneutical philosophy, defines hermeneutics as "the theory and practice of understanding and bringing to language the alien, the strange, and whatever has

How to do Research Using Hermeneutic Approach", sums up the evolution of Hermeneutics as a research method. "Schleiermacher widened the domain of Hermeneutics not only to sacred or legal texts but to all human documents and modes of communication. Heidegger shifted the focus of Hermeneutics from interpretation to existential understanding. Gadamer and Ricoeur finally stated that hermeneutics could be applied to all human activities." So, he states that "in Social Science, the domain of Hermeneutics has been gradually extended to the study of every act or process involving interpretation: verbal and non-verbal communication, as presuppositions, pre-understandings and so on. Nowadays, relying on phenomenological and constructivist epistemologies, Hermeneutic has finally become a social research method." Cf. Felice Addeo, "Hermeneutic as a Research Method: How to do Research Using Hermeneutic approach," p. 10, available from https://www.academia.edu/3735850/Hermeneutic_as_a_Research_Method; accessed on 11 December 2018.

Cf. Joseph Dorairaj, *Philosophical Hermeneutics* (Chennai: Satyanilayam, 2011), pp. 12-13.

2 Paul Ricoeur, "The Task of Hermeneutics," translated by Pellauer, *Philosophy Today* 17.2 (1973), 112-128, p.112.

become alien."[3] Resonance to Gadamer's definition, Riceour would say, "To make one's own what was previously foreign remains the ultimate aim of all hermeneutics."[4] Gadamer further explains the scope of hermeneutical understanding in his *Truth and Method*: "It is not only the written tradition that is estranged and in need of new and more vital assimilation; everything that is no longer immediately situated in a world that is all tradition, whether art or the other spiritual creation of the past: law, religion, philosophy, and so forth-is estranged from its original meaning and depends on the unlocking and mediating spirit."[5] Thus, hermeneutic inquiry uncovers the relevance of the meanings and intentions that are, in a sense, hidden in the text.[6]

'The alien, the strange, and whatever has become alien' is the hermeneutic situation. This situation is the context where the text has to be interpreted. Thus, the objective of the hermeneutical understanding is to understand the text in context. The understanding process is enacted through a series

---

3 Hans-Georg Gadamer, "On the Natural Inclination toward Philosophy," *Reason in the Age of Science,* trans. F. G Lawrence (Cambridge, M.S, & London: The MIT Press, 1982), P. 149.

4 Paul Ricoeur, *Interpretation Theory: Discourse and the Surplus of the Meaning* (Texas: The Texas Christian UP, 1976), p. 91.

5 Hans-Georg Gadamer, *Truth and Method*, translated by Joyel Weinsheimer and Donald G. Marshall, London (New York: Continum, 2004^{2}), p. 159. (Hereafter, Hans-Georg Gadamer, *Truth and Method*).

6 Cf. M. Crotty, *The Foundations of Social Science Research* (St. Leonards, NSW, Allen & Unwin, 1998), p. 91. Cf. Joy Higgs and Margo Paterson, "Using Hermeneutics as a Qualitative Research Approach in Professional Practice," *The Qualitative Report*, 10 (2005), 339-357, p. 344, available from https://www.researchgate.net/publication/228640854_Using_Hermeneutics_as_a_Qualitative_Research_Approach_in_Professional_Practice; accessed on 25 November 2018.

of hermeneutic spirals. The hermeneutic spiral is a composite of three philosophical assumptions in Gadamerian terminology: 'the fusion of horizons of the text and the interpreter', 'dialogue through questions and answers', and 'the hermeneutic circle that shares with the interpreter who repeatedly is moving between the part and the whole of the text'. The interpretive and comparative aspects of hermeneutical understanding bring these alien and strange concepts to have an encounter with each other, which allow mutual sharing of their vibes and creativity and apply their implications in the contextual needs to find out nuances of concepts. Hence, hermeneutical understanding helps to understand the hidden meaning of the text in a particular context. Thus, its scope lies beyond mere apprehension of similarities and differences.

The hermeneutic spiral impeccably states that this understanding is not a mere reconstruction of history. It is true that reconstructing the conditions of the past accelerates the understanding, but "it consists not in the restoration of the past but thoughtful meditation with contemporary life."[7] Gadamer asserts that "understanding here (in law and scripture) is always application."[8] The application of a concept to a given context enhances the hermeneutical process. Therefore, understanding, interpretation, and application are an integral part of hermeneutical understanding. Such understanding brings the possibilities of fresh readings and nuances for the concepts and text.[9] Brice R. Wachterhauser rightly observes the nature of hermeneutical understanding as "historically situated, lingusticaly mediated, contextualist,

---

7 Hans-Georg Gadamer, *Truth and Method*, P. 161.

8 Hans-Georg Gadamer, *Truth and Method*, P. 275.

9 The term text refers to any aspect of the phenomenological world being interpreted. In this research, it represents the *yogi-pratyakṣha*, as the phenomenon that being investigated.

and antifoundationalist."[10] Succinctly, the hermeneutical understanding of concepts implies a contextual-reflective interpretation of the text.

Elizabeth Anne Kinsella, in her research paper "*Hermeneutics and Critical Hermeneutics: Exploring Possibilities within the Art of Interpretation,*" draws an introductory overview of the hermeneutic approach. This overview highlights the procedure of a hermeneutic understanding: "(a) seeks understanding rather than an explanation, (b) acknowledges the situated location of interpretation, (c) recognizes the role of language and historicity in interpretation, (d) views inquiry as conversation, and (e) is comfortable with ambiguity." [11] These expositions of characteristics are the miniature of hermeneutic understanding. Therefore, the hermeneutic approach claims that every understanding is horizonal to the interpreter and text. Hoy mentions that "the term horizon is an attempt at describing the situatedness or context bound character of interpretation."[12] The dialogical encounter of horizons gears up a new meaning for the text in the contemporary context. It germinates future research explorations. To recapitulate, a hermeneutic approach interprets the text in the context and establishes the relevancy of the text.

---

10 Brice R. Wachterhauser, "History and Langauge in Understanding" in *Hermeneutics and Modern Philosophy,* ed. Brice R. Wachterhauser (Albany: SUNY, 1986), p. 16.

11 *Elizabeth Anne Kinsella*, "Hermeneutics and Critical Hermeneutics: Exploring Possibilities within the Art of Interpretation," *Forum: Qualitative Social Research*, 7 (2006), 1-16, p. 2, available from https://www.qualitative-research.net/index.php/fqs/article/view/145/320; accessed on 29 November 2018.

12 Hoy, *The Critical Circle: Literature, History, and Philosophical Hermeneutics* (Los Angels: U of California Press, 1978), p. 96.

1.2 The Observations of the Research

The observations of the research help to define the research area. These observations, rooted in social and cultural contexts, are essential for hermeneutical study. Since hermeneutical understanding relies on contextual interpretation, these contexts are termed hermeneutical situations. This methodical approach refines the research focus and interest. By analyzing hermeneutical situations and delineating the research area, the study cogently clarifies the research problem and hypothesis.

1.2.1 Hermeneutic Situation

As discussed above, 'the alien, the strange, and whatever has become alien' is the hermeneutic situation. The hermeneutic situation is closely moulding the pre-understandings and prejudices of the concept. The pre-understandings of the present research have evolved from three different contexts. These contexts are the development of western parapsychology, the emergence of new-age movements, and the understandings of Indian philosophical systems. These hermeneutical situations envisage the research problem and hypothesis.

1.2.1.1 The Development of Western Parapsychology

Parapsychology has been thriving as a science under psychical research. But in 1934, the publication of J. B. Rhine's book named *Extrasensory Perception* ushers the research into the scientific understanding of parapsychology. The serious research in the field of parapsychology leads to the installation of a new department at Duke University. There were attempts to analyze the paranormal experiences of individuals with the modern statistical research method. They have established their theories by experiments carried out in the psychological laboratory. These are ratified by the anecdotal events of life.[13] It finally leads to the institution of parapsychology as the objective experimental science. In 1969, the American Association for the Advancement of Science approved parapsychology as science.

Parapsychology is a developing branch of science in psychology, which studies the paranormal psychic phenomenon. It includes telepathy, telekinesis, precognition, clairvoyance, near-death experiences, reincarnation, and other paranormal claims. The paranormal events can be divided broadly into two; firstly, those that refer to the anomalous acquisition of information and secondly, anomalous mind-body interactions.[14] They are known as extrasensory perception and psychokinesis. Telepathy, precognition, post-cognition, retro-cognition, clairvoyance, and all extrasensory cognition come under extrasensory perception. They are closely connected to the psychology of the perception. Telekinesis, which is the spontaneous movement of objects without contact or observable force or energy, belongs to the second category, i.e., psychokinesis. Later, J. B Rhine suggests that the 'Psi phenomenon' as an overarching term which conflates both aspects of paranormal powers. Psi is defined as an unusual process of information or energy, which transfers

---

13 Cf. J. B. Rhine, *New Frontiers of the Mind* (New York: Farrar Rhinehart, 1937); J. B. Rhine, *Extra-Sensory Perception after Sixty Years* (New York: Henry Holt, 1940); J. B. Rhine, *The Reach of Mind* (New York: William Sloane Associates, 1947).

14 Cf. K. R. Rao, "Indian psychology, Parapsychology and Spiritual Psychology," *International Journal of Yoga - Philosophy Psychology Parapsychology.* 1 (2013), p. 9, available from https://www.researchgate.net/publication/273812830_Indian_psychology_parapsychology_and_spiritual_psychology; accessed on 30 November 2018. (Hereafter, K. R. Rao, "Indian psychology, Parapsychology and Spiritual Psychology,").

The term 'anamoly' indicates the insufficient understanding of phenomenon, rather than validity of experience.

those are currently unexplained in terms of known physical or biological mechanisms.[15]

C G Jung defines parapsychology as "the science of dealing with those biological or psychological events which show that the categories of matter, space and time and thus of causality are not axiomatic."[16] Psychical research refers to the quantitative study of the paranormal phenomenon. The researches in parapsychology catalyse researches in the field of hypnotism, mentalism, relaxation, absorption, dream telepathy, and ganzfeld experiment. Among these, the ganzfeld experiment has a special status because it demonstrates the presence of paranormal or extrasensory powers in the laboratory. "The ganzfeld is often regarded as the flagship of experimental parapsychology. It is a simple means of reproducing spontaneous psi (psychic) experiences in the laboratory, where controls can be applied to eliminate normal explanations."[17]

But critics considered it as pseudoscience and as the study of apparent mental faculties. They understand it as anomalous cognitive processes that are currently unexplained in terms of known physical or biological mechanisms.[18] James E. Beichler in his article "Physical Theories of Psi: An Investigative Study" admits:

> We have no clear-cut or acceptable theory which collates all of the reported physical, physiological,

---

15 Cf. Robert A. Baron, *Psychology* (New Jersey, USA: Englewood Cliffs, 1996), p. 130.

16 C. G Jung, *Psychology and Occult* (Routledge, New York: Ark Paperbacks, 1977), p. 275.

17 A. Parker, "Ganzfeld," *Psi Encyclopedia*, (2017), p. 1.

18 Cf. D. J. Bem & Honorton, C, "Does psi exist? Replicable Evidence for an Anomalous Process of Information Transfer," *Psychological Bulletin*, 115 (1994), p .4; Cf. K. Ramakrishna Rao, *Experimental Psychology*, pp. 148-149.

> therapeutic and psychological effects of psi In order for progress to be made in any new scientific endeavour and especially so where a new paradigm may be involved, a theory or framework must be set up in which language, experiments, data and such can be used to establish credibility. To this time, parapsychology has been carrying on without this framework and has thus been unable to persuade the skeptics; [...]. The lack of a theoretical framework is the crux or the problem in parapsychology and thus, although it is a science, parapsychology is still a bit premature, in the sense that it has not yet arrived at a paradigm.[19]

That's why K. Ramakrishna Rao remarks the challenge of western parapsychology is that "the [parapsychological] data do not fit into the categories of understanding we are familiar with and the epistemology we subscribe to." He rightly exposes the inability of western parapsychology by saying that "parapsychology, as pursued in the west, will remain forever a study of anomalies rather than science with a specific subject matter and parapsychology may never gain scientific legitimacy as a respectable academic discipline if pursued within the western paradigm."[20] To sum up, even though there is a considerable amount of experience to lend the support for the existence of extrasensory powers and even it is accepted as a scientific fact from not less than a good number of scientists, it has been a matter of ambiguity and uncertainty in the

19 James E. Beichler, "Physical Theories of Psi: An Investigative Study," p. 5, available from: https://www.academia.edu/8200362/Physical Theories_of_Psi_An_Investigative_Study; accessed on 30 December 2018. (Hereafter, James E. Beichler, "Physical Theories of Psi: An Investigative Study,").

20 K. R. Rao, "Indian Psychology, Parapsychology and Spiritual Psychology". pp. 7-8.

western thought. Not because nothing did J.B. Rhine said that evidence of extrasensory perception is good, but the theories are bad.[21] Western psychology desperately seeks a sound theory of extrasensory perception.

1.2.1.2 The Emergence of New Age Movements

The quest for rediscovery of religion (thesis) and anguish over the traditional religious tradition (anti-thesis) in the mid-sixties seminates a new religiosity (synthesis). A holistic approach and a new consciousness of cosmic unity have emerged from it. The new age movement is the offspring of this new religiosity, and new religious movements are the offshoot of this new age movements. This synthesis is the reappraisal of ancient systems in the wake of human science, remarkably in the field of transpersonal psychology. Its scope sprawls from the religious realm to the domain of philosophy, literature, psychology, anthropology, and even topical issues concerning ecology and health. But it is the unequivocal truth that the new age movement retains as a major component of alternative spirituality in the present world. Therefore, it is a complex movement and fluid phenomenon to define because of its wide scope and applicability. Jack Finnegan attempts to define it as: "A major cultural and religious phenomenon, whose basic ideology starts with humanistic and evolutionary assumptions, is global in perspective, is concerned with planetary survival, and emphasis holistic solutions to social and personal problems."[22]

Although there has a scattered organizational set up within the new age movement, there is an overarching conceptual

---

21 Cf. J. B Rhine, *Extra-Sensory Perception after Sixty Years* (New York: Henry Holt, 1940), p. 39.

22 Jack Finnegan, "The New Age Movement: A New Religion," *The Furrow*, 43, no. 6 (1992), p. 351, available from http://www.jstor.org/stable/27662219; accessed on 03 January 2019.

structure. The convergent concepts of new age movement summarise into 'the three worldviews'.[23] They are the fundamental philosophical constructs of new age movements. Three worldviews are; Monism, Wholism and Individualism. Monistic worldview interprets the whole universe in terms of the single boundless spiritual energy. The concept of the unified single spiritual energy is the most celebrating trait of the new age movement. The wholistic worldview resumes traits of pantheism, and it is a philosophical conclusion of the first worldview. It reckons that the universe and individual are constituted of 'many smaller wholes' or 'whole systems'. Individualistic world view sounds the evolution of the soul, which consummates in the perfection of existence, consciousness and bliss. It is the pure and final state of the soul. Thus, the potential power of the soul, the union with the single energy, and the individual transformation are pivotal philosophical concepts of the new age movement.

The humanistic and evolutionary assumptions, in the new age movement, imply a self-determinative phase of unfolding the dormant potentiality of the human being or the inner divine spark within all the human beings, which naturally leads to the sacredness of the total universe through transformation.[24] It is a religion, in terms of the assembly of the people, who believe in the authority and potentiality of the Self. This potential energy of the soul comes under the scope of para-psychological phenomena, and so the scientific studies in the field of para-normal powers are very much influential in the

---

23 New Age Lecture Notes, available from www.ucs.mun.ca/~jporter/New Age Lecture Notes.pdf; accessed on 10 January 2019.

24 Cf. Chrissie Steyn, "The New Age Movement in South Africa," *Journal for the Study of Religion* 7, no. 2 (1994): P. 95, available from http://www.jstor.org/stable/24764191; accessed on 10 January 2019. (Hereafter, Chrissie Steyn, "The New Age Movement in South Africa,").

new age context. It has manifold implications in the religious, spiritual, and cultural life of the people as well. Hence, it brings a holistic and harmonious appearance of the religious, psychic, and mystical experience. At this interactive juncture, pseudo-priests and fake gurus manoeuvre and manipulate supernormal powers for personal gain and temporal achievements. The contemporary society has been witnessing the growth of such popular transnational charismatic spiritual gurus irrespective of religions. Sometimes it confines into 'a superficial label' in unholy religio-commercial bindings and 'a matter of glamour of aura, which emphasis on psychic powers and occult mysteries as well as conspiracies and hidden teachings.'[25]

To gain power, some of the new age spiritual leaders interpret the texts, concerned with supernatural powers, according to their vested interests. It becomes an art of exploitation of spiritual sentiments and aspirations of the common people. Thus, such interpretations derail the spirit of the original teachings. It can be called the politicization of hermeneutics which uses the religious text as a tool to impose hegemony over the people in the name of religion and spirituality. The excessive importance over the psychic powers of the self demeans and discredits the soteriological motif of human existence. Therefore, it is true that the new age movement awakens the charismatic and evolutionary aspect of society and individual; however, to a certain extent, it also succumbs to moral ambiguity, value confusions, and chaotic spirituality.

---

25 David Spangler discusses four stages of evolution in the development of the new age movement: The first is new age as a superficial label in commercial settings, the second is the new age as glamour, which emphasis on psychic powers, the third new age as concerned with transformation, and the fourth is new age as an incarnation of the sacred civilization and celebration of divinity. Cf. David Spangler, *Emergence: the Rebirth of the Sacred* (Delta/Marylord Lawrence, New York, 1984) quoted in Chrissie Steyn, "The New Age Movement In South Africa," pp. 91-92.

1.2.1.3 The Understandings of Yogi-Pratyakṣa in Indian Philosophical Systems

It is a well-accepted truth that parapsychology mediates between our scientific and spiritual worldviews. Therefore, a scientific study of paranormal phenomena seems to be the best way to understand the spiritual existence of the soul. The independent study of psychology and religion somehow fail to suggest a theory that collates all of the reported physiological, therapeutic, psychological and religious effects of extrasensory perception. Therefore, now the psychology and religion rely on philosophy. In the world of philosophies, the spiritual orientation of Indian systems allows a prolific philosophical discussion on these extrasensory powers. Indian philosophical tradition is acquired by intuitive experiences and sustained by logical arguments. James E. Beichler in his article "Physical Theories of Psi: An Investigative Study" admits it: "Even in our language there is no basis for psi in words and concepts commonly used [...] unlike a culture such as the Indian (Hindu), which abounds in words and concepts, which can form a philosophical basis for psi and the supernatural."[26]

Jagannath Prasad Das, in *Consciousness Quest: Where East Meets West*, asserts the place and relevance of the Indian philosophy in the study of self and consciousness where psychology and western philosophy hobble literally. After paraphrasing S. B Klien's statements about the unavailability of the scientific method to analyse self and its variants and reliance on the psychology over philosophy, Jagannath Prasad Das proposes the concern of Indian philosophy as the solution for the problem:

> Back to psychology, while puzzling over the nature of self is in science, Klien (2012) notes that self

26 James E. Beichler, "Physical Theories of Psi: An Investigative Study," p.4.

is essentially an unexplained if not indescribable concept, that the self, as personal experience of the person, is not explained as yet. The first person experience, the self of conscious experience, is not yet amenable to scientific analysis through the methods that are currently available (Klien 2012). So what can be done, asks Klien? How can an individual study his or her self by self-generated thoughts? Klien retreats to philosophy and hopes that it may play a useful role in psychology. Perhaps Klien stopped short of accepting the Eastern wisdom traditional writings on self! As is widely acknowledged, the nature of individual self or soul and its relation to the cosmic self has been a deep concern in Eastern philosophies.[27]

Regarding the existence of the extrasensory phenomenon, Indian tradition is rather free from all sorts of uncertainty and ambiguity. The classical Indian philosophical systems, both orthodox and heterodox, intelligently assume such phenomenon in their respective philosophies. In Indian tradition, *yogi-pratyakṣa* is a generic term for the experience sans the mediation of sense organs. It encompasses different references and terminologies like *Arśa-Pratyakṣa*, *Siddha-Darśana*, *Mukti-jñāna*, *Pratibha*, *Yogaja*, *Siddhis*, *Avadhi*, and *Manaḥaparyaya* etc. *Yogi-pratyakṣa* is the composite of two words; *yogi* and *pratyakṣa*. *Yoga* comes from the Sanskrit root *Yuj* which has multiple meaning in philosophical literature. The root, *yuj* is used in the sense of concentration (*yuj-samādhi*) and the sense of connecting juncture (*yujir-yoge*). Hence, the word *yogi* is the one who possesses concentration and union. The concentration necessarily is ensued from the suppression of activities of the senses (*indriya*) and the restriction of

27 J. P Das, *Consciousness Quest: Where East Meets West on Mind, Meditation, and Neural Correlates* (New Delhi: Sage Publications, 2014), p. 27.

modifications of the mind (*manas/citta*). *Pratyakṣa* is the combination of two Sanskrit words *prati* and *akṣa*, which means 'before' and 'sense organs' respectively. Conventionally, it denotes the object present before sense organs. But, in the absolute sense (*akṣa* stands here for the Soul or Self), it implies direct or immediate knowledge without the mediation of any other means of knowledge. Therefore, the etymological translation of *yogi-pratyakṣa* is 'the direct perception of the ascetic or saint who has unified with the Reality in deep concentration'. Since the perception is without the assistance of sense organs, those perception and experience have been called extrasensory. The scientific world would prefer the term 'extrasensory perception' other than 'supernormal perception'. According to J. B Rhine, the precedence to the term 'extrasensory' is due to the oblivious nature of the term 'supernormal'.[28] Therefore, the present research translates *yogi-pratyakṣa* as the extrasensory perception.

Peter Balcerowicz, in his article "Extrasensory Perception (*yogi-patyakṣa*) in Jainism, Proofs for its Existence and its Soteriological Implications", calibrates the scope of *yogi-patyakṣa* from similar terms and concepts:

> In general, what was known as *Yogi-Pratyakṣa* was claimed to be possessed only by adepts of yoga, mystics or ascetics by virtue of some accomplishment

28 Cf. J. B Rhine, preface to *Extrasensory Perception*, p. ii.
The common understanding of extrasensory perception has echoed in five senses. Firstly, as the quality possessed genetically from the birth by virtue of the past deeds (previous birth); secondly, as the power acquired by application of drugs or medicines; thirdly as the quality possessed by meditation and certain moral practices; fourthly, as the competence acquired by constant repetition of *Mantras* and by consequent well-developed will; and fifthly, as the power through yogic concentration and the removal of ignorance. The research is restricted itself to the last sense of extrasensory perception.

(usually accompanied by some kind of moral superiority) gained through spiritual practice, either meditation or contemplation (*bhāvanā* or *dhyāna*) or asceticism (*tapas*). Its scope was agreed by a range of thinkers to encompass past (*atīta*) and future (*anāgata*) objects, as well as things (especially those present) which are subtle (*sūkṣma*), concealed from sight (*vyavahita*, *dūra*) and distant (*viprakṛṣṭa*).[29]

The pre-fifth *Nyāya-Vaiseṣika*, *Cārvāka* and *Mīmāṃsā* systems are sceptic about the existence of *yogi-pratyakṣa*. Although the concept of extrasensory perception is absent in early *Nyāya-Vaiseṣika* texts, the latter *Nyāya-Vaiseṣika* admits the existence of extrasensory perception and inscribes it into their system. Both *Cārvāka* and *Mīmāṃsā* systems are sceptic about the epistemological and metaphysical validity of *yogi-pratyakṣa*. *Cārvāka* holds that perception is the only means of knowledge, and therefore, they shun the possibility of *yogi-pratyakṣa*. The fundamental philosophical assumption of *Mīmāṃsā*, which categorically asserts the eternity (*anādi*) and auhorlessness (*apoureṣeya*) of *Veda*, advocates the superiority of *Veda* as the means of knowledge. There are no ways of knowing *Dharma* except through *Veda*. Therefore, according to *Mīmāṃsā*, the claim of adherents of *yogi-pratyakṣa* about the cognition of all things is logically inconsistent. At the same time, they have no objection in the acceptance of supernatural perception as a limited perception.

The adherents of *yogi-pratyakṣa* yield not only a detailed account of the nature of *yogi-pratyakṣa* but also prescribe practical means of acquiring them too. For *Nyāya*, the

29 Piotr Balcerowicz, "Extrasensory Perception (*yogi-pratyaksa*) in Jainism, Proofs of Its Existence and Its Soteriological Implications," ed. Key Chapple, *Yoga in Jainism*, Routledge Advances in Jaina Studies (Oxon–New York: Routledge, 2016), p. 52, (Hereafter, Piotr Balcerowicz, "Extrasensory Perception (*yogi-pratyaksa*) in Jainism, Proofs of Its Existnence and Its Soteriological Implications,").

supernatural perception is an extraordinary (*alaukika*) contact (*sannikarṣa*) or the operative relation through meditation or yoga. It is due to 'the particular connection of the self and the mind in the self, and there arises perception of the self as well as due to the contact of the self, sense organ, mind and object.'[30] In *Sānkhya* system, Vijnanabhikṣu suggests that the mind of the yogin can come in contact with distant and hidden objects by virtue of the peculiar power (*atiśaya*) acquired by meditation and followed by the complete suppression of inertia (*tāmasic guna*) of the mind. The third chapter of *Yogasūtra* discusses the manifold supernatural powers. According to *Yoga*, *Dhārana*, *Dhyāna* and *Samādhi* (taken together is called *samyama*) leads to the mutation of the activities of the mind and effected in direct cognition of all the objects. It leads to the cognition of subtle, hidden, distant, and super-sensible objects, the knowledge of the past, present, and future as well as the knowledge of other minds. It can be defined in one word as 'the getting beyond the sphere of perception in all sense' or 'intuitive hearing, feeling, seeing, tasting and smelling'.[31] The objective of *Advaita Vedānta* is to realize the eternal Brahman (*Aparokṣanubhūti*) and,

30 Cf. *Nyāya-bhūṣaṇa*: 1.1.3; Cf. Bhāsarvajña, *Śrīmad-ācārya-Bhāsarvajña-praṇītasya Nyāya-sārasya svôpajñaṃ vhyākhyānaṃ Nyāya-bhūṣaṇam*, edited by Yogīndrānanda, Ṣaḍ-darśana-granthamālā 1 (Vārāṇasi: Ṣad-darśana Prakāśana Pratiṣṭhānam, 1968): *Vaiśeṣikasūtra*: 9.13; *Vaiśeṣikasūtra*: 9.15; Cf. Kaṇāda Muni Jambuvijaya (Hrsg.), *Vaiśeṣikasūtra of Kaṇāda with the Commentary of Candrānanda*, translation and Introduction by Anantalal Thakur, Gaekwad's Oriental Series (Baroda: Oriental Institute, 1961): *Nyāya-sūtra*: 1.1.3; Cf. Goutama, *Nyāya Sūtra* in *Nyāya Sūtra* of Goutama with *Bhāṣya* of Vātsyāna, translated and edited by Ganga Nath Jha, Vol 1, (Delhi: Motilal Banarsidass, 1984). (Hereafter, *Nyāya-sūtra*).

31 Cf. *Yoga Sūtra*: 3. 16, 21, 25, 33, 36. Cf. Patanjali, *Yoga Sūtra*, edited and translated by Swami Haraharananda Aranya, in *Yoga Philosophy of Patanjali with Bhasvati* (Calcutta: University of Calcutta, 2012). (Hereafter, YS).

therefore, not particular about the supernatural powers as a matter of special attention. But at the same time, the system has impeccable standpoints which prove the perception of super-sensible; "the wise should always think with great care of the invisible, the visible and everything else, as his own Self which is consciousness itself."[32] According to Buddhism, the intuitive perception of Yogin is produced by the constant meditation on the four noble truths, and when this constant meditation culminates in the higher stage, it is endowed with "the most distinct, clear, vivid and indeterminate intuition of an object present here and now".[33] For Jainism, it is "the full manifestation of the innate nature of a conscious self, emerging on the total cessation of all obstructive veils", and it is neither assisted by sense organs nor the mind.[34]

In Indian systems, this extrasensory perception is considered as the immediate apprehension of objects, events or information, which is hidden, subtle, and remote. The resultant cognition is independent of sense cognition. The apex of such cognition is the state of perfect bliss, purity, and existence. Thus, it is interpreted as the highest degree of perception, and such excellence in perception is an achievable end because there are definite ways to realise it. Henceforth, for Indian philosophical systems, the extrasensory experience is not an anomaly, but it exists and it is oriented towards liberation or Self-realisation.

---

32 *Aparokṣanubhūti*: 141. Cf. Sankaracharya, *Aparokṣanubhūti*, translated and edited by Swami Vimuktananda (Almora: Advaita Ashrama, 1938). (Hereafter, *Aparokṣanubhūti*).

33 *Nyāyabindu*: pp.14, 20. Cf. Dharamakirti, *Nyyāybindu* (Banares: Chowkhamba Sanskrit Series, 1954).

34 Cf. *Pramāṇamīmāṁsā*: 1.1.15. Cf. Hemacandrasūri, *Pramāṇamīmāṁsā*, translated with critical notes by Satkari Mookerjee in collaboration with Nathmal Tatia (Varanasi: Tara Publication, 1970). (Hereafter, PM).

1.2.2 Jain Philosophy and Yogi-Pratyakṣa

The quest of the context for a reliable theory for extrasensory perception (*yogi-patyakṣa*) finds its solace in Indian philosophy. Most of the classical Indian systems unanimously accept extrasensory perception (*yogi-pratyakṣa*). But the inclusion of it in the cognitive process and the soteriological process became most conspicuous and pronounced in Jain philosophy because there is an impeccable correlation between epistemology and soteriology. For Jaina, the cognitive actuality is tantamount to liberation. Nathmal Tatia has made a general evaluation of ethical and epistemological concepts of Jainism. According to him, even though Jainism has contributed much in the field of ethical and social life, the "attitude of Jainism is more to its rational consciousness" than any other thrusts, and he continues to say, "Jainism presumes infinite capacity for spiritual progress in every individual. Infinite knowledge and joy is the innate character of every soul. What is needed is non-interference from outside. Given the freedom of development, every individual is bound to progress."[35] The perfection in extrasensory perception or omniscience is the culmination of this progression of the Self. Jainism reiterates the validity of extrasensory perception with its epistemological and soteriological underpinnings. Different from other Indian systems, Jain philosophy maintains a rational approach towards *yogi-pratyakṣa*.[36] Therefore, Jain philosophy is the field of

35 Nathmal Tatia, *Studies in Jain Philosophy* (Varanasi: P. V Research Institute, 1951), p. 21. (Hereafter, Nathmal Tatia, *Studies in Jain Philosophy*).

36 There are different approaches to supernatural perception and omniscience in Indian tradition and philosophy. Ram Jee Singh (1974) pigeonholed it into six approaches. The first one is the devotional approach, which is based on the Bhakti traditions. Here, God is endowed with qualities of omniscience, omnipresence, and

research. Slightly different from the general flow of Indian philosophy, Jaina ascribes a new dimension of the meaning of the term '*yoga*'. Jaina philosophical literature has used *yoga* in two senses: *yoga* as the activity, which stimulates karma,[37] and *yoga* as the contemplation with a motif of emancipation. Ācārya Haribhadra in *Yogaviṁśika Kārikā* elucidates the term *Yoga* in the sense of "what leads one to emancipation."[38] In similar to Ācārya Haribhadra's definition for *yoga*, Ācārya Pūjyapāda and Hemacandrasūri conceptulaise and interpret yoga in their

---

omnipotence and the wholly depended devotee will be blessed with his divinity. The second approach is self-knowledge, which advocates self-knowledge as the path of liberation. One who perceives self perceives everything. It is rather a metaphysical approach that has less importance with lower grades of supernatural perception. The third one is the practical approach, which lashes out the necessity of knowing everything and lavishes on the knowledge of what is desirable to attain liberation. The fourth approach is the most celebrating Yogic approach, which promotes the attainment of yogic powers through yogic efforts such as meditation and abnegation. The fifth one is the approach of faith, which is the response of the common people to the revelation of divinity. It may not even have satisfied logical coherence and appeals. The last one is the rational approach, which struggles to prove the existence of supernatural perception and omniscience through logical arguments and epistemological backups. It validates all the above-discussed approaches. The Jain tradition embraces the rational approach in their enquiry into *yogi-pratyakṣa*. Cf. Ram Jee Singh, *The Jaina Concept of Omniscience* (Ahemadabad: L.D Institute of Indology, 1974), pp. 36-46.

37 *Tattvārtha Sūtra*: 8. 1. *mithyādarśanāvirati pramādakaṣāya yoga bandhahetavaḥ.*

Cf. Umāsvāti, *Tattvārtha Sūtra*, edited and translated by Nathmal Tatia in *Tattvārtha Sūtra*: *That Which Is, with combined commentaries of Umāsvāti, Pūjyapāda, and Siddhasenagani* (New York: Harper Collins Publishers, 1994). (Hereafter, TS)

38 *Yogaviṁśika Kārikā*: 1. *Mukkhena joyaṇāo jogo savoo vi dhamma-vāvāro.*

Cf. Ācārya Haribhadra, *Yogaviṁśika Kārikā*: 1, quoted in Nathmal Tatia, *Studies in Jain Philosophy*, footnote no. 1, p. 262.

respective philosophical writings.[39] The inscription of the term *yoga* (*sayoga-kevalī* and *ayoga-kevalī*) in the Jaina doctrine of *guṇasthāna* (the fourteen stages of spiritual development) also resonate the soteriological motif of *yoga*. Here, *yoga* represents the embodied state of a perfect soul. Hence, *yoga* in *yogi-pratyakṣa* reckons the second sense. Yogi is the embodied soul who contemplatively engages in the process of emancipation. Jain logicians define perception as "the immediate and lucid cognition".[40] Therefore, according to Jaina understanding, *yogi-pratyakṣa* is the immediate and lucid cognition of an adept of *yoga*. The perception (*pratyakṣa*) of the liberated embodied self (*yogi*) is the purport of *yogi-pratyakṣa*. Here, the Self possesses and occupies complete control over the cognitive activity, which precludes from the operation of the sense organs and mind. Then, the Self (of *yogi*) is to perceive (*pratyakṣa*) itself and everything directly and distinctly.

---

39 Ācārya Pūjyapāda ascribes the term *yoga* for the process of eradication where the transcendental Self is realized through the elimination of lower status of the self. (*Samādhitantra*: 17). Quoted in Nathmal Tatia, *Studies in Jain Philosophy*, pp. 281-282.

evaṁ tyaktvā bahirvācaṁ yajed antar aśeṣataḥ
eṣa yogaḥ samāsena pradhīpaḥ paramātmanaḥ.

Nathmal Tatia enumerates it like this; "The soul before it cuts the knot (*granthi*) and experiences the first dawn of the spiritual vision is the exterior self, and the soul after the vision and before the attainment of omniscience is the interior self. On the attainment of omniscience, the self becomes the transcendental self. One is to eradicate the interior as much as the exterior self in order to realize the transcendental self. This process of eradication is *yoga*,"

Hemacandrasūri conceptualized yoga as the cause of final emancipation and consists of the threefold jewel of the right knowledge, right attitude and right conduct. (*Yogaśāstra*: 1. 15). Quoted in Nathmal Tatia, *Studies in Jain Philosophy*, pg. 289.

caturvarge graṇīr mokṣo yogas tasya ca kāraṇam
jñāna-śraddhāna cārita rūpaṁ ratnatrayaṁ ca saḥ.

40 PM: 1.1. 13. *viśadaḥ pratyakṣam*.

Jaina considers sensory perception and verbal testimony as to the indirect cognition (*parokṣa jñāna*), and clairvoyance (*avadhi*), telepathy (*manaḥaparyāya*) and omniscience (*kevalajñāna*) as the direct cognition (*pratyakṣa jñāna*). *Parokṣa jñāna* is the cognition attained through the mediation of the five sense organs and mind. *Pratyakṣa jñāna* is the cognition directly perceived by the self without the mediation of sense organs and mind. *Pratyakṣa jñāna* comes under the scope of *yogi-pratyakṣa*. *Avadhi* and *Manaḥaparyāya* are comparable to what almost called *yogi-pratyakṣa* in other systems and western psychology. According to Piotr Balcerowicz, "the idea of extrasensory perception connoted two different things. First, it was a generic description for the three types of direct perception, which was neither mediated by sense organs nor by quasi-sense, or the mind [...]. In its second meaning, extrasensory perception is equated with omniscience."[41] In short, the epistemological and soteriological concerns are well substantiated, in Jain philosophy. Therefore, the enquiry into Jain *darśana* is much conducive to the research problem and research objectives.

1.3 Review of Literature

The contextual understanding of extrasensory perception prompts for a contextual interpretation of the Jaina source texts. The review of literature determines the scope and relevance of the present research. There are confusion and ambiguity concerning the chronological arrangement of Jain philosophical literature. Erich Frauwallner admits in *History of Indian Philosophy*: "Consequently, in the attempt to understand the development of Jaina doctrine and to arrange it chronologically the different constituent parts of tradition,

41 Piotr Balcerowicz, "Extrasensory Perception (*yogi-pratyakṣa*) in Jainism, Proofs of its Existence and its Soteriological Implications," pp. 43-44.

great difficulties have grown, and it is no wonder that the research in this in this respect still stands in its initial stage."[42] Indira Chandra Shastri in *Jaina Epistemology* mentions the historical development of Jain epistemology. He divides Jaina philosophical literature into two schools: *Āgama* School and *Tarka* School. The difference between the two schools is not in fundamental concepts and doctrine but the manner of treatment and style of presentation.[43] *Āgama* School presents everything in a dogmatic style. *Tarka* School lends precedence to logical style. *Āgama* School consists of three consecutive traditions: Jain canonical literature, post-canonical literature or the commentaries on the canonical literature, and the group of independent doctrinal literature. The *Tarka* School has two phases. The first phase begins with Siddhasena or Samantabhadra (600 A. D) and lasts up to Hemacandrasūri (1100 A.D). The second phase begins at the beginning of the 18th century with Upadhyaya Yasovijaya who adapted the *Navya-Nyāya* style of Gangesa's *Tattvacintamani* into his works, and it continued with his followers.[44]

The research has woven around the third tradition of *Āgama* school, namely independent doctrinal literature,

42 Erich Frauwallner, *History of Indian Philosophy*, Vol I (Delhi: Motilal Banarasidass, 2008 reprint), p. 197.

43 Cf. Indra Chandra Shastri, *Jain Epistemology* (Varanasi: P. V Research Institute, 1990), p. 4. (Hereafter, Indra Chandra Shastri, *Jain Epistemology*).

44 Cf. Erich Frauwallner, *History of Indian Philosophy*, Vol II (Delhi: Motilal Banarsidass, 2008 reprint), pp. 182-184. Indra Chandra Shastri, *Jain Epistemology*, pp. 1-52: Anupam Jash, "Historical development of Jaina Epistemology and Logic," *Jain Journal*, 49 (2014- 2015), p.59; Devendra Muni Shastri, *A Source Book in Jain Philosophy*, translated by T. G. Kalkhatgi (Udaipur: Sri Tarak Jain Granthalaya, 1980). pp. 22-27, (Herafter, Devendra Muni Shastri, *A Source Book in Jain Philosophy*); Mohan Lal Mehta, *Jaina Philosophy* (Varanasi: P. V Research Institute, 2002), pp. 17-34, (Herafter, Mohan Lal Mehta, *Jaina Philosophy*).

which is the faithful and systematic presentation of *Āgama* doctrines and the first phase of *Tarka* School, which is the logical and philosophical arrangement of *Āgama* doctrines. To be more concentrative, Ācārya Umāswāti's *Tattvārtha Sūtra* from the independent doctrinal literature of *Āgama* school and Hemacandrasūri's *Pramāṇamīmāṁsā* from the first phase of *Tarka* School are the primary sources of research. But these texts are not free from shortcomings. Therefore, they are being perfected and compensated with the writings of Ācārya Kundakunda, Ācārya Samantabhadra and Vādidevasūri. They render a better Jaina understanding and interpretation of *yogi-pratyakṣa*. A short review of some of the recent works in Jaina epistemology and *yogi-pratyakṣa* rightly place the present study in Jaina philosophical literature. Thus, the review of the source texts and recent philosophical contributions reiterates the relevance and uniqueness of the present research.

1.3.1 *Tattvārtha Sūtra*

Ācārya Umāsvāmi (variant: Umāswāti) is the author of *Tattvārtha Sūtra*. It is the first Jain text in Sanskrit aphoristic form. In Jaina tradition, it has two names: *Tattvārthadhigama-Sūtra* (manual for knowledge of true nature of things or realities) and *Mokṣa - Śāstra* (tenets of salvation). The name *Tattvārtha Sūtra* consists of three Sanskrit words: *Tattva* (true nature), *artha* (things or realities) and *sutra* (aphorisms). Therefore, it is 'the collection of aphorisms on the true nature of realities.' This indicates the contents of the text, which is the manual for the understanding of the true nature of things. There are differnts of opininon concerning the time of composition. Analyzing the aphoristic style of literature, the composition of *Tattvārtha Sūtra* also falls in the *Sūtra* period of Indian tradition. The reception of text among two Jaina sects proclaims the authority of the text. There are commentaries and commentaries on commentaries. Ācārya

Umāswāti has himself written a commentary on it, known as *Svopajña Bhāṣhya*. This commentary is commented upon by Siddhesenagaṇin also known as *Svopajña Bhāṣhya Tīkā*. *Sarvārthasiddhi* by Pūjyāpada and *Tattvārta Slokavārtika* by Vidyānanda are the major commentaries of *Tattvārtha Sūtra*. Later, Akalaṅka has written a commentary on *Sarvārthasiddhi*, and it is known as *Rājavārtika*.[45]

Tattvārtha Sūtra describes the major theoretical and practical aspects of the Jain system. It has collected scattered canonical dogmas into a structured system. It is akin to the teachings of *āgama* school. The structure of the *Tattvārtha Sūtra* sets in ten chapters with 344 aphorisms. The soteriological motif of Jaina doctrines shins forth from the right beginning of the text. "It is based on the premise that the goal of human life is the liberation which is defined as perfect knowledge, perfect intuition, and eternal bliss."[46] Therefore, the book begins a description of the path of liberation (*mokṣa*) with the exposition of the enlightened world view (*samyag-darśna*), the enlightened knowledge (*samyag-jñāna*), and the enlightened conduct (*samyag-cāritraṇi*).[47] The whole treatise is an attempt to understand the true nature of things. In the first chapter, the text enumerates and interprets the seven categories of truth and the five faculties of cognition. In another way, it is the exposition of metaphysical and epistemological

45 In this research work, we consider two English translations of *Tattvārtha Sūtra* as referential texts; Nathmal Tatia (1994) translation and K. K Dixit (2000) translation of Pt. Sukjlaji commentary on *Tattvārtha Sūtra*. Both these books are the compendium of all the commentaries mentioned above.

46 Nathmal Tatia, Introduction to *Tattvārtha Sūtra*: *That Which Is, with combined commentaries of Umāsvāti, Pūjyapāda and Siddhasenagani* (New York: Harper Collins Publishers, 1994), p. xvii.

47 Cf. TS: 1.1 "*samyag-darśna-jñāna-cāritraṇi mokṣamārgaḥ*" (The Enlightened world view, enlightened knowledge and enlightened conduct are the path to liberation.).

credentials of Jaina thought system. *Tattvārtha Sūtra* exerts to understand the categories of truth through the valid means of cognition (*pramāṇa*) and the philosophical standpoints (*naya*). Following the *Āgamic* classification of the *pramāṇa*, *Tattvārtha Sūtra* also distinguishes two means of cognition: *pratyakṣa* (direct) and *parokṣa* (indirect). The illumination of the innate nature of the soul is the criteria of calibration. The self-illumination of the soul is limited and obfuscated by karmic obscurities. Since the sense organs and mind is the product of this karmic matter, the direct perception of the soul inevitably demands the exclusion of sense organ in the faculty of direct cognition. Therefore, the direct cognition of the soul, i.e., the illumination of the innate nature of the soul, is known as the cognition independent of senses. Therefore, it is called extrasensory perception (*yogi-pratyakṣa*) in *Tattvārtha Sūtra*. The limited cognition endures in the partial philosophical standpoints (*naya*). The second chapter is the detail exploration of the innate nature (consciousness) and characteristics of *Jīva* or Soul substance, and various modes of the soul (*jīva*). The innate nature of the soul manifests in the form of consciousness drive (*upayoga*) and on the ground of the possession of senses (*indrīya*), the soul is classified into various modes.

The third and the fourth chapters engage in the proper cosmology, which has less philosophical thrust. The fifth chapter lays logical and doctrinal ground of the Jaina thought system, by establishing the existence and the nature of the triune relationship of the substance, qualities and modes, which are the constituent elements of Jain metaphysics. Based on the discussion of the triune nature of reality, Jaina explains the nature of the subject and the object. After the discussion of the nature of the subject (*jīva*) in the previous chapter, this chapter understands the nature *ajīva* (non-soul substance). It facilitates the nature of the object of knowledge. The opacity of the soul's (*jīva*) innate nature is due to the karmic matter, which are the modifications of matter (*ajīva*). Therefore, the Sixth, seventh and eighth chapters deal with the various types of karmas, their manifestations, the inflow of karmas, the observance of vows, which determine the variety of the karmic inflow, and the bondage of the karmas. The ninth chapter elucidates the stoppage of incoming karma and wearing off the karmas. It brings different states (*guṇasthana*) of laddering soul towards liberation. Owing to the degrees of suppression and annihilation of karma, one attains the direct perception (*pratyakṣa*), which is beyond the capacity of senses (*yogi-pratyakṣa*). Therefore, *Tattvārtha Sūtra* claims that *pratyakṣa* is equivalent to *yogi-pratyakṣa*. The tenth chapter describes the complete liberation of the soul. The complete liberation necessarily implies the complete annihilation of karma and the total manifestation of the self-luminous soul. It is the perfection of perception and intuition.

It is the miniature of all *Āgamic* doctrines, and therefore, it functions as the referential text in the research. The research is heavily depended on Umāswāti's *Tattvārtha Sūtra*. In the matter of controversies or confusions regarding doctrines, *Tattvārtha Sūtra* remains an unflappable source text and sole arbitrator in the research. On the one hand, the concise aphoristic presentation embraces the entire range of dogmas and doctrines of Jainism, but on another hand, the dryness of structure and style misses the enthusiasm among the readers. The book repeatedly stresses the equal importance of metaphysical, epistemological and ethical aspects with a motif of liberation. But in presentation, it fails to do justice to the epistemological understandings of the doctrines. On some occasions, philosophical thoughts come in them very briefly. Besides, it enters incomparably at great length into things which philosophically of only little interest.

1.3.2 *Pramāṇamīmāṁsā*

Hemacandrasūri is the author of *Pramāṇamīmāṁsā*. Belonging to the tradition of *Tarka* School, Hemacandrasūri enriches Jaina literature with his philosophical works. *Pramāṇamīmāṁsā* is a composition in the form of aphorism with the self-commentary of the author. The self-commentary enhances the value of the work. *Pramāṇamīmāṁsā* and two *Dvātriṁśikās*; *Anyayoga-vyavaccheda- dvātriṁśikās* and *Ayoga-vyavaccheda-dvātriṁśikās* are his works on philosophy. The date of composition is approximately in the eleventh century, and his works follow the style and characteristics of *Tarka* School.[48] The subject matter and objective of the work is pointed out in the commentary of the first aphorism as "the problem of emancipation together with means of realization and its opposites, after a thorough evaluation of the objects of valid knowledge by means of *pramānas* and *naya*."[49]

According to the commentary and critical notes of *Pramāṇamīmāṁsā*, the work has divided into five books (*adhyāyas*) and each consisting of a group of lectures (*āhinkas*). They consist of discourses (*prakaraṇas*), and each discourse is made of a group of aphorisms (*sūtras*). Each aphorism

48 Indra Chandra Shastri, in *Jain Epistemology*, points out the general characteristics of Tarka School. 'It is mainly based on independent works, of which one of them is discussed just above, dealing with the subject logically. Knowledge is considered as a means to ascertain reality. The main problems and subject matter of discussion are the criteria of validity of knowledge, the methods of ascertainment, the sources of knowledge, and its relation with the object. The literature of this period is an attempt to defend Jain views from external attacks and at the same to refute non-Jaina views. Hence, it tries to maintain a logical style of presentation. Sanskrit overpowers as a medium of philosophical discussion. The problem of objective validity becomes a serious concern of the study.' Cf. Indra Chandra Shastri, *Jain Epistemology*, pp. 4-6.

49 PM: 1.1.1.6.

composite of inflected words (*padas, and* each of which in its turn composed of some syllables (*varṇas*). The biggest limitation of the available book is that it remains incomplete. Hence, the entire vision of the author is unavailable. The incomplete *Pramāṇamīmāṁsā* contains two books. Of them, two lectures are in the first book and one lecture in the second book. The methodology of the work composes in the traditional threefold way, i.e., enumeration, definition, and examination.

Yogi-pratyakṣa and its epistemological back up are discussed in the first lecture of the first book. The first lecture contains forty-two aphorisms. After setting the objectives and methodology of the text, Hemacandrasūri clarifies the meanings of technical terms such as *pramāna* and *pratyakṣa*. The self-commentary enumerates and examines the content with logical definitions and etymological explanation. *Pramāṇamīmāṁsā* is keen to explain the constituents of epistemology; the subject of knowledge (*pramāta*), the object of knowledge (*premeya*), the means of valid knowledge (*pramāna*), and fruits of valid knowledge (*phala*). Being the subject of cognition, the self-illuminative soul cognizes the object, which is the substance possessed of permanent qualities and impermanent modes. Therefore, the resultant of cognition is the illumination of the object and that which needs no other agency to illuminate itself. *Pramāna* is defined as 'the authentic and definitive cognition of an object' and divided into two as *Tattvārtha Sūtra*: '*pratyakṣa* and *parokṣa*'. The text stands as an authoritative Jaina treatise on *pratyakṣa.* Perceptual cognition is defined as that which 'qualified by immediacy and lucidity,' and that which lacks this defining characteristic can be defined as non-perceptual cognitions. The sensuous cognition (*abhinibodha/ mati*) and testimonial cognition (*śruta*) are earmarked as the indirect cognition (*parokṣa*) because they are mediated either by a sense organ or mind, or both. Direct cognition (*pratyakṣa*) comprises three varieties of cognition. They are; clairvoyance (*avadhi*), telepathy or mind-reading (*manaḥparyaya*), and the omniscience (*kevala*) in which the Self directly perceives object independent of sense organs and mind. Since they cognize the objects without the mediation of senses, they are called in a wider sense as extrasensory perception (*yogi-pratyakṣa*).

Distinct from other Jaina philosophical literature, Hemacandrasūri attempts to prove the existence of *yogi-pratyakṣa* with logical arguments. These arguments are the collection of Jaina traditional arguments. Having presented some of the positive proofs for the existence of *yogi-pratyakṣa*, he intelligently repudiates the opponents' view by delineating the lack of contradictory proofs to disprove the existence of *yogi-pratyakṣa*. The systematic arrangement of these set of arguments is the highlight and uniqueness of *Pramāṇamīmāṁsā*.

This work has contributed much to the development of Jaina epistemology. It is one of the standard text-books of Jain epistemology and logic. *Pramāṇamīmāṁsā* deals with the fundamental problems of epistemology logically and presented comprehensively. Because of its simple manner of presentation, it enjoys wide popularity among the readers of philosophy. In the introduction to *Pramāṇamīmāṁsā*, Satkari Mookerjee states: "He had no original theory of his own to offer to the readers and his purpose for writing the work was to give a rounded exposition and treatment which would satisfy the needs of average students who would learn all that was essential without unnecessary exertion." [50] Obviously, it doesn't bring a new contribution to the Jain doctrinal system. But, its popularity saps its shortcomings.

The epistemological thrust, which is not much developed in the discussions of *Āgamic* and independent works, gets its

50 Satkari Mookerjee, Introduction to *Pramāṇamīmāṁsā*, p. xi.

abode in this work. It is the logical exposition of doctrines discussed in independent works. In the commentary of the first sūtra, Hemacandrasūri acknowledges the reverence towards Umāswāmi. His works are the logical explanations of Ācārya Umāswāti's aphorisms. The aphorisms of Umāsvāmi and logical explanations of Hemacandrasūri provide the right combination to tackle the philosophically important problems at hand. A close connection between independent works and the works of *Tarka* period signifies the importance of *Pramāṇamīmāṁsā* in the research. All the relevant problems of epistemology and logic have secured adequate and just treatment in this literature. Therefore, Hemacandrasuri's *Pramāṇamīmāṁsā* renders a logical and comprehensive analysis of the research hypothesis and objectives.

1.3.3 *Samayasāra* and *Pravacanasāra*

In the period of independent doctrine, Ācārya Kundakunda animates to lay the foundation for Jain epistemology. He is one of the finest and the earliest Jaina logicians to discuss the *Āgamic* doctrines logically. At the same time, his works are not a mere reproduction of *Āgamic* literature. They are the intelligent response to the general development of philosophy. Thus, they catalyzed the easy transmission of *Āgamic* doctrines into the *Tarkic* logic. Holding the fundamental tenets of *Āgama*, Ācārya Kundakunda laid the foundation for the *Tarka* period. Among the stupendous contributions of him, *Samayasāra* and *Pravacanasāra* earn much philosophical importance. They are originally composed in *Prākṛit*, and these works have been commented upon in Sanskrit by Ācārya Amṛtacandra. Jaina tradition considers that the date of composition of his works is before Ācārya Umāsvāmi.

The ten chapters of *Samayasāra* are a philosophical treatise on Jaina concept of soul, consciousness, and Karma. It is described through the treatise of the Jaina categories of

Truth. The identical and indissoluble relationship between the soul and consciousness and the beginningless but terminative relationship between the soul and Karma are the nexus of these chapters. It animates the doctrinal ground for the Jain epistemology in general. Therefore, the spillover of these logical treatments of the principle themes of epistemology leverages the conceptual framework of *yogi-pratyakṣa*.

The purport of *Samayasāra* is the philosophical exploration of the nature of the Self. Here, *Samaya* represents the Self. *Samayasāra* assumes two viewpoints in its discussion of the self: *Niścayanaya* (transcendental point of view) and *Vyavaharanaya* (transactional point of view). Having defined the nature of the Self from both perspectives, *Samayasāra* elaborately analyses the relationship of the Self with its essential qualities and changing modes. Regarding the essential quality, the Self is defined as a pure conscious substance, which is the subject as well as the mean of direct and valid knowledge. Concerning the changing modes, the Self is undergoing various degrees of modification, which is characterised by indirect and limited knowledge. Ensued from these understandings, *Samayasāra* prompts to define *yogi-pratyakṣa* as a pure perception of the self. The identical relation between the self and consciousness entails him to say that the perfection of *yogi-pratyakṣa* is self-cognition, which manifests all objects simultaneously. Thus, the cognition of the self is identical to the cognition of the entire universe.

Ācārya Kundakunda's *Pravacanasāra* is the compendium of Jaina metaphysics, epistemology and ethics. The epistemological and soteriological aspects of omniscience are explicitly placed and vividly explained in it. Therefore, it inscribes a huge reverence among the intelligentsia and the common people. Ācārya Amṛtacandra (*Tattvapradīpikā*) and Ācārya Jayasena (*Tātparyavṛtti*) have written commentaries on *Pravacanasāra*. Āchārya Amṛtacandra calibrates the teachings of it under three headings: Reality of knowledge (*jñānatattva*), Reality of object of knowledge (*jñeyatattva*), and Reality of conduct (*cāritratattva*). The crux of *Pravacanasāra* is that the self by own nature (*svabhāva*) and by own effort (*svayambhū*) is omniscient. Thus, the three sections of the work are a philosophical reflection of the nature of omniscience from the perspective of the subject, object and liberation, respectively. The identity of soul and pure cognition and happiness, the difference of pure cognition and auspicious cognition, the nature and existence of the object of knowledge, the distinctive features of an omniscient (*śramaṇa/muni/yogi*), and the path of conduct to achieve the omniscience are some of the profound concepts discussed in the treatise. The direct and simultaneous perception of the soul independent and beyond of senses (*atīndriya*) is presented in this work as a logical necessity of Jaina epistemology. Thus, omniscience is claimed to be the state of liberation. The distinction of an imperfect omniscient and perfect omniscient is the unique contribution of *Pravacanasāra*. Extricated from the influx of karma, a perfect omniscient engages in pure cognition. Affected by the influx of karma, an imperfect omniscient is still striving to attain pure cognition. Abnegated all the attachments, infatuations, delusions and activities, a perfect omniscient is progressively endowed with the perfect cognition (*jñāna*) and intuition (*darśana*).

The dogmatic presentations of *Āgamic* knowledge in *Tattvārtha Sūtra* and the logical presentation in *Samayasāra* and *Pravacanasāra* are working in tandem in the research. Indeed, the problems of proper epistemology are not the prime concerns of his works, and these works are weak in the construction of the argumentative structure. But it sets frames for the later development of Jaina epistemology. Hence, resonations of Ācārya Kundakunda's works can be seen in the *Tarka* period of Jaina epistemology

1.3.4 *Āpta-Mīmāṁsā*

Ācārya Samantabhadra's *Āpta-Mīmāṁsā* is a monumental work in Jaina tradition. According to Digambara tradition, Āpta-Mīmāṁsā is the introductory portion of the commentary to Ācārya Umāsvātī's *Tattvārthasūtra.* Ācārya Samantabhadra's commentary to *Tattvārtha Sūtra* is known as *Gandhahasti Mahābhāṣya.*[51] There is a divergence of opinion regarding the time of Ācārya Samantabhadra. But, according to the general understanding, he flourished after Ācārya Umāsvātī and Ācārya Kundakunda and before Ācārya Pūjyapada. The influence of Ācārya Umāsvātī and Ācārya Kundakunda is vivid in his philosophical literature. Akalaṅka, Vidyānandī, and Vasunandī have written commentary on it; *Aṣṭaśai*, *Aṣṭasahasrī*, and *Vṛtti,* respectively. The first word of *Āpta-Mīmāṁsā* begins with the verse '*Devāgama*', and so, it is also known as *Devāgama Stotra*. *Āpta* literally means 'he who has attained or achieved', and practically it is defined as 'the trustworthy'. The word *Āpta* in *Āpta-Mīmāṁsā* is meant for the omniscient being. Ācārya Kundakunda presents the essential characteristics of omniscience. But Ācārya Samantabhadra engages in establishing omniscience by logical reasoning. It expounds the Jainas concept of omniscience philosophically and logically. In *Āpta-Mīmāṁsā*, Āchārya Samantabhadra attempted to justify the existence of omniscient being, refuting the view of those who deny omniscience. In other sense, it is an examination of the existence of omniscient being based

51 Unfortunately, the commentary in full has not been found out. The tradition and some of the references in other Jainas works corroborate the existence of such commentary written by Āchārya Samantabhadra. Āchārya-Chandra Sūri in his *ṭīkā* on the *sūtra Upajñāte*, Malliṣeṇa-sūri in his *Syādvādamañjarī*, Dharmabūṣaṇa in his *Nyāyadīpikā* refers that Āchārya Samantabhadra as the author of *Gandhahasti*. Cf. Saratchandra Ghoshal, 'Introduction to Ācārya Samantabhadra', in Āpta-Mīmāṁsā, edited and translated by Saratchandra Ghoshal (New Delhi: Bharatiya Jnanpith, 2010^2), p. 7.

on the Jaina theory of *Nayavāda* and *Syādvāda*, repudiating the absolutistic (*ekānta*) views of reality. The first chapter logically reckons certain arguments to prove omniscience and impeccably explain the presuppositions of the arguments. The following nine chapters critically examine and quash theses of absolutistic point of view. Finally, it establishes the existence of an omniscient being who can perceive the manifoldness of reality at once. The metaphysical and epistemological notions, as well as problems of Jaina philosophy, are cogently dealt with in this literature. In that way, *Āpta-Mīmāṁsā* is the quintessential textbook for the study of *yogi-pratyakṣa* from the perspective of the omniscience. The close relation to the teachings of Ācārya Umāsvātī and Ācārya Kundakunda places this text as the interpretive text to understand their works.

1.3.5 *Pramāṇa-Naya-Tattvālokālaṃkāra*

Emphasis on omniscience and its refutations precludes Āpta-Mīmāṁsā from entering into the depths of proper epistemology. This shortcoming is compensated by Vādidevasūri, in his philosophical compendium, *Pramāṇa-naya-tattvālokālaṃkāra*. As the name indicates, it is a prompting treatise on Jaina categories of *Pramāṇa* (valid means of knowledge) and *Naya* (partial judgement). It is considered an encyclopaedic work on the Jaina medieval logic, psychology and epistemology. Apart from an exhaustive commentary of Vādidevasūri (*Syādvādaratnākara*), there are commentaries of Ratnaprabha (*Ratnākarāvatārikā*), Rajasekhara (*Pañjikā*) and Jñānacandra (*Ṭippaṇa*). Vādidevasūri was a living contemporary to Hemacandrasūri. Jaina tradition considers him as one of the prominent Jaina medieval logicians. *Pramānamīmāṃsa* of Hemacandrasūri has taken similar manner of presentation and style of Vādidevasūri's *Pramāṇa-naya-tattvālokālaṃkāra* and its commentary. The lucid and elegant treatment of the problems of epistemology renders an elaborative analysis of the concise and cryptic discussions of *Pramāṇamīmāṃsa*. At the same time, the encyclopaedic style and scope of the work may not entertain people. It is divided into eight chapters. With regard to the concept of *yogi-pratyakṣa*, Vādidevasūri sets the epistemological backup cogently. A logical and comprehensive definition, enumeration and examination of *pramāṇa, premeya, prama* and *pratyakṣa* enhance the formation of philosophical constructs in the research. Incidentally, the arguments of the rival Indian schools are developed and refuted in this work. Therefore, *Pramāṇa-naya-tattvālokālaṃkāra*, with its close affinity towards *Pramāṇamīmāṃsa* of Hemacandrasūri, substantiates the arguments of the research.

1.3.6 Recent Development of Literature

In the Jaina stream of thought, extrasensory perception is usually dealt with in the context of perception (*pratyakṣa*) or in the context of the 'epistemic ladder' that culminates in the perfect cognition, i.e., omniscience (*kevala*). Therefore, even in the recent kind of literature, the study of *yogi-pratyakṣa* is mainly discussed with other problems of epistemology. Indra Chandra Shastri (1990) in *Jain Epistemology*, Hari Mohan Bhattacharyya (1994) in *Jaina Logic and Epistemology* and Pushpa Bothra (1996) in *The Jaina Theory of Perception* furnish the study of Jain epistemology with special reference to the theory of perception. Nathmal Tatia (1951) in *Studies in Jain Philosophy*, Devendra Muni Shastri (1980) in *A Source Book in Jain Philosophy* and Walther Schubring (2000) in *The Doctrine of the Jainas* provide a doctrinal back up of the Jain theories. T. G Kalghatgi (1961) in *Some Problems in Jain Psychology* and Mohan Lal Mehta (2002) in *Jaina Psychology* initiate the researchers into the psychological aspects of Jain epistemology. But, it is the research and study of Piotr Balcerowicz (2016) and his articles; 'Extrasensory Perception (*yogi-pratyaksa*) in Jainism, Proofs of Its Existence and Its Soteriological Implications' and 'Extrasensory Perception (*yogi-pratyakṣa*) in

Jainism and Its Refutations' are the direct attempts to have a serious study on the Extrasensory Perception in Jainism. To understand the concept of omniscience, the attempts of Ram Jee Singh (1974) is commendable because his work has engaged in the philosophical and logical explorations on the concept of omniscience. The present research sucks up the doctrinal, epistemological and psychological aspects of previous studies and tries to understand the extrasensory perception with its contemporaneity.

1.4 Conclusion

An enquiry into the hermeneutical understanding of *yogi-pratyakṣa* is the fusion of the pre-existing contextual knowledge and textual interpretation. Western psychology is uncertain about the cognitive value of extrasensory perception, while the new age movements often belittle the soteriological value extrasensory perception. Indian systems, although less affected by these issues, generally view *yogi-pratyakṣa* as a matter of dogma and faith. In contrast, Jain philosophical texts clearly render discussion on the cognitive and soteriological value of extrasensory perception. When this abridged form of expressions in old texts encounters culture, other philosophies, time, and praxis, it gets new nuances and expression. Here, hermeneutical interpretation excels. Therefore, this treatise is an enquiry into the hermeneutical understanding of *yogi-pratyakṣa* in Jain philosophy.

The research problem centers on interpreting the nature and function of *yogi-pratyakṣa* within a contemporary context. The study is guided by two hypotheses: first, that *yogi-pratyakṣa* is an interdisciplinary subject, and second, that it possesses both epistemological and soteriological dimensions. The objective of the research is to understand and elucidate the key features of *yogi-pratyakṣa* and to interpret them through specific hermeneutical principles. This approach aims to safeguard religion, psychology, and philosophy from the distortions introduced by pseudo-prophets and pseudo-scientists. Consequently, the research focuses on the contextual interpretation of the text.

The limitation of the research is the collection of material about the extrasensory perception, which is scattered in various Jaina works. There is hardly any text, which is solely devoted to the topic of extrasensory perception. To emphasize the logical and epistemological foundations of *yogi-pratyakṣa*, the research has drawn from a wide range of philosophical literature within the Jain tradition, referencing relevant texts as needed to ensure a thorough and well-documented study. Another limitation is the incompatibility between modern psychology and traditional Indian psychology, which restricts the scope of comparative analysis. Despite this, the research focuses on the epistemological validity of *yogi-pratyakṣa* and the alignment of epistemology and psychology within the Jain tradition. This focus highlights potential advancements in the cognitive psychological aspects of Jainism. Additionally, the research has not employed qualitative hermeneutic methods such as interviews, data collection, or detailed interpretation, leaving this as a potential area for future exploration.

A research effort to establish an epistemological foundation and soteriological implications for extrasensory perception (*yogi-pratyakṣa*) underscores the relevance of this study. The scientific approach of the research supports the possibility of grounding *yogi-pratyakṣa* in epistemological and logical terms. Conversly, the right understanding about the soteriological underpinnings of *yogi-pratyakṣa* helps counteract the misuse of revealed texts and doctrines for personal, political, social and economic gain. The forthcoming chapters will use specific hermeneutical tools to understand and interpret the concept of *yogi-pratyakṣa* in Jainism.

CHAPTER 2

Metaphysical Credentials of Yogi-Pratyakṣa: *Jīva-Upayoga-Karma*

In Indian philosophy, metaphysics has generally preceded epistemology. Metaphysics explores the fundamental nature of reality while epistemology investigates the methods for acquiring true knowledge of that reality, ultimately guiding the path to liberation or realization. In this context, the concept of *Jīva* or soul connects metaphysics, epistemology, and soteriology. This chapter is an enquiry into the nature of the soul in Jain philosophy, focusing on its essential quality, consciousness (*upayoga*) and its impediment, *karma*. Having analysed the triad of *dravya*, *guṇa* and *paryāya*, the chapter attempts to define and examine the doctrines of *j*īva, *upayoga*, and *karma*. The interpretive understanding of the metaphysical credentials brings forth ontology of the functional relationship between soul and consciousness. The objective of the chapter is to investigate the metaphysics of knowing that governing in the occurrence of *yogi-pratykṣa*. Thus, it is a bird's eye view of the concept of *yogi-pratykṣa* in the Jain thought system.

2.1 Major Credentials

The metaphysical position of Jainas is a corollary to the problem of Reality. According to Jainas, Reality is a composite of *dravya*, *guṇa* and *paryāya*. Through the right understanding of the nature and relationship between the triad, Jainas resolves the contentious problem of metaphysics and epistemology, such as 'permanence and change', 'universal and particular' and 'identity and difference'. The following concepts lay the philosophical ground for Jain metaphysics and epistemology.

2.1.1 Dravya-Guṇa-Paryāya

According to Jainas, *dravya* or substance is the self-existent reality. The defining attribute of *dravya* defines the nature of *dravya*. As the norm, the defining attribute must be presented in all its instances and absent from all instances other than it. Observed the gauging principle, existence is the definitive characteristic of the substance. Hence, the substance is defined "*sad drvayalakṣaṇam*".[1] Here, '*sat*' denotes 'existence'. The Jain thought system has a unique understanding and interpretation for the philosophical jargon '*sat*'. *Tattvārtha Sūtra* defines it as "*utpāda vyaya dhrauvyayuktaṃ sat*."[2] The existence consists of origination (*utpāda*), decay (*vyaya*), and permanence (*dhrauvya*). "Not to give up one's specific nature is the *dhrauvya* or permanence that characterises all substance whatsoever, to originate and perish in the form of a different transformation every moment is the *utpāda-vyapa* or origination-cum-destruction that characterises them."[3] Thus, Jaina explains the evolution of self-existent reality by the triad

---

1 TS: 5.29.

2 TS: 5.29;

Ācārya Kundukunda in his *Pravacanasāra* also defines existence in same way PS: 2.3-13.

Cf. Ācārya Kundukunda, *Pravacanasāra*, translated by Vijay K. Jain (Dehradun: Vikalp Printers, 2018). (Hereafter, PS)

3 Pt. Sukhlalji, *Commentary on Tattvārtha Sūtra of Vācaka Umāsvāti,* translated By K. K Dixit (Ahemadabad: L. D Institute of Indology, 2000^2), p. 205. (Hereafter, Pt. Sukhlalji, *Commentary on Tattvārtha Sūtra*)

of dialectical movement. It interprets the nature of existence is the combination of permanency and impermanency. The enumeration of the triune relation of *dravya*, *guṇa* and *paryāya* expunges the apparent contradiction of permanency and impermanency.

Ācārya Umāswāti in *Tattvārtha Sūtra* gives a stipulative definition of *Dravya*, "*Guṇa-parya*̄yavad *dravyam*."[4] The definition states that that substance (*dravya*) is possessed of qualities (*guṇa*) and modes (*paryāya*). Qualities (*guṇa*) are the essential, permanent, and inseparable nature or attribute of a substance. Modes (*paryāya*) are the changing and accidental nature (*paryāya*) of a substance. A substance has an independent objective existence. Here, Jaina scholars render an instructive analysis of the nature of the object. Ācārya Kundakunda observes in *Pravacanasāra* "The existence of an object can only be established with the existence of all three -the substance (*dravya*), the quality (*guṇa*), and the modes (*paryāya*)."[5] An object is not the substance aloof from qualities and modes and is not mere qualities and modes sans the substance. Thus, *dravya* as an object can be defined as a permanent substance that runs through different modes. It sets forth the characteristics of change and permanence. Hemacandra reiterates the real existence of an object and

4 TS: 5. 37.

The Vaisesika influence is evidently felt on the Jaina conception of *Dravya*. *Vaiśeṣika* defines *Dravya* as "*Kriyāguṇavat samavāyikāraṇamiti dravyalakṣaṇaṁ*" (*Vaiśeṣika Sūtra*., 1.1.14). Karma of the *Vaiśeṣika* is equivalent to *paryāya* of Jain philosophy.

Cf. Kaṇāda, Muni Jambuvijaya (Hrsg.), *Vaiśeṣikasūtra*, in *Vaiśeṣikasūtra of Kaṇāda with the Commentary of Candrānanda*. With the Introduction by Anantalal Thakur. Gaekwad's Oriental Series, (Baroda: Oriental Institute1961).

5 PS: 1.10.

ṇātthi viṇā pariṇāmam attho attham viṇeha pariṇāmo
dvvaguṇpajjayattho attho atthittaṇivvatto.

describes the nature of it in *Pramāna-Mīmāṃsā* as that which 'is real and has the nature of substance and modes.'[6]

The *guṇa* or qualities are the essential and eternal attributes of a substance. It permeates over the evolving stages of a substance and responsible for the idea of generality or continuity. Concerning the substance, *guṇa* is a differentia because it is the defining attribute of the substance. Concerning the modes, *guṇa* is the identical link because it shows the existence of a substantial continuity amidst of changes. The substance remains as the substratum (*dravya*) of the qualities (*guṇa*), and qualities are inseparable from the substratum. Yet, the substance is not the same as qualities. Thus, the nature of quality is defined "*dravyāśrayā nirguṇā guṇāḥ*".[7] It means that the substance is the substratum of qualities, and at the same time, qualities are not the substratum of any other qualities. It shuns the danger of the fallacy of the *infinite regressum*. Since the substance is infinite, qualities also should be infinite. If qualities were not infinite in their own kind, it could not be the expression of the substance.

Modes (*paryāyas*) are the transformations produced by qualities.[8] The term *paryāya* etymologically denotes what has the characteristics of coming into existence and ceasing to be in succession. What originates and disappears is the mode. According to Jaina, the successive stages through which a substance passes are known as modes. Modes exist in substance and qualities. *Dravyaparyāyas* are modes of substance and *guṇaparyāya*s are modes of qualities. *Dravyaparyāyas* are two; *Samānajātīya* and *Asamānajātīya*. *Samānajātīya* is the mode by the union of atoms of the same class of substance; whereas, *Asamānajātīya* is the mode by the union of different

6 PM: 1.1.30. *pramānasya viṣayo dravyaparyāyātmakam vasthu.*

7 TS: 5.40

8 Cf. Pt. Sukhlalji, *Commentory on Tattvārtha Sūtra*, p. 214.

classes of substances. *Guṇaparyāyas* are also two; *Svabhāva* and *Vibhāva*. *Svabhāva* is the mode by the transformation of the substance of the soul with its intrinsic qualities; whereas, *Vibhāva* is the mode by the interaction of the qualities of one substance with other substance.[9] A *dravya* has its essence in *guṇas*, and *paryāyas* have their essence in *dravya* and *guṇas*. Thus, *paryāyas* are the manifestation of *dravya* and *guṇa*. Ācārya Kundakunda in *Pravacanasāra* affirms the indissoluble union of modes and the substance in existence, "Substance does not exist without the mode."[10] The modes are the cause behind the changes. Both the qualities and modes are relatively different and identical with the substance. As there are innumerable numbers of qualities in the substance, so there are innumerable numbers of modes.

Hence, the substance, qualities, and modes constitute three objective aspects of the same reality. Qualities evince substantial continuity amidst modification and change, as like forms and shades of colour may change but the thread and colour remain intact. To sum up, the discussion of triad union of *dravya guṇas* and *paryāyas* with the statement of Ācārya Kundakuda: "that which does not ever leave its own-nature of existence endowed with origination, destruction, and permanence, and has qualities and modes, is a substance."[11] The substance is the object of knowledge, according to Jainism. The substance in the form of origination, annihilation and persistence is the nature of objects.

---

9 Cf. Vijay K. Jain, Explanatory notes to *Pravacanasāra* 2.1.

10 PS: 1.10.

ṇātthi viṇā pariṇāmam attho attham viṇeha pariṇamo
dvvaguṇpajjayattho attho atthittaṇivvatto.

11 PS: 2.3

apariccattashāveṇuppādvvayadhuvattasambddam
guṇvam ca sapjjāyam jam tam davvatti vuccamiti.

2.1.2 The Permanence and Change

The triplicate process of origination, annihilation and permanence validates the nature of a self-existent and self-evolving reality. It substantiates in the tri-union of the substance, quality, and mode. The constitution of the triad evidences the nature of an object is not the absolute permanency, nor the absolute change. Instead, it is permanency and change. According to Ācārya Umāsvāti, the criterion of permanence is that 'not leaving self-essence'.[12] That which neither leaves its existent essence at present nor will leave it in the future is permanent. Jainas interprets eternity and immutability of the substance in order to endorse the permanent character of the substance. Eternity represents the specific nature of a particular substance, and immutability constitutes the non-assuming nature that belongs to some other substance.[13] It suggests that the substance retains its own nature even in the midst of changes. The substance has permanence on account of its own nature (*Svabhāva*) even in its modifications. *Svabhāva* or the own nature of substance, according to Ācārya Kundakunda, 'is the existence (*sat*) in the form of origination, annihilation, and permanence.'[14] The differentia of substance, that is existence, undergoes modifications from one to another. It is clear that the substance, in this sense, is an effect when assumes a new modification by giving up the old. The effect-hood of the substance consists of its undergoing varied modifications. The real existence is not a state of static

---

12 TS: 5.30.

13 Cf. Pt. Sukhlalji, *Commentory on Tattvārtha Sūtra*, pg. 176

14 PS: 2.17. The substance is never deprived of defining attribute, existence. Here, Ācārya Kundakunda two logical questions are commendable; "How can something that is non-existent be a substance or how a substance can exist remain as existence without the nature of existence?" He concludes; therefore, the substance is of the nature of existence. Cf. PS: 2.13.

and permanent existence or stationary and changing existence. Therefore, both permanency and change are inseparable from an existing entity because there is no independent existence of the quality and the mode without the substance and the substance has its own nature, the attribute of existence.[15] The difference between the change and permanence is a matter of point of view.[16] From the point of view of modes, the reality is always changing; whereas, from the point of view of the substance, the reality is permanent.

The nature of the substance is *arthakriyākāritva*. It means that activity with a purpose. When the 'causal efficiency or the capacity for the practical consequence remains as the criterion for the reality', the permanence-in-change is conducive than the absolute permanence and absolute change.[17] Even in the state of liberation, the substance is in its state of change, but it is a homogenous change. Transformation or change (*pariṇāma*) means the continuity of one's own nature (*tadbhāva*) through change. It means that the change into the same kinds of states.[18] Therefore, the nature of change is defined as "*tadbhāvaḥ pariṇāmaḥ*"[19] The continuity, together with the surrender and appropriation, of the preceding and succeeding determinations constitute the defining characteristics of change. It is the causal efficiency of the object.[20] The idea is that the substance and qualities retain their specific nature and yet assuming ever new states depending on the conditions available. In this way, Jaina has quelled the adherences of absolute permanency or absolute impermanency and considered the nature of the object as

15 Cf. PS: 2.19.

16 Cf. PS: 2.20.

17 Cf. PM: 1.1.31-32.

18 Cf. Nathmal Tatia, *Studies in Jain Philosophy*, p. 229.

19 TS: 5.41.

20 Cf. PM: 1.1.33; 30-32.

permanent-cum-transitory. Hence, it does not predicate being without becoming or becoming without being.

2.1.3 Identity cum Difference

The permanence and change indicate the problem of identity and difference. It entails the conclusion that the nature of an object, at a given moment, is conceived as identity and difference. This conception is the perennial problem of epistemology. The existence is the defining nature of the substance (the object) with essential qualities and changing modes. However, with regard to the space points (*pradeśa*), there is no difference (*pṛathaktva*) between the substance and quality. The difference between the substance and quality is the difference in self-identity (*anyatva*). Ācārya Kundakunda cogently declares it: "The substance is of the nature of the existence, the quality is of the nature of the existence, and the mode is of the nature of the existence. Such is the extent of existence. The cause of difference between the existence of the substance, the quality and the mode is certainly the self-identity of all these."[21] Thus, there is no distinct existence (*pṛathaktva*) of either the quality or modes without the substance. The differentia (*guṇa*) of the substance has endowed with a twin role. Concerning *dravya*, *guṇa* is the differentia on which substance is based. Concerning *paryāyas*, *guṇa* serves as the uniting link and shows the existence of substantial continuity.

The logical and metaphysical ground of this mode of relationship is that "they (*dravya*, *guṇa*, *paryāyas*) do not express themselves independently of each other, and there is no third substance that unites them."[22] There is an identity

21 PS: 2.15

saddvvam sacca guṇo sacceva ya pajjao tti vitthāro
jo khalu tassa abhāvo so tadbhāvo atbbhāvo.

22 Devendra Muni Shastri, *A Source Book in Jaina Philosophy*, p. 42.

that unites the substance and its qualities and modes. At the same time, they are different in their self-identity. That is to say, from the subjective point of view in thought, *dravya*, *guṇa*, and *paryāyas* are different from one another. From the objective point of view, they are non-different from one another.[23] On account of the identity, they are never perceived separately. Owing to the difference in self-identity, they can be defined differently. The quality is to represent co-existent relations, and modifications are to represent successive relations as compared with a substance, which really the substratum of qualities and modes.[24] Jainas hold that quality is not merely a chain of successive stages but a constant identity factor undergoing various changes. It is the same permanent qualified substance that undergoes various modifications. The cognition of the object is the apprehension of this co-existent and successive relation.

2.2 Jīva and Ajīva

Whatever exists independently and becomes the substratum of qualities and modes, they are substance. It widens the scope of substance to conscious and non-conscious objects as well. They include the categories of truth.[25] Jaina divides the substance

---

23 Cf. TS: 5.37.

24 Cf. Hari Mohan Bhattacharya, *Jaina Logic and Epistemology* (Calcutta: K. P Bagchi & Company, 1994) p.5.

25 *Tattvārtha Sūtra* says, "To possess enlightened world view is to believe in the categories of truth." (TS: 1.2 *tattvārthaśraddhānaṃ samyaṃgdarśanam*). These categories of truth are called *tattva* in Jainism. The belief in categories don't mean leap into darkness but categories are "which reason and scripture have established as true." (*Tattvārtha Sūtra*: *That Which Is*, trans. By Nathmal Tatia, p.6). The seven categories of truth are necessitated by the consideration of the problem of liberation or emancipation. They are; Soul or sentient entity (*jīva*), non-sentient entities (*ajīva*), the inflow of karmic particles to the Soul (*asrava*), binding of the karmic particles to the Soul *bandha*, stopping the inflow of karmic particles (*saṃvara*), the

into two: *jīva* and *ajīva*. They have a real existence, and they are possessed of qualities and modes. The definitive criterion (*guṇa*) of *jīva* and *ajīva* is consciousness (*cetanatattva*) and unconsciousness (*acetanatattva*), respectively.[26] *Ajīva* has five categories, *Pudgalāstikāya* (matter), *Dharmāstikāya* (the medium of motion), *Adharmāstikāya* (the medium of rest), *Akāśāstikāya* (space), and *Addhāsamaya* (time).

Since *ajīva* has endowed with certain non-material categories, *ajīva* widens its scope beyond matter. Among these substances, only *Pudgalāstikāya* (the matter) has gross form and hence, it is *rūpin* (form). All other substances, including *Jīva*, are *arūpin* (formless). With regard to the extension of substances or possession of *predeśās*, there is one more classification.[27] The first four *ajīva* substances and *jīva* are *astikāya*[28] and *addhāsamaya* (time) comes under *anastikāya*. Thus, there are three categories:

1. That which is purely conscious and has no form.
2. That which is unconscious and has got some form.
3. That which is unconscious and has no form.[29]

---

falling away from the karmic particles (*nirjarā*), and liberation from worldly or karmic bondage (*mokṣā*). The first two are existential, and the rest five are the conceptual realities. The categories of truth can be capsulated under the three titles; sentient entities, non-sentient entities, and the interaction (Karma) of Sentient and Non-Sentient.

26 The definition of a particular substance is through its differentia that is the special quality not found in other substances. *Tattvārtha-śloka-vārtika* articulates it like this, "*Parasparavyatireke sati yenānvyatvaṁ lakṣyata tallakṣanaṃ*" (p. 318).

Other Indian systems of thought, except the monistic materialism of *Cārvāka* and the monistic spiritualism of *Vedānta*, agree to the two aspects of the Reality; *cetanatattva* and *acetanatattva*.

27 Cf. *Dravya Sangraha*: 27. Cf. Muni Nemichandra Siddhantideva, *Dravya Sangraha*, translated and edited by Saval Chandra Ghoshal (Bombay: Shri Chandraprabha Digambhara Jain Mandir Trust, 1986). (Hereafter, DS)

28 Cf. DS: 24.

29 Cf. Mohan Lal Mehta, *Jaina Philosophy*, p. 66.

Jainism classifies substances as the sentient and non-sentient, and again corporeal and non-corporeal. *Ajīva* is non-spiritual or non-sentient. In the non-spiritual, Jaina has non-corporeal substances like *dharma* and *adharma*: and corporeal substance *pudgala*. The unconscious but immaterial category of substance is one of the unique contributions of the Jain thought system. It should be kept in mind that 'corporeal' and 'unconscious' does not necessarily correspond to 'the materialistic nature of reality', in Jainism, because from the phenomenal point of view, *jīva* is corporeal but spiritual and sentient; whereas, the categories of *ajīva* except *pudgala* are unconscious but immaterial.

2.3 The Jīva as the Substance

Jīva is commonly translated as the Soul, Sentient entity, and Self. In Jaina metaphysics, the soul has sounded in two senses; noumenal (*niśchaya*) and phenomenal (*vyavahāra*). The noumenal point of view denotes a pure state of the Soul. The phenomenal point of view offers the soul with empirical qualifications. From the noumenal point of view, the Soul (*jīva*) is Right conduct (*cāritra*) Faith (*darśana*) and Knowledge (*jñāna*), and it is the pure soul (*svasamaya*).[30] From the phenomenal point of view, the Soul is described as the possessor of four *prāṇas* - *indriya* (senses), *bal* (force), āyu (life), and *ana-prāṇa* (respiration)-, the lord, the doer, the enjoyer, corporeal but spiritual and associated with karma in equal extension to the body. [31] All the *vyavahāra* forms of the Soul are the *paryāyas* of the self-same unitary *dravya*, i.e., *Jiva*. Both views are not absolutely different or identical. Thus, it is necessary to understand the distinction to assimilate the concept of the Soul or Self in Jainism.

---

30 SS: 2. *Jīvo carittadaṁsanaṇāṇaṭṭhido taṁ hi sassamayaṁ jāṇa.* Cf. Ācārya Kundakunda, *Samayasāra*, translated and edited by A. Chakravarti (New Delhi: Bharatiya Jnanpith, 2008[5]). (Hereafter, SS)

31 Cf. DS: 3-14; SS: 7-8.

Later, Jaina scholars conflate both views in a single frame to form a comprehensive definition of *Jīva*. Vādidevasūri in *Pramāṇanayatattvāloka* enumerates the nature of the soul in the following manner: "The Soul which is proved by direct experience (*pratyakṣa*) etc. is the knower (*pramātā*). It is essentially conscious (*caitanyasvarūpaḥ*), changing (*pariṇāmī*), agent (*karttā*), direct enjoyer (*sākṣābhoktā*), equal in extent to its own body (*svadehaparimāṇaḥ*), different in each body (*pratikṣetraṁ bhinnaḥ*), and the possessor of material karma (*paudagalikādṛṣṭavaṁscāyam*)."[32] Nemichandra Siddhantideva in *Dravya Sangraha* defines the nature of the Soul almost the same manner: "Jīva is characterised by *Upayoga*, is formless, and an agent has the same extent as the body, is the enjoyer of the fruits of karma, exists in *samsāra*, is *Siddha* and has characteristics of upward motion."[33] These definitions have rightly emerged in the wake of the logical development of other systems. They establish and communicate squarely a logical and philosophical view of *Jīva*.[34] Thus, the interpretive

---

32 PNT: VII: 55, 56.

Pramātā pratyakṣādiprasiddha ātmā.
Caitanyasvarūpaḥ pariṇāmī karttā
sākṣābhoktā svadehaparimāṇaḥ pratikṣetraṁ
bhinnaḥ paudagalikādṛṣṭavaṁscāyam.

Cf. Vādi Devasūri, *Pramāṇa-Naya-Tattvālokalaṃkāra*, translated and edited by Hari Satya BhattĀcārya (Bombay: Jain Sahitya Vikas Mandal, 1967). (Hereafter, PNT).

33 DS: 2.

Jīvo uvaogamao amutti katta sadehaparimano
Bhotta sansarattaho siddho so vissasoddagai.

34 The Soul is the spiritual entity and not the modifications of matter that raises criticism over *Cārvaka*. It is a real existing entity and not an aggregate of material forms, etc. or mere illusion is the refutation over Buddhism and *Vedānta*, respectively. The soul is the active agent and the enjoyer that refutes *Saṅkhya* and Yoga system. Soul as the substance is possessed of the attributes and modifications are direct criticism over *Nyāya-Vaiśeṣika* views. Cf. Hari Satya Bhattacharya,

dimensions of these definitions bolster to differentiate the Jain conception of *Jīva* from that of other systems. Responding to the general development of Indian systems, these definitions have both didactic and refutative purposes. Constrained to the objective of the research, the present treatise refrain from an attempt to analyse them in detail, which is a vast area that later to be exposed. Significantaly, Jainas concept of the soul has never taken the reality of the soul as pure identity, nor as pure differences or bundle of emotions, but always as reality realising itself in and through qualification and modifications, which are of the same essence.

The defining attribute scrutinises the nature of *jīva*. To differentiate *j*īva from non-*jīva*, 'the Consciousness' or *cetana* (*cetanāguṇamasaddaṁ*) identifies as the defining attribute.[35] As there are modifications of the quality (*guṇaparyāya*), the consciousness manifest in three psychological activities of cognition: the process of knowing, the process of emotion, and the process of activity or conation. These triple cognitive and psychic activities are considered as *cetana paryāya*.[36] Correspondingly, it is said that the soul is the Knower, the Enjoyer, and the Actor. Without barring other natures of the soul, the knowing nature (*upayoga*) stands distinct due to its direct relation to *cetana*. Ācārya Kundakunda in *Samayasāra* proclaims "its nature as the Knower (*jñāyakasthu*) is unique

---

Reals in the Jaina Metaphysics (Bombay: The Seth Sant Das Khestsy Trust, 1966) pp. 270-289. (Hereafter, Hari Satya Bhattacharya, *Reals in the Jaina Metaphysics*); J.C Sikdar, *Jaina Theory of Reality* (Varanasi: P.V Research Institute, 1991), pp. 231-254. (Hereafter, J.C Sikdar, *Jaina Theory of Reality*)

35 Cf. SS: 49.

36 Cf. A. Chakravarti, "Introduction to Ācārya Kundakunda's *Samayasāra*," in Ācārya Kundakunda, *Samayasāra*, translated and edited by A. Chakravarti (New Delhi: Bharatiya Jnanpith, 2008[5]) pp. 150-151.

and self-identical."[37] As a competent and exclusive *lakṣaṇa*, *upayoga* present in all the cases of the soul, in all the three phases of time, and absent in all the cases what is other than the soul. The admission of *upayoga* as *lakṣaṇa* does not denigrate other aspects of the soul. Different from *upayoga*, other natures have evolved from the direct or indirect relation to *karma*, and so, they have been conferred the status of *upalakṣaṇa* or indicative mark, not *lakṣaṇa* or defining characteristic.[38] Hence, Umāsvāmi states in *Tattvārtha Sūtra* the nature of the soul: "*upayogo lakṣaṇam.*"[39] *Upayoga* is the defining attribute (*lakṣaṇa*) of the soul. *Jīvatva* or being a soul is identical to *upayoga*. Ācārya Kundakunda in *Samayasāra* echoes the same by saying, "*sarvajñānadrṣto jīva upayogalakṣṣanaṃ nithyam*"[40] 'The nature of the soul is permanently associated with its quality called *upayoga*.'

'Attention', 'function or application of consciousness', 'cognitive operation', and 'sentience' are the close translations of the term *upayoga*. Towards a cognitive analysis, it places as 'a tendency of the consciousness with purpose or drive'. The identity of the soul and *upayoga* and its causal activity corroborates a causal and effectual state of *upayoga*. The causal state is a state of permanency. The effectual state is a state of change and modification. Therefore, it is the tendency of the consciousness arising out of the relation of the soul and a tendency to attend to the object of knowledge.[41] It propels

---

37 SS: 6.

ṇavi hodi appamatto ṇa pamatto jāṇago du jo bhāvo
evaṁ bhaṇaṁti suddhā ṇādā joso du so ceva.

38 Cf. Pt. Sukhlalji, *Commentary on Tattvārtha Sūtra*, pp. 80-81.

39 TS: 2.8.

40 SS: 24. *Jīvo uvaogalakkhaṇo ṇiccaṁ.*

41 *Upayoga* has been interpreted as an expression of cognition and as the resultant of consciousness. It is interpreted as a psychological term stating that as karmic energy, which is primarily responsible for the

that *upayoga* has a subjective as well as an objective side. Indra Chandra Shastri observers the reason behind taking *upayoga* as the essential definition of the soul:

> We cannot separate it from the latter. There is no soul without *upayoga*, and there is no *upayoga* without the soul. Yet, we cannot say that they are absolutely one and same thing. *upayoga* is only a part of the psychical function. Other functions are feeling, willing etc, which according to Jainism are not included into *upayoga*, which is the activity of cognition only, a particular expression of consciousness which covers the entire range of psychical life. [42]

In the broader sense, the definition of the Soul as "*upayogo lakṣaṇam*" definitely explains the identity cum difference in the relationship between the Soul as *dravya*, the causal state of consciousness as *guṇa* and the effectual state of the consciousness as *paryāya*. To recapitulate the enquiry into the nature of the Self, it is appropriate to refer to the concluding remarks of *Samayasāra* with regard to the discussion of the Self: "As the characteristic of the soul is o be always knowing, therefore the soul is certainly the subject of knowledge, the Knower, par excellence. It should be understood that knowledge and the knower cannot be differentiated from each other."[43]

2.4 Upayoga as the Defining Quality

Upayoga assumes a causal and effectual state of existence.

---

expression of varieties of cognition. Cf. T. G Kalgatgi, *Some Problems in Jaina Psychology*, pp. 30-32: Hari Mohan Bhattacharya, *Jaina Logic and Epistemology*, p. 27.

42 Indra Chandra Shastri, *Jain Epistemology*, p. 143.

43 SS: 403.

Jamhā jāṇai ṇiccaṁ tamhā jīvo du jāṇao ṇāṇī
ṇāṇaṁ ca jāṇayādo avvadiritaṁ muṇeyavvaṁ.

The causal state of *upayoga* is equivalent to the concept of consciousness in other systems of Indian philosophy. Depended on the metaphysical relationship of the soul and consciousness, Indian systems have manifold understandings and interpretations about consciousness. The prominent views have calibrated into five:

1. Consciousness does not exist.
2. Consciousness is a combination of material elements.
3. Consciousness is the accidental quality or action of the soul.
4. Consciousness is eternal and pure reality.
5. Consciousness is the inseparable and permanent quality of the soul.

Mādhyamika school of Buddhism denies the eternity of consciousness as part of their crude denial of the permanency. The material realist, the *Cārvaka* system, accepts consciousness as a phenomenal fact but considers it as the combination of material elements and not eternal. For *Nyāya-Vaiseṣikas*, the consciousness inheres in the soul as the accidental quality. *Advaita Vedānta* and *Sāmkhya-Yoga* hold that consciousness is identical (*svarūpa*) to the pure substance. Some others, like Ramanuja advocates consciousness, are the inseparable quality of the substance. Different from other systems, Jaina ascertains that consciousness exists as the essential quality of the soul, and it is not totally different or totally non-different from the soul. The nature of the relationship between the soul and consciousness enumerates the metaphysics of cognition in the Jain thought.

2.4.1 Consciousness as the Essential Quality of the Soul

The consciousness, being the quality, depends on the substratum for its existence. Indian philosophical systems, except *Mādhyamika* school of Buddhism and *Cārvāka*, accept the soul is the substratum of consciousness. Having upheld the theory of interconnected aggregates and the theory of dependent origination, the *Mādhyamika* school of Buddhism propels the theory of the denial of the absolute existence of the soul and consciousness. They accept the soul and consciousness. But they dismiss the conception that the soul is an eternally conscious entity. By their subtle dialectical reasoning, they approbate the changing and indefinable nature of everything. It proclaims the psychic life of an individual as a bundle of successive but unconnected states. Hence, consciousness is an ever-flowing but the unconnected stream of becoming. Jaina dismays the concept of ever-changing reality bereft of permanence. 'Becoming is not possible for what is not being.' If it is not so, the admission of *smṛti* (memory) *pratyabhijñā* (recognition), and *pratyanmārgaṇa* (anticipation) and the removal of ignorance will be in turmoil.[44] Similar to Buddhists, Jaina approves causal efficiency (*arthakriyākāritva*) as the nature of reality. But, Jaina exposes the voidness of Buddhists tortuous argument by shunning 'the possibility of causal efficiency in a momentary reality manifesting itself either in a gradual or in simultaneous production of an effect.'[45] Jaina scholars, therefore, acclaims the essential connection between consciousness as quality and soul as permanent substratum is inevitable in the formation of a solid epistemology.

Indian materialism, *Cārvāka* holds that consciousness is something new property through the combination of material elements in a peculiar way. As the cause of fermentation exists in the yeast, the cause of consciousness exists in the particular combination of material elements. It is inherent

44 Cf. Āpta-Mīmāṃsā: 41-45. Cf. Ācārya Samantabhadra, Āpta-Mīmāṃsā, translated and edited by Saratchandra Ghoshal, New Delhi: Bharatiya Jnanpith, 2010[2]. (Hereafter, AM).

45 Cf. Hari Mohan Bhattacharya, *Jaina Logic and Epistemology*, p. 18.

(*svabhāva*) in the matter. Thus, the potential subtle element is the material cause of consciousness. Then, Jaina interrogates whether the subtle element belongs to the same class as that of consciousness or the different one. If it is the same, the material elements fail to be the cause of the consciousness and hence, one has to admit the existence of the self or something spiritual as the substratum of the consciousness. If it is different, it contradicts the very logical concept of material cause.[46] The psychic activities are to be substantial and immaterial. It is the logical necessity to concede that the subtle element of the consciousness is the spiritual entity. Therefore, Jaina divulges that the immaterial soul is the substratum of the immaterial consciousness.

Having placed the soul as the substratum of consciousness, the research moves to analyse the mode of relationship between the soul and consciousness. Is it an accidental or permanent relationship? Along with Jainism, *Nyāya* and *Vaiseṣika* systems accept consciousness as the quality of the soul, and the soul is the substratum of consciousness. But, *Nyāya* and *Vaiseṣika* hold the consciousness as the adventitious quality or accidental phenomenon of the soul, and it resides in the soul through the eternal relation of inherence (*samvaya*).[47] It indicates that the self is an unconscious self-existent reality. The appearance of consciousness depends on external factors. These external factors are not possible in the state of liberation. Therefore, liberation is a state of the soul bereft of consciousness. According to *Nyāya-Vaiseṣika*, the nature of the soul is distinct from the quality, i.e., consciousness. Jaina

---

46 Cf. Indra Chandra Shastri, *Jain Epistemology*, pp. 95-96; Vādi Devasūri commentary to PNT: VII. 55, p. 542.

47 Cf. *Bhāṣa Paricchedа*: 49. Cf. Visvanātha-Nyāya-Pancānana, *Bhāṣa Pariccheda*, translated and edited by Swami Madhavananda (Uttarakhand: Advaita Ashrama, 1940, 6th impression). (Hereafter, BP)

asserts the identity of essence between soul and consciousness. Such an absolute separation, as *Nyāya* holds, between soul and consciousness will exacerbate 'chaos to the origin and condition of all determination.'[48] Here, the problem arises that the consciousness behaves as the stranger to the soul. They try to compensate for the rift between them by the advent of the theory of inherence. The soul is not conscious of itself, but it becomes so through the category of inherence. The inherence is the separate category of eternal relation, according to them. Henceforth, one would have to explain again how the relationship between consciousness and inherence happens. It demands another category of relationship, and the demand remains endlessly. It would lead to the fallacy *ad infinitum regressum*.

The Kumārila *Mimāṁsā* considers consciousness as the modal change of the self. Based on the relation between the soul and consciousness, it is defined as the act (*avasthā*) of the self.[49] It implies a distinction between the soul and the consciousness as an agent and the act. Unlike the *Nyāya* system and like Jainas, Bhatta *Mimāṁsā* regards consciousness as a fundamental attribute of the soul. But in agreement to *Nyāya* system and polemic to Buddhist, *Mimāṁsā* propels that the self is a pure substance, which is devoid of consciousness and qualities in the state of liberation. The conscious reality sunder from its own conscious modification is a haphazardous position. A conscious real is a conflation of the origin and function. Therefore, Jaina boldly asseverates consciousness is essential to the soul.

For *Sāṇkhya*, *Vedānta* and Jaina systems, consciousness is the essential quality of the soul. *Sāṇkhya* and *Vedānta*

48 Cf. PNT: VII.11-12; The commentary to PNT: VII. 56, pp. 561-568.

49 Cf. Hari Mohan Bhattacharya, *Jaina Logic and Epistemology*, pp. 25-26.

consider that consciousness is the very stuff of the self, and there is no perception of the difference between the substance and the quality. They are identical. But their conception of the modification of consciousness is different from Jaina. It will be discussed later in this chapter. *Tattvārtha Sūtra* definition of the soul depicts the unique picture of the inalienable relationship between the soul and the consciousness. The relationship is not absolute non-difference or absolute identity. Jainas tradition reckons the soul is coextensive with knowledge (*jñānam*).[50]

Āchārya Kundakunda defends it like this: "If the soul is not coextensive with knowledge, it must be conceded that the soul is either smaller or larger than knowledge. If the soul is smaller than knowledge, knowledge becomes insentient and loses its ability to know. If the soul is larger than knowledge, how will it know without knowledge?" He encapsulates the discussion as; "The knowledge (*jñānam/ṇāṇaṁ*) is the soul (*atma/appa*). Without the soul, there is no existence of knowledge (*jñānam/ṇāṇaṁ*). Therefore, knowledge is the soul, and the soul is knowledge, besides other qualities."[51]

It cogently corroborates that the consciousness is identical with the soul. At the same time, the self-luminous

---

50 Cf. PS: 1.23. The term knowledge (*jñānam*) is used here as more in general sense which is equivalent to consciousness (*cetana*). The operation of cognition is denoted with the term '*upayoga*' or '*uvayoga*' in Jaina tradition.

51 PS: 1.24-25.

ṇāṇppamāṇmādā ṇa havadi jasseha tassa so ādā
hīṇo vā adhgo vā ṇāṇādo havadi dhuvmeva
hīṇo jadi so ādā *taṇṇāṇmacedaṇam ṇa jāṇādi*
adhigo vā ṇāṇeṇa viṇa kaham jāṇādi.

PS: 1. 27.

ṇāṇaṁ appa tthi madam vaṭṭadi ṇāṇaṁ viṇā ṇa appāṇaṁ
tamhā ṇāṇaṁ appā appā ṇāṇaṁ va aṇṇaṁ va.

consciousness as the eternal quality of the soul is manifested through the operation of cognition (*upayoga*). Thus, when the soul behaves as *karta* and consciousness behaves as the *karana* in the practical sense, they are taken to be different. In the absolute sense, the soul, consciousness and operation of cognition are identical.

Jain system accepts the identity and difference in the relationship between the soul and consciousness and squashes the possibility of the third category that joining them. Indra Chandra Shastri in *Jain Epistemology* correctly observes it like this: "The consciousness is the essence as well as a faculty of the soul which is neither absolutely different nor absolutely identical with its substratum."[52] Therefore, the Jain system holds that the soul is essentially conscious not partially or the adventitious quality or action of the soul and the consciousness is not absolutely identical or absolutely different in the relationship with the soul. Liberation or the pure state of the soul is not devoid of consciousness; instead, it is the state of omniscience or absolute knowledge. Thus, consciousness is the eternal and essential quality of the soul.

2.4.2 Consciousness as the Self-Luminous Quality

The soul is the substratum of consciousness, and there is an eternal and inseparable relationship between them because consciousness is the essential quality of the soul. Consciousness is the source of all operations of cognition (*Upayoga*). It stirs up a perennial question of epistemology, i.e., the cognition of consciousness. There are four possible alternative answers; consciousness may remain as unrevealed, it is cognised by the second cognition, it is inferred from the object of cognition, and it reveals itself. Can the consciousness be remained as unrevealed? No, because it is contradictory

52 Indra Chandra Shastri, *Jain Epistemology*, p. 120

to our common experience. If consciousness is cognised by another consciousness as *Nyāya* says, and then it is a cataclysmic position because the consciousness is manifested by a second entity since the latter, too, being equally is cognised by the third and the process continues without an end. It will lead to the fallacy of *regressum ad infinitum*. The consciousness cannot be manifested by the object as well. Can consciousness depend on the object or the content of the objects for its manifestation? If it is so, the ground of the object and the cause of the consciousness would be the same. The prevalent question is whirling around that how the material object becomes the source of immaterial consciousness. Further, the position that claims consciousness is known only after the object is known and the object cannot be known unless the knowledge is known will end up in the fallacy of logical see and saw.[53]

In agreeing with Jainas, Bhatta *Mīmāṃsā* regards consciousness as the attribute of the soul. In contrast to Jainas, Bhatta *Mīmāṃsā* rejects the notion of self-luminosity of consciousness and advocates consciousness is inferred indirectly through the cognizedness of the object. It can reveal neither itself nor the subject, i.e., the self. Instead, it can reveal only the object. To say that knowledge is not self-revelatory and nevertheless to validate their position is self-contradictory. Because an explanation of the meaning of a theory or position is an endeavour at knowing it, and this knowing, if not-self-revelatory will not be intelligible.[54] It is nasty to say that consciousness knows everything but cannot know itself. Jainas criticises this position vehemently and propels that which is self-luminous cannot help but illuminating object and subject.

Jaina holds that consciousness is self-illuminative. Jain philosopher Hemacandrasūri in *Pramāṇa-Mīmāṃsā* defines

53 Cf. PM: 1.1.1. no.12

54 Cf. Ram Jee Singh, *The Jaina Concept of Consciousness*, p. 79.

pure and transcendent perception based on the self-illuminative nature of the soul. "The full manifestation of the innate nature of a conscious self (*mukhyaṃ cetanasya svarūpāvibharyāvo*)" [55] substantiates the manifestation of the luminous nature of the soul, i.e., consciousness. It is unconscionable to say that the omniscient knows everything other than his consciousness. The omniscient should have known his consciousness. Otherwise, he should not be omniscient. In order to know his consciousness, another consciousness is not needed. It is self-illuminative. Vādidevasūri emphasises the clear illumination of consciousness in certain knowledge.[56] Therefore, consciousness is self-revealing. Jainas reiterates that consciousness when it reveals objects does not require itself to be revealed by anything else. The knowing process does not generate self-luminous nature and self-consciousness, but the consciousness is generated at its genesis with the nature of self-illumination.[57] Hence, the cognition of consciousness is not the act of revealing itself. Instead, consciousness is self-illuminative or self-revelatory by nature. Thus, when it illuminates, it also illuminates itself to the substratum, the soul. The self-luminous nature of consciousness shuns the possibility of the third entity for its revelation. The implications of the self-luminous nature of consciousness in the operation of cognition will be dealt in the subsequent chapter.

2.4.3 Soul, Consciousness and Cognition

According to Jain metaphysics, substance and quality exist in identity and difference. It frames Jaina philosophical constructs that the identity of the self and consciousness

---

55 PM: 1.1.15.

tat sarvathāvaraṇvilaye cetanasya
svarūpāvibharyāvo mukhyaṃ kevalaṃ.

56 Cf. PNT: 1.16.

57 Cf. PNT: 1. 17.

and difference in modifications. It is generally accepted philosophical norm that whatever is produced from a substance has the same attributes as those of the substance. The soul is eternally conscious, and the consciousness is manifested in the form of cognition. Therefore, there would be an identical relation between the soul and cognition. Ācārya Kundakunda says, 'the cognition is the principle nature of the soul, besides other nature and there is no existence of the knowledge without the soul.'[58] Therefore, the soul (*dravya*), consciousness (*guṇa*), and cognition (*paryāya*) are identical.[59]

The cognition has endowed with the features of the self-conscious soul. The content of knowledge is not something different from the self-conscious soul. Vidyānanda and Jinabhadra enumerate the three equivalent sense of the term *jñāna*. They are; apprehension (*paryāya*), the power of apprehension (*guṇa*) and the cognisor (*dravya*).[60] In the logical or epistemological sense, they can be demarcated from one another. In the absolute or ontological sense, they are identical in their existence. It is the relation between identity

---

58 PS: 1.27.

Akalnka states that consciousness has two forms, the cognition form and the object form. The cognition form is substantial continuity in all the operation of cognition. The objective form represents different apprehensions. The cognition form as the state of pure consciousness is not a metaphysical state. On the discursive level, Jainas also hold that consciousness cannot appear alone without modifications. Cf. Indra Chandra Shastri, *Jain Epistemology*, pp. 156-157.

59 Cf. SS: 309.

jīvassājivassa du je pariṇāmā du desiyā sutte
taṁ jīvamajīvaṁ vā tehimaṇaṇṇaṁ viyāṇāhi.

SS: 403.

Jamhā jāṇai ṇiccaṁ tamhā jīvo du jāṇao ṇāṇī
ṇāṇaṁ ca jāṇayādo avvadiritaṁ muṇeyavvaṁ.

60 Cf. Vidyanandi, *Tattvārhaślokavārika* (the Commentary on *Tattvārtha Sūtra*) (Bombay: Nirnaya Nagar Press, 1918), p. 58.

and difference. The soul as the substance has its essence in qualities, and cognition as modification has its essence in soul and consciousness. The consciousness is differentia and the ground of co-existent successive relations in cognition. Hence, according to Jainism, cognition is the cognitive manifestation of the self-luminous consciousness, which has the self-conscious soul as the substratum.

Nyāya-Vaiśeṣika defines cognition as the adventitious attribute of the self. It denotes an apprehension (*upalabdhi*), knowledge (*jñāna)*, and cognisance (*pratyaya*).[61] The *Mīmāṃsā* and Bauddha systems agree in describing the cognition as an activity, a transitive process.[62] These systems accept consciousness as the accidental quality or activity of the self and cognition as the adventitious under certain conditions. For *Sāṇkhya*, *Vedānta* and Jain, the consciousness (*cetanā*) is an intrinsic or essential nature of the soul, which is inseparable from the soul, and this consciousness manifests in the form of cognition through a certain process. The causal state of the soul is consciousness, and the manifested state of the soul is cognition.[63] However, they vary in the formation and function of the effectual state of cognition.

For *Sāṇkhya*, *puruṣa* is the pure consciousness but inactive, and therefore, the cognition happens in relation to *prakṛti*, which is active but unconscious.[64] Strictly speaking, it

---

61 Cf. *Nyāya Sūtra*: 1.1.15. Cf. *Nyāya Sūtra* of Goutama with *Bhāṣya* of Vātsyāna, translated and edited by Ganga Nath Jha, Vol 1 (Delhi: Motilal Banarsidass, 1984).

62 Cf. *Sāsṭradipika*: p. 56; *Nyāyabinduṭika*: 1. Quoted in Satischnadra Chatterjee, *The Nyaya Theory of Knowledge* (New Delhi: Rupa Publications, 2015), p. 12.

63 Cf. Indra Chandra Shastri, *Jain Epistemology*, p. 141.

64 Cf. *Sāṁkhya Kārikā*. 20. Cf. Vācaspati Miśra, *Sāṁkhya-Tattva-Kaumadi: Commentary on Sāṁkhya Kārikā*, translated by Mahamahopadhyaya Ganganath Jha (Delhi: Chaukhamba Sanskrit Prathishthan, 2004), p.88

is through the unconscious *buddhi*, the first evolute of *prakṛti*, the cognition evolves. *Buddhi* through the contact of sense organs with the objects takes the form of the objects called *vṛtti*, and the wrong reflection of *puruṣa* in *vṛtti* is recognised as cognition. Hence, *Yoga* -the counterpart of *Sāṇkhya*- aims at "*citta-vṛtti-nirodhaḥ*,"[65] which means the suppression of the modifications of the *buddhi* (*vṛtti*) to realise the principle of Pure Self. It implies that the noumenal consciousness is represented by *puruṣa*; whereas, the phenomenal consciousness or cognition is represented by *buddhi*. The logical conclusion of this would be the consciousness does not observe or perceive objects directly. The external objects are never apprehended by the cognisor. In the process of cognition, *buddhi* plays an active part where *puruṣa* remains passive. It suggests that the substratum of consciousness is different from the substratum of the act of cognition. To be conscious and devoid of cognition is an absurdity and so, Jain view criticises *Sāṅkhya* position. Jain reiterates that cognition and consciousness are not separate entities, and cognition is the direct apprehension of pure consciousness. It does not mean creation or reflection, but the illumination of the already existing objects.[66]

Advaita Vedanta accepts that the soul is pure consciousness, and the soul and consciousness are identical. Consciousness has transcendental and transactional dimensions. The transcendental consciousness is the principle of pure knowledge, and transactional consciousness is the principle of empirical knowledge. Advaitin advocates that the pure conscious soul present in all modes of consciousness (attributive-transactional knowledge) as a witness consciousness (*sākṣi*). Since it is indifferent and inactive, the transcendental consciousness is unaffected by the cognitive

65 YS: 1. 2.

66 Cf. PM: 1.1.2-4.

process of the transactional sphere. Thus, when the advaitin says that the soul is identical to the pure consciousness, it totally precludes from transactional modes of consciousness, which is the principle of empirical cognition. Thus, the modes of consciousness do not have a real existence. They (*vyavahārikasatta*) are illusion in comparison with the pure absolute existence (*pāramārthikasatta*) of consciousness. For Jaina, the Advaitin view that the pure knowing is identical with the soul and empirical knowing is aloof from it seems to be untenable and logically unsound. If it is so, the operation of cognition cannot really be considered 'as having cognitive value and as owned by the soul.'[67] For Advaitin, *anthakaraṇa vṛitti*, which is the cause of attributive knowledge, is essentially physical. Jaina alleges that how material or physical becomes the source of knowledge, which has a spiritual nature.

According to Jainas, the self-luminous soul is immanent in all its modes and forms. The soul as the substance exists in changes, and so, attributive knowledge as the modification is identical in essence with the soul. The consciousness and the soul are not absolutely identical in Jainism, and they are not absolutely different also. Consciousness and cognition have the same substratum but different in their state of existence because the causal state of cognition is consciousness, and cognition is the manifested state of consciousness. The causal state and its manifestation are not physical or material transformation. Jaina would say that 'both the consciousness and the cognition exist in one eternal, but changeable reality and both are equally real.'[68] Therefore, according to Jainism, cognition is the self-modification of consciousness to illumine itself and the object.

---

67 Hari Mohan Bhattacharya, *Jaina Logic and Epistemology*, p. 31.

68 Indra Chandra Shastri, *Jain Epistemology*, p. 156.

2.5 Modes of the Soul

All souls are of one but of the same kind insofar as the possession of the essential nature, i.e., the consciousness. However, the possession of modes demarcates souls into two: Worldly souls (*saṃsāra)* and Liberated souls (*mukta).*[69] The worldly souls are souls in bondage. They have embodied life in the concrete world under the influence of karma. The liberated souls exist in the pure and free-state of the soul. They are emancipated from the clutches of karma and attained the soul's pristine nature of intrinsic purity. The worldly souls have to undergo transmigration from one birth to another, but liberated souls have no more transmigration. In general, there are three types of classification of worldly souls; according to the place of their existence, according to the possession of the mind and according to the mobility of the soul.

2.5.1 Modification according to the Abode of Soul's Existence

The worldly souls have divided into four, according to the abode of their existence. They come into existence physically by three ways; by manifestation, by coagulation, or by generation.[70]

1. *Devagati-* the class of gods living in the abode of gods.
2. *Manusyagati-* the human being living in this world.

---

69 TS: 2. 10. *Saṃsāriṇo muktāś ca*.

70 Cf. TS: 2. 32-36. The manifestation means the creation without any material basis such as the heavenly and hellish bodies. The coagulation takes place out of existing matter. The sub-human creatures up to five sensed beings belong to this group. All five sensed beings including human beings come into existence partly coagulation and partly by generation. Cf. Walther Schubring, *Doctrine of Jaina*, translated by Wolfgang Beurlen (Delhi: Motilal Banarasidass, 1962), p. 140. (Hereafter, Walther Schubring, *Doctrine of Jaina*).

3. *Triyagati-* the sub-human creatures including botanical kingdom living in this world.
4. *Narakagati-* the infernal or beings living in hell.

2.5.2 Modification according to the Mobility of the Souls

According to the mobility of the souls, they are divided into two;

1. *Trasa-* Mobile
2. *Sthāvara* -Immobile

Mobile beings can move from one place to another. Immobile beings cannot move from one place to another. The movement here means voluntary movements and not automatic movements for the maintenance of life.[71] All immobile beings are one-sensed organisms such as earth-bodied, water-bodied, fire-bodied, air-bodied and plant-bodied beings. Mobile beings are those with two or more sensed organisms such as two-sensed (worms, leeches, molluscs, etc.), three-sensed (ants, fleas, centipedes, etc.), four-sensed (wasps, flies, butterflies, etc.), five-sensed (fish, birds, humans, infernals, gods, etc.) beings.

2.5.3 Modification according to the Possession of Mind

Among these five-sensed souls, there is distinction of soul according to the possession of the mind. Based on the possession of mind, souls are divided into two:

1. *Saṁjñi* - Souls those have the possession of the mind
2. *Asamjñi* - Souls those have no possession of the mind.

71 Cf. *Tattvārtha Sūtra*: *That Which Is*, trans. By Nathmal Tatia, p. 42.

Mind has two aspects; psychic mind (*bhāva-manas*) and physical mind (*dravya-manas*). The psychic mind is the spiritual capacity, and the physical mind is a cluster of atoms. The possession of mind implies the souls which possess both aspect and exclusion of one are considered to be souls without mind.[72]

2.6 Karma

Notwithstanding the pristine nature of the soul is identical to the intrinsic purity of consciousness, the impure and imperfect worldly existence of the soul presupposes the corruption that has crept into the original nature of the soul. The source of corruption of the soul is its association with karma. Karma impedes the nature of the soul. This corruptive element assumes different names in different systems, such as unseen potency (*adṛṣṭa*, *apūrva*), predisposition (*vāsanā*), energy (*śakti*), trap (*pāśa*), and illusion (*māyā*). Further, Karma behaves as a *modus operandi* in the interaction between the sentient and the non-sentient substance. Here, the study investigates the nature, characteristics, types, and function of karma.

2.6.1 The Nature and Cause of Karma

Tattvārtha Sūtra defines Karma as: "The material particles attracted to the soul are a cause of nature of karma, enter from all sides, cause bondage qualified by the activities of the soul, are subtle clusters of matter, are in the space occupied by the soul, are stationary, are assimilated by all the units of the soul, and are constituted of infinite times and infinite number of atoms."[73] It is the limpid explanation about the origination,

72 Cf. *Tattvārtha Sūtra*: *That Which Is*, trans. By Nathmal Tatia, p. 40.

73 TS: 8.25.

nāmapratyayāḥ sarvato yogaviśeṣāt sūkṣmaikakṣetrāvagāḍhasthitāḥ sarvātmapradeśeṣv anantānantapradeśāḥ.

formation, nature and characteristics of karma. *Pudgala* (subtle matter) is *ajīva* (substance) that exists independently and eternally. Of these material particles, some (cluster of subtle matter) have inherited the capacity (*yogyta*) of transforming into the form of karma. The fine matter which can become karma permeates in the entire cosmos, which is equal to space (*pradeśā*) occupied by the soul.[74] Through the vibrations of the soul, which is caused by its activity (*yoga*) and motivated by passions (*kaṣāya*), the capable material particles are attracted and drawn to unite themselves to Jīva. Then, they become *karman* and enter into union with a *Jīva*.[75] It is the state of the karmic bondage. *Tattvārtha Sūtra* put forward five conditions of karmic bondage; '*mithyā-darśana* (perverse attitude), *avirati* (non-abstinence), *pramāda* (spiritual inertia). *kaṣāya* (passions), and *yoga* (activity).'[76] It propels that the nature of the dispositions of the soul catalyzes the bondage of karmas.

Karma has two aspects; physical karma (*dravya-karma*) and psychic karma (*bhāva-karma*). The former is āvarna (cover), and the latter is *doṣa* (defects). *Doṣa* obliterates the capacities of the soul. *Āvarana* veils and project the karmic bondage in action. Both are mutually related as cause and effect, each of the other.[77] The *dravya-karma* consists of the material particles and *bhāva-karma* is the mental attitudes and conditions which facilitates the flow of these material particles. In this sense, karma is produced by the activity and passions of which the soul is the cause. Is the Soul, the cause

74 Cf. PS: 2.76; TS: 8.2.

75 Cf. TS: 8.2-.3.

76 TS: 8.1.

77 Cf. AM: 4.

Samayasāra also illustrates this relation to the relation of artisan and pot. As the artisan translates his mental thought of the object into the physical form by his activity, so the soul remains as the cause of the *bhāva-karma* or mental thought of material karma. (SS: 350-354).

of Karma? *Samayasāra* clears the ambiguity and ascertains that "the soul is the substantial cause of its own modifications, but is not the substantial cause of any of the modifications of karmic matter."[78] 'The matter is active, and its combinations and disintegration are produced on account of its nature of change. Thus, the matter changes into the karmic matter by its own merit and respective nature.'[79] So, Karma is not the quality of the soul as *Naiyayikas* holds.[80] Nemicandra presents the Jaina position in the following pregnant verse in *Dravya Sangraha*: "According to the practical standpoint, the soul is the cause of karma modifications. According to the imperfectly ontological standpoint, the soul is the cause of its own conscious dispositions. According to the purely metaphysical view, the soul is the cause of its own pure essential states."[81] To sum up, from the transcendental point of view *pudgala* or matter is the material cause and the *bhāva-karma* is the determining cause of the karmic particles and karmic bondage, and *Jīva* is neither the agent nor the cause of karma. However, from the phenomenal point of view, *Jīva* is the agent and cause of karma.

2.6.2 Relation between Karma and Soul

The nature of Karma is the fine material and subtle particles. It instils into the soul and causes corresponding changes in the soul. It implies that the soul's concrete association

---

78 SS: 82.

edeṇa kāraṇeṇa du kattā ādā *saeṇa bhāveṇa*
poggalakammakadāṇaṁ ṇa du kattā savvabhāvāṇaṁ.

The causality is further explained in 45, 100, and 313.

79 Cf. PS: 2. 75-78.

80 Cf. J.C Sikdar, *Concept of Matter in Jain Philosophy* (Varanasi: P.V Research Institute, 1987) p. 85. (Hereafter, C Sikdar, *Concept of Matter in Jain Philosophy*).

81 DS: 8.

with karmic matters becomes a fabric of a real modification of the active soul.[82] It is an indubious fact that the realistic view of Jainas endorses concrete identity between soul and karmic matter in the state of karmic bondage. Nevertheless, the soul is different from the karmic matter. Here, the modification of the soul has to be understood as the continuity of one's own nature (*tadbhāva*) through change. It reckons that the soul as the substance retains its specific nature and yet assuming ever new states depending on the conditions available.

In fact, there is a beginningless mutual determination between the states of the soul and the depending conditions. Akalanka comments on the definition of the bondage (*Tattvārtha Sūtra*: 8.2) casts light on this beginningless relationship: "the passionate living beings intake matters capable of transformation into karmas. This intake is called the bondage."[83] *Samayasāra* admits that the intrinsic nature of the soul associated with karmic delusion from the beginningless time.[84] Nathmal Tatia interprets it as, "the soul has a number of potencies, and each moment of its existence is an integration of those potencies. The nature of the karmic body, at any moment, is determined by the integrated existence of the soul."[85] He elaborates this mutual relationship between karma and the soul like this:

> The soul is ever-changing by its own nature and, in the state of worldly existence; this change is

82 According to *Sankhya-Yoga* philosophy, the relation of Karma is not with the soul but with the mind or *antaḥkaraṇa* and this *antaḥkaraṇa* is the modification of *prakriti*. Cf. .C Sikdar, *Concept of Matter in Jain Philosophy*, pp.87-89.

83 N. L Jain, *Jaina Karmology: English Translation with Notes on Chapter Eight of Tattvārtha-Rāja-vāartika of Akalanka* (Varanasi: P. V Research Institute, 1991), p. 54.

84 Cf. SS: 89, 313.

85 Nathmal Tatia, *Studies in Jain Philosophy*, p. 223.

> determined by the nature of the karmic matter that is associated with it. The nature of the association of karmic matter is determined by the nature of passions of the soul, the nature of the passions of the soul is determined by the nature of the karmic matter, this mutual determination has no beginning in time, and this explains the apparent difficulty of the first beginning of the process.[86]

Through a series of practices, the *Jīva* must suspend the absorption of new karma (*saṃvara*) and eliminate the already accumulated karma before they come to the realization (*nirjarā*). Constant practice suppresses and annihilates the karmic remnant. Significantaly, it leads to the manifestation of the pristine nature of the soul. It is the state of liberation (*mokṣā*). Having overcome all obstacles, the soul manifests innate capabilities and potentialities.

2.6.3 Four Forms of Karmic Bondage

Passions (*kaṣāya*) and vibrations (*yoga*) of the soul stimulate the flow of karma. Every inflow of karma is followed by the binding of karmic particles to the soul. Bondage is due to the association of the soul with karma. These karmic bondages are in the following four forms:

1. *Prakṛti bandha* - According to the manner of their effect.
2. *Sthiti bandha* - According to the duration of their effect.
3. *Anubhāva bandha* - According to the intensity of their effect.
4. *Pradeśa bandha* - According to their quantity, i.e., according to the number of their *pradeśas*.[87]

86 Nathmal Tatia, *Studies in Jain Philosophy*, p. 226.

87 Cf. TS: 8.4.

The karmic matter obscures the essential nature of the soul. The binding of the nature of the soul is known as *prakṛti bandha*. It disrupts the qualities of the soul. The duration that karmic matter attaches to the soul before it produces the result, is called *sthiti bandha*. The duration of the karmic binding remains until the time of karmic fruition. The fruition of karma demarcates karma from the soul. Again, the *karmaphala* or fruition of karma is determined at the time of attachment by varying degrees of the soul's passions. The varying degree of depth of karmic fruition is known as *anubhāva bandha* and or *rasa bandha*.[88] It naturally undergoes a corresponding quantitative distribution that is drawn towards the soul for attachment. This quantum of the assimilated material particles refers to *pradeśa bandha*. All these karmic bondages are due to either through the activity or the passions of the soul through which it attracts and assimilates karmic particles. Of the above-discussed types of bondage, *prakṛti bandha* and *pradeśa bandha* depend on the degree of the activity concerned, and *sthiti bandha* and *anubhāva bandha* depend on the degree of the passions concerned, respectively.[89]

2.6.4 Types of Karma

The infusion of karma into the soul concurrently procures various repercussions in the soul. All these repercussions confer opacity over the nature of the soul. This obfuscation finds expression in the imperfect existence of the soul. It foils the soul away from its supreme state of perfection and purity. These distorting karmic obscurities are classified into eight.[90]

---

88 Cf. Jaina: Federation of Jain Associations in North America (2020), "The philosophy of Karma and Jain Tattvas." p.3. available from https://www.jaina.org/page/KarmaTattvas; accessed on 11-April 2019.

89 Cf. DS: 33. Pt. Sukhlalji, *Commentary on Tattvārtha Sūtra*, pg. 295.

90 Cf. TS: 8.5-8.13. Cf. Walther Scubring, *The Doctrine of the Jainas*, pp. 179-182; Nathmal Tatia, *Studies in Jain Philosophy*, pp. 232-252

1. ***Jñāna-varaṇiya karma***— It conceals the soul's essential nature, i.e. the consciousness. It disrupts the source of discriminative knowledge. Forayed karmic energy is responsible for the flawed modification of consciousness. The consequential expression of karmic energy obfuscates cognition in five forms. Therefore, there are five sub-types of knowledge covering karma. They are; *matijñāna-varaṇiyakarma* (veiling karma of empirical knowledge), *srutajñāna-varaṇiyakarma* (veiling karma of articulate knowledge), *avadhijñāna-varaṇiyakarma* (veiling karma of clairvoyance), *manahparyayajñāna- varaṇiyakarma* (veiling karma of mind-reading), *and kevalajñāna-varaṇiyakarma* (veiling karma of omniscience).

2. ***Darśana-varaṇiya-karma***— It conceals the soul's power of perfect intuition or indeterminate cognitions. It obliterates the cognition in which one apprehends the generality of an object. There are nine subtypes of *darśana-varaṇiya-karma*. Among these first four the shroud of *cakṣurdarśana* (visual intuition), *acakṣurdarśana* (non-visual intuition), *avadidarśana* (clairvoyant intuition), and *kevaladarśana* (omniscient intuition). Furthermore, it consists of five types of sleep; *nidra* (dozing), *nidrānidra* (sleeping), *pracala* (drowsing), *pracalāprachala* (sleep-walking), and *styānagrdhi* (torpidity).

3. ***Mohṇīya karma***— It engenders delusion in the soul concerning its own true nature. This delusion is theoretical and practical. It is responsible for the cycle of birth and death. It deludes the right vision and right conduct, and thus, there are *darśana mohṇīya karma* (vision deluding karma) and *cāritra mohṇīya karma* (conduct deluding karma). It blurs the right world view and thwarts activity leading to the right conduct, respectively. There are three kinds of *darśana mohṇīya karma* and twenty-five kinds of *cāritra mohṇīya karma*.

4. *Antarāya karma*— It obstructs the inherent energy of the soul. This prevents the soul from attaining liberation. It also restricts the spiritual and ethical progress of the soul. The five varieties of *antarāya karma* arrest the soul's energies of beneficence, gain, satisfaction, comfort and power, respectively.

5. *Vedṇīya karma*— Detaining the original bliss of the soul, *vedṇīya karma* stimulates earthly pleasure and pain. It is the object of sense-mind perception. It engenders the experience of comfort and discomfort. *Satavedaṇīya* (pleasant feelings) and *asatvedaṇīiya* (painful feelings) are the two subtypes of *vedṇīya karma*. These two feelings are related to the body and mind.

6. *Nāma karma*— It distorts the non-corporeal existence of the soul. It determines the realms of birth (hell, lower animal, human and heaven) and different formulations of the body with its limitations, qualities, and faculties (species of being, five types of body, parts and limbs and logistics of the body). Thus, *nāma karma* functions as a constitutive element in the formation of the embodiment of the soul. The forty-two sub-types of *nāma karma* calibrate the shape of the body and inhabitants of those realms of birth.

7. *Gotra karma*— It disrupts the equal status of the soul. It determines the caste, family, society, lineage, personality and the high as well as low status of an individual. *n*āma *karma* and *gotra karma* are related to each other because they are associated with the forms and the state of the body and the mental states.

8. *Āyuṣ karma* – It delineates the span of life in one birth. It constrains the eternal existence of the soul and curtails the longevity of birth. To the fructifying of this karma, the being succumbed to death. The consequential distinctions of āyuṣ *karma* represent the life span of infernal beings, sub-human beings, human beings, and heavenly beings.

2.6.5 *Ghāti* Karma and *Aghāti* Karma

Eight karmas are classified into two groups; *Ghāti* karma and *Aghāti* karma. *Ghāti* karmas include *jñāna-varaṇiya karma, darśana varaṇiya karma, mohṇīya karma,* and *antarāya karma.* They obliterate the pure nature and capacity of the soul. It enervates the inherent qualities of the soul (Infinite knowledge, infinite intuition, infinite bliss, and infinite energy). Among these obscuring karmas, some are completely obscuring, and some are partially obscuring. For example, of the sub-types of *jñāna*-varaṇiya *karma*, *kevala* is the completely obscuring karma; whereas, all other four come under the partially obscuring karmas. The function of the former is 'to cover the wholeness or the fullness of knowledge,' and the function of the latter is 'to effect privation of the remainder knowledge.'[91] *Aghāti* karmas are *vedṇīya karma, nā*ma *karma, gotra karma*, and āyuṣ *karma*. They do not obliterate the original nature of the soul. However, they associate with the material nature of the soul. When a person destroys all of his *ghāti* karmas, one attains *kevalajñāna*. At that time one is known as *Arihant*. One continues to live one's human life until all *aghāti* karmas are destroyed, and it is the state where the soul is freed from material existence.

2.7 Soul and Body

The interaction between the soul (*jīva*) and non-soul (*pudgalāstikāya*) is responsible for the worldly existence of the soul.[92] Through the association of the matter, the soul gets a

91 Nathmal Tatia, *Studies in Jain Philosophy*, pg. 240

92 In Jain metaphysics, *Ajīva* cannot be translated simply as the matter alone, since it has endowed with certain non-material categories also such as *Dharmāstikāya* (the medium of motion), *Adharmāstikāya*

form, i.e., the body. Thus, the body is a composite of material and spiritual nature. Consciousness is the spiritual basis of the body. Owing to the different kinds of *nāma-karma*, there are different formations of the body.[93] Ācārya Kundakunda deliberates the procedure of the formation of the body: "The cluster (*skandha*) of matter (*pudgala*) bound earlier with the soul (*jīva*) in form of material-karmas (*dravya-karma*), certainly transform themselves into the body, as the soul (*jīva*) adopts a new body on change of its mode (*paryāya*)."[94] On account of their nature of formation and functions, there are five types of bodies. They are *audārika*, *vaikriya*, āhāraka, *taijasa* and *kārmaṇa*.[95]

Audārika or gross body is the perceptible material body. The external physical actions leave their imprint on the gross body. It can experience external and internal objects through the operation of the sense organs. *Vaikriya* or transformation bodies avail the power of invisibility and the capacity to transform their shapes. It is the type of body that can assume various forms, such as subtle, huge, light, heavy, one, and many.

(the medium of rest), *Akāśāstikāya* (space), and *Addhāsamaya* (time). Among these substances, only *Pudgalāstikāya* has gross form and hence it is called *rūpin*, the substance that has form.

93 Karma obscures and distorts the attributes of the soul, is classified into eight types. Among these eight, *nāma karma* obscures the non-corporeal existence of the soul, and produces the body with its limitations, qualities, faculties, etc. There are forty-two sub-types of *Nāma karma*. Cf. TS: 8.12.

94 PS: 2.79.

orālio ya deho deho veuvvio ya tejasio
āhāraya kammio poggladavvappgā savve.

95 TS: 2.37. "*audārika-vaikriyā-hāraka-taijasa-karmaṇāni* śarīrāṇi"
The explanation of five types of bodies is mainly based on the text *Tattvārtha Sūtra* (2.37-49.). Cf. Pt. Sukhlaji's commentary on *Tattvārtha Sūtra* (2000) and Nathmal Tatia, *Tattvārtha Sūtra: That Which Is* (1994).

It is formed at birth by descent and acquired by the potential power through practising spiritual austerities. The āhāraka or translocation body (conveyance body) is made from the clusters of non-obstructive and non-obstructed matters that are auspicious, white, and pure[96]. This body is linked to the super-ordinary powers of a monk who is well versed in the fourteen *Purva* texts.[97] This body has two purposes; seeking knowledge on subtle problems from the distant omniscient one and avoiding injury to subtle living beings. The *taijasa* is made of fiery particles (*taijasa*) and formed by the power of potential. It has two functions; ordinary and extra-ordinary. The ordinary function of it is 'to digest food for the nourishment of the gross body.' The extra-ordinary function performs 'through certain austerities.' It inherits the capacity of transmitting hot rays to burn or cold rays to cool an object at a distance.' *Kārmaṇa* body is the inner subtlest body that forms the basis of all the mental and physical activities. It is known as the basket that contains all the karmic particles of the soul. It constitutes the occasioning cause of all bodily functioning whatsoever.

Modes have the character of impermanence and change. Hence, the relation between the bodies with matter and the soul is not eternal. Although all bodies except the gross one are closely linked with the soul, the infinite-fold, beginningless association with the soul and non-resisting yields a unique status in the last two bodies.[98]'The five bodies are progressively

96 Non-obstructed matters-The clusters of matter have free impeded movement. Auspicious-The clusters of matter are pleasant in colour, odour, touch and taste and those they produce merit. White and pure-The clusters of matter are transparent, shiny and conducive to harmless conduct.

97 Cf. TS: 2.49; śubhaṃ *viśudham avyāghāti cāhārakaṃ pramattasaṃyatasyaiva*.

98 Non-resistance means that it gains entrance everywhere and suffer no

finer or subtler.[99] The term finer or subtler and grosser indicates the looseness and tightness of the construction. Thus, *audārika* is the grossest one, and *kārmaṇa* is the subtlest form of the body. All five types of body are clusters of matter. [100] Among these, the latter number of the cluster of the matter in one body is innumerable and larger than the former body. The possessions of atomic aggregates of the five bodies are progressively bigger.[101]

They perform some direct and indirect functions.[102] The chief purpose of the body is to be the instrument of functioning. The first three bodies have cognitive organs to experience pleasure and pain. They are capable of accumulating fresh karma and suppressing past karma. The fiery body inflicts curse and bestows benefit from its spiritual potentiality. Although the *kārmaṇa* body cannot serve any of the direct purposes like others, it is the underlying cause for all the instrumentality. *Kārmaṇa* body is devoid of any direct instrumental purposes, but it remains as the cause of all-purpose. Thus, it has an indirect instrumentality. The specific bodily existence of the individual consists of more than one body. There are two-body combination, three-body combinations, and four- body combinations. According to Jainism, a worldly soul can possess

---

resistance anywhere in the world. Some Jain learners would say that there is no beginningless association of the worldly soul with *taijasa*, because its production from labdhi or mental faculty commencing with luminous and Karmic body, up to four bodies can be had simultaneously by a single soul. Cf. TS: 2.44; J.C Sikdar, *Concept of Matter in Jain Philosophy*, p. 191; Walther Schubring, *The Doctrine of Jainas*, p. 139.

99 Cf. TS: 2.38; *paraṃ paraṃ sūkṣmam.*

100 Cf. PS: 2.79. *pudgaladravyātmakaḥ sarvaṃ.*

101 Cf. TS: 2.39-40.

pradeśato 'saṃkhyeyaguṇaṃ prāk taijasāt.

anantaguṇe pare.

102 Cf. TS: 2.45.

four at the most, and it cannot possess all the five of them.[103] Therefore, the study on the constitution and function of the body exhibits the ordinary and extraordinary potentiality or capacity (*yogyata*) of the body.

2.8 Conclusion

The interpretive exploration of the metaphysical foundations of Jaina philosophy establishes a framework for understanding *yogi-pratyakṣa*. In Jain thought, substance (*dravya*) has endowed with innumerable qualities (*guṇa*) and modes (*paryāya*). Both the soul (*jīva*) and non-soul (*ajīva*) are considered substances that exist independently and eternally. That which exists is the object (*artha*) of knowledge, possessing essential qualities and accidental modes. The consciousness is the essential quality and defining attribute of the soul. This consciousness drive (*upayoga*) is the operational source of all types of cognition. In other words, cognition is the manifestation of objects by the self-luminous Self through its faculty of knowing. Thus, the soul is, as the substratum of consciousness, the subject as well as the instrument of cognition. However, this manifestation of identity is impeded by different degrees of karmic influences. It results in different degrees of cognition and enhances the possibilities and potentialities of an embodied soul. Thus, the inheritance of higher degrees of cognition is the ramification of the absolute removal of Karma and manifestation of the pure nature of the Soul. In summary, this chapter provides a comprehensive view of the metaphysics of cognition as it operates in *yogi-pratyakṣa*, highlighting how the process of knowledge and its manifestations are influenced by the state of the Soul and its karmic encumbrances.

103 *Vaikriya* and āhāraka formation are never exercised simultaneously because the formation of the former one is in a state of negligence whereas the formation of the latter one is in a state of lack of negligence ensures on account of the possibility of spiritual purification. Cf. Walther Schubring, *The Doctrine of Jainas*, p. 139.

CHAPTER 3

The Psychological and Epistemological Backup of Yogi-Pratyakṣa: *Pramāna-Pratyakṣa-Yogi-Pratyakṣa*

Jaina epistemology is deeply intertwined with Jaina psychology, illustrating how an understanding of cognitive processes also addresses psychological concerns. Knowledge in Jain philosophy is defined by three fundamental elements: the subject, the object, and the means of knowledge. Building on previous discussions about the metaphysical nature of these components, this chapter critically examines the means of knowledge (*pramāṇa*) that connect the subject and object. It also explores the outcomes or results of knowledge (*prama*). In Jainism, the operative force (*pramāṇa*) is integral to both cognitive and psychological aspects of experience. *Yogi-pratyakṣa* is included in the classification of *pramāṇa*, highlighting its role in this framework. Therefore, this chapter investigates the epistemological and psychological foundations of *yogi-pratyakṣa*. The chapter begins with an interpretive analysis of Jaina concepts of *pramāṇa* and *pratyakṣa*, progressing to substantiate the cognitive and psychological implications of *yogi-pratyakṣa*. The objective is to validate *yogi-pratyakṣa* as a legitimate and effective component of the cognitive process.

3.1 Cognition as Pramāna

The knowledge (*jñāna*) can be right or wrong. In Indian epistemology, the right knowledge is *prama*, and wrong knowledge is *aprama*. Jaina defines *prama* as 'the right determination of the nature of reality'.[1] Reality is that which has the objective and independent existence (*sat*). The source and the means of the right judgement of the nature of reality is *pramāṇa*. The term *pramāṇa* has derived from the root '*mā*', which means 'to measure' with the prefix '*pra*', which has an intensive sense, and by adding suffix *yut* or '*anat*' in the instrumental sense. Collectively, it suggests a means of the right measurement. All means or causes are not *pramāṇa*. Only the efficient cause (*karaṇa*) becomes *pramāṇa*. For valid knowledge, the immediate cause is the efficient cause (*karaṇa*) and specific condition, other than the causes (*kāraṇa*) like the subject and object. Jaina logicians, Vādidevasūri and Hemachandrasūri, admit the operative and instrumental nature of *pramāṇa*.[2] It is the operative cause and the instrumental for the cognition because that is the instrument with regard to an act, which is being used by an agent, that act is unfailingly accomplished, and otherwise, that act is never accomplished, for instance, axe with regard to cutting. Thus, *pramāṇa* is the organ or source of the right knowledge. "There cannot be any right understanding of thing except by means of *pramāna*. A subject arrives at the valid knowledge of objects by means of *pramāna*, for the existence and nature of objects are to be ascertained only by such cognitions as are

1 PM: 1.1.1. no. 5.

2 Cf. PM: 1.1.8.26; PNT: 1.5.

based on *pramāna*."[3] *Prama* is the right determination of the nature of the object, and therefore, *pramāṇa* is the mean for the determination of the nature of the object.

Indian epistemology has dealt with the two streams of thought with regard to the nature of *pramāṇa*. The first view considers *pramāṇa* as physical contact, and the second view upholds *pramāṇa* as purely psychic grasping. *Ny*āya and Jaina are the forefront adherents of these views, respectively. Like the Jaina logicians, Annaṁbhaṭṭa, the *Ny*āya logician, reiterates that the competency of *pramāṇa* remains in its capacity of being the efficient condition of right knowledge.[4] The old *Nayāyika* School conflates the function (*vyapāra*) as well as the object that has the function (*vyapārāvat*) in the calibration of *karaṇa*. Later *Nayāyika* lends emphasis on the functioning object in the conception of *karaṇa*. Annambhaṭṭa in *Tarkasaṅgraha* states: "*Vyāpāravat asādharanam kāraṇam karaṇam.*"[5] *Pramāṇa* is an operative special cause in every instance of knowledge. Valid knowledge should appear as a natural sequel. An operative cause devoid of the nature of *vyapārāvat* can never become *karaṇa*. Thus, there is indistinguishable unity between the cause and the function. *Nayāyika* would say that the sense-object contact (*sannikarṣa*) becomes the special cause (*asādharanam karaṇam*) in perceptual cognition and so, sense-object contact is *pramāṇa*. Udyotakara defines *pramāṇa*, "*upalabdhihetuḥ pramāṇam.*"[6] It means that the cause of valid

---

3 Satish Chandra Chatterjee, *The Nyāya Theory of Knowledge* ((New Delhi: Rupa Publications, 2015), p. 57. (Hereafter, Satish Chandra Chatterjee, *The Nyāya Theory of Knowledge*).

4 Cf. *Tarkasaṅgraha*: 42, 43, 46. Cf. Annambhaṭṭa, *Tarkasaṁgraha-Dīpikā* on *Tarkasaṁgraha*: translated and elucidated by Gopinath BhattĀcārya (Kolkatta: Sri Kamal Mitra for Progressive Publishers, 2009 reprint). (Hereafter, *Tarkasaṁgraha*).

5 *Tarkasaṅgraha*: 42.

6 *Nyāyavārtika*: 1.1.1.

cognition is *pramāṇa*. Different from other *hetu*, *pramāṇa* has a distinguishing feature, i.e., *atiśaya*, which is the highest efficiency. It is termed as *sādhkatamatva* (the most efficient ground). Vacaspatimiśra stands for this the highest efficiency of pramāṇa-hood. Jayanta Bhaṭṭa endorses *kāraṇasāmagrivāda* or the doctrine of the assemblage of causes on which pramāṇa depends. He demarcates the nature of *pramāṇa* like this: "*Avyabhicārinimasaṁdigdhāṁ arthopalabdhaṁ. vidadhati bodhābodhasvabāvā sāmagri arthopalabdham.*"[7] It denotes that the valid cognition of object (*arthopalabdham*) is definite (*asaṁdigdhāṁ*) and should be free from contradiction and inconsistency (*avyabhicāri*). It consists of both conscious (*bodha*) and unconscious (*abodha*) elements. The conscious element is the substratum of conscious activity, i.e., the soul and its quality, i.e., the consciousness. The unconscious elements are sense-organs, mind, and everything relevant to the generation of knowledge. It signifies the inclusion of physical and psychical elements in the cognitive process. Hence, *pramāṇa* is the complex of physical and psychical conditions that are actually operative in bringing about a valid and definite cognition of objects. In this regard, 'it is the assemblage of specific conditions, other than the subject and the object, which does not normally fail to produce valid knowledge.'[8] To encapsulate *Nyāya darśana* discussion of *pramāṇa*, there are three distinct but correlated views; (i) *pramāṇa* as sense organ (*indriya*), (ii) *pramāṇa* as the contact or proximity (*sannikarṣa*) of sense organ and object, and (iii) *pramāṇa* as the assemblage (*sāmagri*) of different conscious and unconscious elements.

---

7 *Nyāyamanjari*: p. 19. Jayanta Bhaṭṭa, *Nyāyamañjarī of Jayanta Bhaṭṭa with the Commentary of Granthi-bhaṅga by Cakradhara*, edited by Gaurinath Sastri, Part 1–3, M. M. Śivakumāraśāstri-Granthamālā 5 (Vārāṇasī: Sampūrṇānand Saṃskrta Viśvavidyālaya, 1984). (Hereafter. *Nyāyamanjari*).

8 *Nyāyamanjari*: p. 15.

Jaina and *Nyāya* unanimously promulgate *pramāṇa* as the operative condition for the right determination of an object. Concerning the nature of *pramāṇa*, Jaina has a different view from *Nyāya*. Jaina holds that the self and cognition are identical in nature, and valid knowledge is cognition of the self and not-self.[9] Jaina excoriates the unspecific definition of *pramāṇa*, which states that *hetu* of the knowledge is *pramāṇa*, because it has over coverage (*ativyāpti*). All the antecedent conditions are not *pramāṇa*, such as *akaśa* for pot. Thus, specifically, *pramāṇa* is the immediate, antecedent and efficient condition for *prama*. For Jainism, the cognition is *pramāṇa*. Therefore, they dismiss the sense organ, proximity, and assemblage of elements as valid means of knowledge (*pramāṇa*). Hemachandrasūri enumerates the inefficiency of these elements like this: "Now, that alone is the instrumental case of cognition on the operation of which the object is immediately known. It is a fact that cognition of object does not occur even in the presence of such conditions as sense-organ, its contact, if the cognition is absent."[10] Thus, these elements are not *pramāṇa*.

According to Jainism, the sense organ cannot be *pramāṇa* because they are unconscious and material. Vādidevasūri in *Pramāṇa-Naya-Tattvālokālaṃkāra* vindicates the definite instrumentality of the conscious self in the cognition by explaining the constitution and function of the two aspects of the senses; *drvyendriya* and *bhāvendriya*. Of these, *drvyendriya* is caused "by the manifestation of the corresponding nāma-karma", and *bhāvendriya* is brought into being "by the

9 The self is the subject of knowledge, and the not-self is the object of knowledge. In the realm of Jaina epistemology, the not-self is not *Ajiva* or non-self, which is the substance bereft of consciousness. The not-self can be conscious and unconscious objects of knowledge (*artha*).

10 PM: 1.1.8.25.

subsidence and destruction of the obscuring karma and obstructive karma frustrating the relevant capacity."[11] *Drvyendriya* is 'the clusters of matter (*pudgala*) possessed of a particular form and definite shape (*niyathākārām*)', and *bhāvendriya* is 'the modes of the soul possessed of the nature of consciousness (*upayoga*).'[12] *Draveyendriya* is the material sense organ, and cannot be the cause of the knowledge without its spiritual counterpart (*bhāvendriya*). *Bhāvendriya* has endowed with psychic functions. The revelatory power of the spiritual counterpart (*bhāvendriya*) of the sense organ is conferred by consciousness only. Accepting *bhāvendriya* as the *pramāna* is equal to accept Jainas contempt of inability of the material sense organ as the *pramāna*. Since it is unconscious, it cannot be an invariable instrument for cognition. Whatever is unconscious cannot be the instrumental cause as in the case of pot or cloth. The constituent element of Indriya (sense organ) is matter, which is unconscious by nature. The unconsciousness of an instrument of cognition is a contradictory condition (*bādha*) to the constitution of any valid cognitive process. Unconscious and material sense organ and the proximity cannot be the immediate cause of the cognition that which is conscious and spiritual by its nature.

A conscious *pramāna* implies self-illuminating or self-manifesting *pramāna*. The unconscious sense organ and the proximity of the sense organ are inefficient conditions to be the immediate cause or operative cause for the cognition of self. Pure self is without any sensory qualities and is characterised by consciousness, and thus, the self is entirely beyond sense

---

11 PM: 1.1. 21. no. 77.

12 Cf. TS: 2.15; PM: 1.1. no. 22-23.
draveyendriyaṁ niyathākārāḥ pudgalāḥ
bhavendriyaṁ labdyupayogai.

perception.[13] *Pramāṇa-naya-tattvālokālaṅkāraḥ* declares that the unconscious thing, whether the sense organ or the proximity, "is not the instrument of determining the Self, as it is unconscious like a pillar; nor for determining the object as that which is incapable, as a pitcher, of determining the self is incapable of that also."[14] What is not conscious cannot manifest itself and objects. Thus, the sense organ is not the operative and immediate cause. Jaina contempts *Nyāya* views by reiterating that the object-revealer should be the self-revealer. The contact or the proximity (*sannikarṣa*) of the sense organ with the object is also unconscious. Whatever is unconscious cannot be the instrumental cause as in the case of pot or cloth. Proximity cannot generate knowledge of the object. The *Nyāya* contention, that proximity can reveal the object without being the self-revealer, is repudiated by Jaina by indicating the challenge of the fallacy, i.e., *infinitum regressum*. The need for another lamp-light to reveal the present lamp light will unendingly demand another.[15] Therefore, they can never become instrumental in the production of valid knowledge about self. The proximity falls short to produce valid knowledge invariably.

The sense organ is unconscious and cannot reveal the object. According to Jaina doctrine, an object has innumerable aspects. Even though sense organ is instrumental for the manifestation of some aspects of an object, it cannot manifest the totality of an object. The innumerable aspects of an existent object are not cognisable for sense organs, and therefore, it cannot rightly determine the nature of an object. They

---

13 Cf. SS: 49.

14 PNT: 1.5

> *na khalv asya svanirṇītau karaṇatvam staṃbhāder ivācetanatvāt;*
> *nāpyartha niścitau svaniścitāv akaraṇasya kumbhāder*
> *iva tatrāpy akaraṇatvāt.*

15 Cf. PNT: p. 28.

are not instrumental in the procuration of valid knowledge about itself and other objects. Hence, sense organs are not *Svanirṇayaḥ* and *paranirṇayaḥ*, which implies that they never become *pramāṇa*.

Hari Mohan Bhattacharyya in *Jaina Logic and Epistemology* summarises the inability of sense organs, mind, and the contact of sense organs to be *pamāṇa* for a valid cognition:

> For, to the Jaina the nature of the object is *aprakāśa*, unconscious and unrevealing and, as such, cannot determine what is *svaprakāśa*, which *jñāna* is. The senses are no better off. They are evidently *jada* and must, therefore, be ruled out of court as in any determinant of knowledge; and manas as kin of the senses must share the same fate. And lastly, *sannikarṣa* or sense-object contact, the much vaunted instrument of Naiyāyika, which not only does not bear scrutiny by the Jaina either as a case of samyoga or as a case of samvaya or as a case of their permutation and combination, but also fails miserably as an instrument of *pamāṇa*, being a relation of whatever sort it may be, between elements that are themselves unconscious and unrevealing, cannot have anything to do with the effectuation of *pamāṇa* which, as *jñāna*, is self-revealing and self-generating.[16]

Pramāṇa cannot be the assemblage of different elements. Prabhācandra logically dismays this precarious philosophical position.[17] According to Jainas, an aggregate of unconscious

16 Hari Mohan Bhattacharyya, *Jaina Logic and Epistemology*, p. 78.

17 Cf. *Premeyakamalamārtaṇḍa*: p. 2. Cf. Prabhacandra, *Premeyakamalamārtaṇḍa*: the Commentary on Manikyanaṇdi's *Pariksāmukha* (Bombay: Nirnaya Nagar Press, 1941). (Hereafter, PKM).

elements cannot become the most efficient of *prama*, which is conscious in nature and existence. Another objection of him is that whose intrinsic nature has already established can only serve as a means of a proof; otherwise, it has no right to be called as *pramāṇa*. Therefore, the complex of different elements cannot fulfil the function of *pramāṇa*. In this regard, Jaina impeccably declares that sense organs, the proximity of sense organ, and the assemblage of different elements can never invariably produce valid knowledge.

Here, Jaina put forward a unique conception of *pramāṇa*. Siddhasena Divakara, in *Nyāyavatāra*, renders a classical definition of *pramāṇa*: "*Pramāṇam svaparābhāsi jñānaṁ bādhavivarjitam*."[18] '*Pramāṇa* is the knowledge which illumines itself (*sva*) and other objects (*parā*) without any obstruction (*bādha*).' Vādidevasūri in *Pramāṇa-naya-tattvālokālaṅkāraḥ* defines *Pramāṇa* as "*sva-para vyvasāyi jñānaṁ pramāṇam*."[19] '*Pramāṇa* is that which manifests itself (*sva*) and manifest the true nature of objects (*para*).' Jaina critique of *Nyāya* logically asserts that the sense organ, the contact or proximity and the assemblage are insufficient instruments to reveal itself and other. Therefore, Jaina endorses cognition as *pramāṇa*. The cognition is self-revelatory (*sva*) and object-revelatory (*para*). 'Being the modification of the conscious self, the cognition partakes of its own nature and also determined by it.'[20] To determine the multifaceted nature and existence of reality, Siddhasena claims the exclusivity of the cognition as *pramāṇa,* where other unconscious and limited instruments crumble. He says, "Owing to the impossibility of all phenomena being invalid, cognition as *pramāṇa* is evidently

18 *Nyāyavatāra*: 1. Cf. Siddhasensa Divaraka, *Nyāyavatāra*, edited with introduction and notes Satya Ranjan Banarjee (Calcutta: Sanskrit Book Depot(P) Ltd, 1981). (Hereafter, NV).

19 PNT: 1.2.

20 Hari Mohan Bhattacharyya, *Jaina Logic and Epistemology*, p. 42.

a determinant of Self and other things, and serves to establish both."[21] Since cognition is the means of right determination of the nature of reality, Jaina claims cognition as *pramāna*. Hemachandrasūri enumerates cognition as *pramāṇa* after referring to the definition of *pramāṇa* like this:

> That which is the instrument of authentic cognition is the organ of knowledge, the insertion of the word instrument is intended for the exclusion of the subject and the object, and thus ends in proving that the organ of knowledge is none other than the instrumental case. Such being the case, the most effective condition is certainly none else than the cognition, in as much as it is immediately followed by the effect and so that the cognition alone should be accepted as the organ of knowledge.[22]

An instrument is that which is being used by an agent and without which the act remains unaccomplished. The instrumental application of *pramāṇa* definitely assumes an act of cognition. The cognition is *pramāṇa* on the operation of which the object is immediately known. Vādidevasūri asserts it like this: "Because of the instrumentality of the cognition in bringing about certain knowledge regarding the Self and not-self, it is *sadhana* or the instrument, that which effects."[23] In this sense, the cognition is *pramāṇa*.

Pramāṇa is valid knowledge because pramāṇa-hood cannot be met with otherwise. Pramāṇa-hood (*hetu*) of cognition is not unproved, not contradictory and not doubtful. Positively, it is proved, compatible, and clear. It

---

21 NV: 7. *pramāṇaṁ khānyaniścāyi dravyasiddhvo prasidhyathi.*

22 PM: 1.1.8. no. 26.

23 PNT: 6. 15.

pramāṇaṃ hi karaṇākhyaṃ sādhanam,
sva-para vyvasitau sādhakatamatvāt.

contains no matter (*vipakṣa*) that invalidates the existence of valid knowledge. Therefore, wherever valid knowledge is absent, there is the absence of the pramāṇa-hood. Also, wherever there is pramāṇa-hood, there is valid knowledge.[24] Vādidevasūri cogently claims that the cognition satisfies the conditions of a *pramāṇa*. Cognition as *pramāṇa* functions 'to accept agreeable objects, to reject the disagreeable objects and to make indifference towards negligible objects.'[25] The object is placed under three heads; what is to be avoided, what is to be accepted and what is to be ignored. Cognition distinguishes objects as acceptable, avoidable and ignorable.[26] Thus, cognition as *pramāṇa* makes one to accept, discard and indifferent towards the object.

Sidhhsena Divāraka and Vādidevasūri acclaim that the calibration of desirable and undesirable or acceptable and ignorable is the mediate effect of ordinary cognition. The immediate effect of both transactional and transcendental cognition is 'the removal of ignorance'. However, the mediate effect of absolute cognition (*kevala*) is 'bliss and equanimity'.[27] The material sense organs, including the mind and the contact or proximity (*sannikarṣa*), are insufficient to produce such a result. Henceforth, they miserably fail to be instrumental in the production of valid knowledge.[28]

Thus, cognition as *pramāṇa* is the extraordinary cause of the manifestation of self and object. And also, cognition

---

24 Cf. PNT: pp. 17-22.

25 PNT: 1.3.

abhimatānabhimata-vastu svīkāra-tiraskāra-kṣamaṃ hi pramāṇam ato jñānam evedam.

26 Cf. PM: 1.1.2. no. 10.

27 Cf. NV: 28; PNT: 6. 2-5.

28 Cf. PNT: 1. 4.

na vai saṃnikarṣāder ajñānasya prāmāṇyam upapannam, tasyarthāntarasyeva svārtha vyavasiyau sādhkatamat vānupapatteḥ.

as *pramāṇa* is free from contradiction and inconsistency because it 'determines the nature of an object free from doubt, error, and inattention. It is opposed to all forms of false apprehension.'[29] The right judgement is the prerequisite for the right knowledge (*prama*). Thus, the resultant of cognition is "the illumination of the object" (*artha prakāśa*), i.e., the cognition of the object, and "the cessation of the ignorance" (*ajñānivaṛthi*).[30] It highlights the constitutional characteristics of *pramāṇa*. A *pramāṇa* must be self-revelatory (*sva*), other-revelatory (*parā*) and bereft of contradictions and obstructions (*bādhavivarjitam*). *Svanirṇayaḥ* and *paranirṇayaḥ* function as positive conditions for *pramāṇa* and *bādhavivarjitam* stand as the negative condition of *pramāṇa* in the absence of which valid knowledge arises.

3.1.1 Cognition as Manifestation of the Object

Pramāṇa connects between the knowing subject and the knowable external object. Regarding the constitution and function of *pramāṇa*, there are three precarious stands in the epistemology; cognition as the modification of the subject, cognition as the modification of the object and cognition as a physical grasping. These positions are untenable, according to Jainism. The first theory considers all properties are subjective, and therefore, they negate the existence of the external object. Hence, there is no difference between the object and cognition. The second view defines valid knowledge as the identity of content between cognition and the *cognitum*.[31] Here, the object gives the datum, which determines the object and cognition of it. The third theory promulgates that cognition arises only after the contact of the sense organ with

---

29 PNT: 1.6. *tad vyavasāya svabhāvaṃ samāropa paripanthitvāt pramāṇatvād.*

30 Cf. PM: 1.1.34; 37; 38.

31 Cf. Satish Chandra Chatterjee, *The Nyāya Theory of Knowledge*, p. 62.

the object. For Jainism, cognition is not absolutely identical with the subject or Pure Consciousness and not identical with the content of the object as well as the contact of a sense organ to the object is not the necessary condition for the cognition.

Advaitins claims the subject of empirical cognition is the Pure Consciousness limited by mental modifications (*anthakaraṇavṛtti*).[32] This mental modification limits pure consciousness. Having obtained apparent identification with pure consciousness, the unconscious mental modification becomes a conscious force in the empirical cognition of the object. Rejecting the real existence of the object, Advaitin states that *anthakaraṇavṛtti* takes the form of the object. Jaina exposes the incompatibility of Advaitains in presenting the unconscious *anthakaraṇavṛtti* as the conscious force in cognition. Jaina would say that the cognition occurs in the self-modification of the Pure Soul as the conscious drive (*upayoga*), and it is not by any external agency.[33] Different from Advaitin, Jaina upholds the independent and absolute existence of the object. The external objects and the world of appearance are not an apparent modification of reality, but they are real. So, Jaina interprets pure cognition, not in negative terms as the absence of non-intelligence. They interpret cognition in positive terms as 'the self-illumination and illumination of the object' because "the soul has the nature of self-revealing its own self as well as the object which is other than the soul."[34] It means that cognition includes the cognition of the subject and the object. Retained in the respective status of subject and object (self-conscious soul as the subject of knowledge and all substances as the object of knowledge), the soul never inheres

32 Cf. *Vedānta Paribhāsha*. p. 15. Cf. Dharmaraja Adhvarindra, *Vedānta Paribhāsha*, translated and annotated by Swami Madhavananda (Kolkata: Advaita Ashram, 2011). (Hereafter, VP).

33 Cf. PS: 1.35.

34 PM: 1.1.42.

into the nature of the object or other way.[35] The knower and known do not become one at any level of cognition.

According to Kumarila, identity cannot be the relation between cognition and cognised object. Instead, it is the relation of objectivity consists of the object bearing the result of the cognitive process. Jaina repudiates it with their fundamental metaphysical postulate that the self is of the nature of consciousness and non-self is bereft of consciousness, and therefore, there has no 'knowledge content' in non-self.[36] The epistemological position of Buddhists confers form for the knowledge because knowledge arises from the objects. Jaina expunges this position. The knowledge cannot take the form of the object because knowledge is immaterial, and what is immaterial cannot take the form of material, as in the case of the *Ākaśa*.[37] The identity of knowledge and object would lead to absurdity because of assuming an object as a form of knowledge. Then, one would feel 'I am the jar'; instead of 'I know the jar'.[38]Thus, it is clear that the knowledge is apprehended as the knowledge of the object and not as the form of the object. They hold that the object is presented to the subject directly.

The subject relates to the object, is not a physical grasping through sense organs, as *Nyāya* holds. Having taken the function (*vyapāra*) and functioning object (*vyapāravat*) together, *Nyāya* constitutes the contact (*sannikarṣa*) of sense organs as *karaṇa* of cognition. The limited size of the soul scotches the

35 Cf. PS: 1. 28-30.

36 Cf. PS: 1. 36.

37 Cf. Pushpa Bothra, *The Jaina Theory of Perception* (New Delhi: Motilal Banarsidass, reprint 1996). p.3. (Hereafter, Pushpa Bothra, *The Jaina Theory of Perception*).

38 Cf. PKM: p. 106.

theory of physical grasping in Jainism.[39] According to Jaina doctrines, the self and self-luminous cognition is identical in nature. Thus, there is no difference between the subject and the instrument of cognition. Here, cognition manifests the object and quashes the possibility of any intermediary physical condition to reveal the object. For Jainism, the subject and object, and their modifications, are being known through the instrumentality of consciousness. It is the manifestation of the object. It is not modification, resemblance, reflection, and material contact. In the manifestation of cognition, neither the object comes to the agent nor does the agent goes to the object. It is that the knowledge itself manifests the object without the assistance of any other agents.[40] Thus, the resultant of cognition is "the illumination of the object" (*artha prakāśa*), i.e., the cognition of the object, and "the cessation of the ignorance" (*ajñānivaṛthi*).[41] Therefore, Hemacandrasūri rightly defines *pramāṇa* as "*samyagarthanirṇayaḥ pramāṇam*".[42] *Pramāṇa* is 'the authentic definitive cognition of an object.' The inclusion of the object in the definition of cognition releases it from the clutches of absolute idealism.

3.1.2 Cognition of Cognition

Cognition of cognition is also a part of the Jaina definition of *pramāṇa*. However, there is a just and inevitable dubiety of the cognition of cognition. The *Mīmāṁsa* School considers cognition as an activity of the self. They hold that cognition manifests the object, but cognition is not the object

39 Cf. Indra Chandra Shastri, *Jain Epistemology*, pp. 173-174.

40 Cf. PNT: 1.3.

41 PM: 1.1.34; 37; 38.

42 PM: 1.1.2. The self-cognition is also a characteristic of cognition. However, Hemacandrasūri does not consider self-cognition as a defining attribute of cognition because self-cognition is even common to such erroneous cogniton also. Cf. PM: 1.1.3.

of perception. It is powerless to reveal itself. It can be known by inference after the cognition of the object.[43] In other words, the act of cognition is presumed from the cognizedeness of the object. Bhāṭṭa school of *Mīmāṁsa* later philosophically defend this position to approbate their crude realism. Bhāṭṭa sasys that "there is no apprehension of cognition but its existence is presumed to explain the cognizedeness of the object."[44] The self-luminosity of cognition entails a logical conclusion that the object is the pure manifestation of cognition, which shred off the real existence of the object. Thus, Bhāṭṭa is a staunch critic of the cognition of cognition. *Nyāya* criticises Bhāṭṭa view and upholds that cognition is an object of perception, and it is perceived by other cognition through internal perception. *Sāṁkhya*, *Advaita Vedānta* and Jaina advocate that cognition is perceived directly by itself.

According to Jaina, the subject of cognition (*pramātr*), the means of cognition (*pramāṇa*), and the resultant of cognition (*pramiti*) are the object of cognition (*prameya*).[45] "Whatever is revealed in our experience is cognized, and whatever is cognized is an object of consciousness."[46] It is an irrevocable experiential truth. There is no stringent rule that whatever is perceived must be perceived as an object of perception, for example, the perception of the self. The self can be perceived as a subject of cognition and not perceived as an object of cognition. In the empirical judgement, "I know the Jar," the subject, the object and knowing, the fact of the act of cognition is revealed. Therefore, cognition also may be perceived not as

43 Cf. Govardhan P. Bhatt, *The Basic Ways of Knowing: An In-depth Study of Kumarila's Contribution to Indian Epistemology* (Delhi: Motilal Banarsidass, 1989), p. 51. (Hereafter, Govardhan P. Bhatt, *The Basic Ways of Knowing*).

44 Govardhan P. Bhatt, *The Basic Ways of Knowing*, p.51.

45 Cf. PS: 1. 34-36; 2. 16.

46 PKM: p. 31. *pratīyamānatvaṁ hi grāhyatvaṁ tadeva karmatvam.*

an object of perception but as an instrument of perception.[47] Hemacandrasūri mentions that "it is not possible that the cognition of an object can happen to a subject who does not intuit the act of cognition".[48]Whatever is not self-revealing is not the cognition of the object, as in the case of a jar or pot.

It implies that cognition is an operative process of which the knower is conscious, and the knowledge is self-conscious. The Bhaṭṭa school of *Mīmāṃsā* holds that the knowledge is never known directly, but it is inferred through the quality of knowness. The act of cognition is inferred to have taken place in the self by the fact that the object has become cognized.[49] Therefore, a clear knowledge of the object is the function of the object. Jaina contempt this position and raise the question: whether this function of the object is the unconscious or conscious process? If it is unconscious, it will be a precarious position because the conscious apprehension of the object is the categorical imperative for clear knowledge. If it is conscious, then the other two possibilities will be there, i.e., self-conscious or cognised by another mode of cognition. If it is self-conscious, then it is self-contradictory to their contention over self-illuminative knowledge and if it is cognised by other cognition, then it will end up the fallacy of *infinitum regressum*.[50] The incompatibility of *Mīmāṃsā* arguments vividly exposes their haphazard position.

Nyāya is conducive to accept the self-cognition of the supreme soul. Jaina argues that as the cognition of the

47 These are Prabhācandra's arguments. Jadunath Sinha collects and logically presents them. Cf. Jadunath Sinha, *Indian Psychology: Perception* (London: Kegan Paul, Trench, Trubner & Co. Ltd, 1934), p. 216. (Hereafter, Jadunath Sinha, *Indian Psychology*).

48 PM: 1.1.1.no. 12.

49 Cf. Chandradhar Sharma, *A Critical Survey of Indian Philosophy*, p. 225.

50 Cf. PNT: 1. 17, pp. 68-70.

supreme soul is the cognition by itself, so why can't apply the same principle to the empirical soul's cognition also? The *Naiyāyika* defend it by raising the issue of the difference between divine cognition and human cognition. "The Jaina contends that this argument is fallacious. Consciousness, by its very essential nature, both manifests itself and other objects; this is the common and essential characteristic of all consciousness; this is not a special characteristic of the divine consciousness."[51] Then, *Nyāya* would say that the cognition is known directly but not by itself; instead, by other cognition. Jainas investigate the possibility of cognition is perceived by another cognition. Jainas concludes with three possibilities. The first one suggests that the unending demand for the second cognition to validate the first cognition succumbs to the fallacy of *regressum ad infinitum*. The second one seeks the possibility of the second cognition arises when the first cognition continues to exist. But it is impossible because, according to the *Nyāya*, cognitions are always successive and are never simultaneous. The third one seeks the possibility of the second cognition arises when the first cognition is destroyed. But it is also impossible because if the second cognition arises when the first cognition is no longer in existence, then what will be cognized by the second cognition. [52] Thus, Jainas asserts that cognition is the object of cognition directly by itself as well as it quashes the existence of the second cognition to cognise the first cognition. The cognition manifests itself and the subject. The concept of self-manifestation does not necessarily mean that cognition is a pure subject without any form of being an object. But on the contrary, it means that cognition, when it manifests objects, does not necessitate itself to be manifested by anything else. The manifestation of the object inevitably presupposes the manifestation of cognition to self.

51 Jadunath Sinha, *Indian Psychology: Perception*, p. 215. Cf. PNT: 1.17, pp. 70-72.

52 Cf. Jadunath Sinha, *Indian Psychology: Perception*, pp. 215-218.

Hemachandrasūri quashes out the ambiguity over cognition of cognition. "It is cognition with reference to the object and cognisable with reference to its own self."[53] The cognizability is self-luminous and does not depend upon other cognition. Therefore, it is unleashed from the fallacy of *infinite regressum*. Thus, there is no logical absurdity in accepting the fact that cognition is also cognisable. Critics may question that cognition is also an entity like a jar, and it must be liable to be revealed by another. Hemachandrasūri makes clear the air by differentiating the nature of jar and cognition. "The jar is revealed by a cognition is not due to the fact that it is an entity but because it is other than cognition."[54] But, can the organ and the resultant be identical? In other words, can the cause and effect be the same? Hemachandrasūri resolves it like this: "the activity of knowledge having reference to the objects is the resultant" and "the same activity of knowledge as relates to the subject is the organ."[55] The cognition, as the organ and resultant, has the relation of identity cum difference. Vādidevasūri renders a limpid explanation for this: "They are identical because the same self, through self-evolution, which is modified into the *pramāṇa* is found to be modified into the *phala*. They are different for some conditions because the cognition (*pramāṇa*) and the resultant of cognition (*phala*) appear as 'what effects' (*sādhana*) and 'what is effected' (*sādhya*)."[56] They have the identity because both of them

53 PM: 1.1.1.no. 12.

54 PM: 1.1.1.no. 12.

55 PM: 1.1. 35; 36.

56 PNT: 6. 8-9.

tasyaika pramātṛ tādātmyena pramāṇād abhedavyavasthteḥ pramāṇatayā pariṇatasyaivātmanaḥ phalatayā pariṇati-pratīteḥ.

PNT: 6. 13-14.

kathaṃcit tasyāpi pramāṇād bhedena vyavasthānāt sādhya sādana bhāvena pramāṇa phalayoḥ pratīyamānatvāt.

belong to the self-same cognition and are cognised by the same identical Knower, and their difference is in respect to the relation of determinant and determinatum.

3.2 The Psychology of Cognition

The existent self is identical to the status of the knower because consciousness is the essential quality of the soul. But the knower is not static reality as *Sāṅkhya* and *Advaita Vedānta* holds. The self is self-conscious and self-illuminative and the object is ready to be illuminated. Hence, the function of conscious drive (*upayoga*) of the self is to illumine the object. *Upayoga* resumes the pure relation between the illuminer and the illuminated. It means that *upayoga* functions as the remover of obstruction to manifest the object. The cognitive process, whether internal or external, is limited and oblivated due to the causal aggregate karmic conditions over the individual soul. The karmic condition obscures cognition externally and internally. The external depends on the difference of the objects, instruments of knowledge, place and time, and the internal depends on intensity or the mildness of karmic influences, respectively.[57] Thus, the conscious drive (*upayoga*) subsists in all the souls without exception, but the operation of it varies, owing to the external and internal possession of and extrication from karmic obfuscations. It implies that cognition is progressively manifested, according to the scale of the internal and external suppression and annihilation of karmic veils.

Cognition is the self-modified conscious drive (*upayoga*) of the soul, which manifests in the apprehension of the self and objects. This conscious drive is the nexus of psychic experiences. T. G Kalghatagi, in *Some Problems in Jaina Psychology*,

---

Hemacandrasūri sounds similar statement about the identity and difference in the relation between the cognition and the resultant of cognition. Cf. PM: 1.1.37. no. 141.

57 Pt. Sukhlalji, *Commentary on Tattvārtha Sūtra*, pg. 81.

has taken initiatives to compare *upayoga* to the 'horme' of modern psychology.[58] This 'horme' or internal conscious force determines the experiences. There are determinate and indeterminate experiences. Some of the Jaina literature names them as *sakāra* (determinate) and *anākāra* (indeterminate) experiences. The internal experience is indeterminate and formless, and the external experience is possessed of form. The cognitive process conflates both in cognition. One implies the other, and seclusion of the one distorts the act of cognition.

An indistinguishable state of indeterminate and determinate nature of the cognitive process refers to the two constituent aspects of *upayoga*; *darśana* (indeterminate intuition) and *jñāna* (determinate cognition).[59] Ācārya Kundakunda concludes the discussion of the soul in *Samayasāra* with this aphorism: "*Ahamekaḥ khalū suddhaḥ darśanajñānamayaṃ sadarūpi*"[60] It means that 'the soul in this absolute purity is having the nature of *darśana* and *jñāna*, and hence, always non-corporeal.' It implies the identity of *jīva*, *darśana* and *jñāna*. *Tattvārtasūtra* commentary defines it as that "the cognition that apprehends the objects concerned in a specific form is determinate cognition or *jñāna*, the cognition that apprehends the same in generic form is indeterminate cognition or *darśana*."[61]

In contrast to the Buddhist view, Jainas realism reiterates that the inevitability of the determinate and indeterminate

---

58 Cf. T. G Kalghatagi, *Some Problems in Jaina Psychology*, p. 30.
Quoted a reference from *Education-Its Data and First Principle* (Nunn, P.T, pp. 28-29), T. G Kalghatagi defines horme as the internal conscious drive: "To this drive or urge, whether it occurs in the conscious life of men and the higher animals we propose to single name-horme."

59 Cf. TS: 2.9.

60 SS: 38.

61 Pt. Sukhlalji, *Commentary on Tattvārtha Sūtra*, pg. 82.

cognition in an experiecne.[62] Vādidevasūri rebuts the Buddhist position in *Pramāṇa-Naya-Tattvālokālaṃkāra*.[63] Jaina dismays the exclusive pramāṇa-hood of indeterminate (*nirvikalpa/darśana*) cognition. One cannot ratify the validity of indeterminate cognition at the time of its generation because, according to the Buddhist view, a valid knowledge precludes from the feelings and ideation and therefore, there should not have the feeling of 'the certain knowledge' (*vyavasāya*) at that time. To validate indeterminate cognition, they must admit the *sva-saṁvedana* or direct self-consciousness. Direct self-consciousness presents itself as *sva-saṁvedana* is a nasty conclusion. The modified perception (*vikalpa*) cannot approbate *sva-saṁvedana* because *vikalpa* is not similar to *nirvikalpa* in the constitution, according to Buddhist thought. Thus, *vikalpa* does not prove the pramāṇa-hood of *nirvikalpa*. The pramāṇa-hood of *nirvikalpa* cannot be substantiated through inference also because *nirvikalpa* cannot account for the revived idea (*vyāptismaraṇa* - mental reproduction or

---

62 AM: 112. *sāmānya vāg viśeṣe chenna sabdārtho mṛṣā hi sā.*
According to Jainas, the universal is not one and ubiquitous class essence as Nyāya holds. There is common character or similarity among the object of knowledge. This likeness is the real universal. "The common characters again, which constitute the real universal, according to the Jaina, are of two kinds, viz. *tiryak sāmānya* and *urddhvatā sāmānya*. By *tiryak samanya* means similar modifications (*sadṛṣapariṇāmastiryak*) e.g. dewlap and the like in cows. By *urddhvata sāmānya* means the permanent substance which abides in the midst of past, present, and future modifications (*parāparavivartavyāpi-dravyamūrddhvatā*) e.g. earth in its various modifications (Mānikyanandi, *Parīkṣāmukhasūtra*, p. 5; PNT: 5. 4-6). So the common characters of an object are constituted by its permanent substance which persists in the midst of all its modifications, and its modifications which are similar to those of other like objects. And these are the real universal; there is no other universal than these common characters (Prabhācandra, *Prameyakamalamartāṇḍa*, p. 136)." (Cf. Jadunath Sinha, *Indian Psychology: Perception*, pp. 173-174).

63 Cf. PNT: 1.6. pp. 28-37; 3. 7, pp. 182-186; 5. 4-5, pp. 369-388.

recollection), which is one of the constituent elements of the inferential knowledge.

The Buddhist repudiates criticism by redefining the nature of certain knowledge. They endorse that *nirvikalpa* is *pramāṇa*, not because it leads to a consistent valid or certain knowledge in itself, but because it entails to producing valid knowledge. Jaina again refutes it by analysing the two possible alternatives; *nirvikalpa* reveal the object at the time of generation of the feeling the validity of cognition and *nirvikalpa* reveal the object as soon as there is *nirvikalpa*. Jaina discards the first alternative on the ground of non-coherence to the general understanding of Buddhist thought because all sensations are momentary and therefore, it is impossible to reveal the object in the second moment after the genesis of *nirvikalpa*. The second alternative denounces the connection of *nirvikalpa* and *vyavasāya*. Buddhist may safeguard their position by claiming *nirvikalpa* procures *vyavasāya* to reveal the object and therefore, the object of *nirvikalpa* and *vyavasāya* is identical. Jaina points out that *nirvikalpa* is the negative apprehension and *vyavasāya* is the positive apprehension of the object. Accordingly, the object of both cannot be identical. The function of valid knowledge is to determine the object. However, for Buddhism, valid knowledge is bereft of any determination. Jaina would say that this position is self-contradictory. The commentary to *Pramāṇa-Naya-Tattvālokālaṃkāra* declares Jaina view like this:

> According to Jaina, it is only a *vikalpa*, attended with *vyavasaya*, i.e., only a valid or certain piece of cognition that can give rise to the certain subsequent *vikalpa* which is the reproduced idea. The absolutely colourless nirvikalpa which is strictly unconnected with all *vikalpa* previous or subsequent to it, cannot

account for *vikalpa* or the revived idea. A true and valid percept only can be remembered and not the *nirvikalpa*.[64]

The cognition of universality (*darśana*) apprehends the indeterminate common characters, and the cognition of particularity (*jñāna*) comprehends the determinate distinctive characters of an object.

There are identity and difference between the cognition of universality and particularity. It is the truth that it may perceive as the successive stages of cognition and not able to demarcate in the process of cognition, but they are distinct, and that distinction is not absolute. *Jñāna* conceives the reality in its complex and universal-cum-particular nature. *Darśana* comprehends universals but not as a rudimentary stage of cognition. Therefore, it need not be taken as 'pure sensation of the existence of objects'[65] because it even exists in the apex state of transcendental perception. It means that *darśana* is not subjugated or subdued in the state of omniscience. Jainas accept the existence of perfect intuition (*kevala darśana*). Thus, it is imprudent to say that *jñāna* apprehends the particular and *darśana* comprehends the universal. The difference between them is with reference to the object of cognition. *Jñāna* engages in comprehending the external reality while *darśana* is engaging in the intuition of the internal self.[66] The internal as well as the external reality is, according to the metaphysics of Jainas, possessed of the characteristics of universal cum particular. The object of both *jñāna* and *darśana* is the composite of universality and particularity.

Brahmadeva's commentary to *Dravyasaṅgraha* (*gātha* 43 and 44) yields a clear understanding of the distinction

64 The commentary to PNT: 1. 6, p. 31.

65 Mehta, *Jaina Psychology*, p. 46; T. G Kalghatagi, *Some Problems in Jaina Psychology*, p. 32.

66 Cf. Nathmal Tatia, *Studies in Jain Philosophy*, pp. 72-73.

of *jñāna* and *darśana* in Jaina philosophical literature.[67] According to him, there are two streams of understanding in Jaina literature: logical (*tarkābhiprāyeṇa*) and scriptural (*siddhāntābhiprāyeṇa*). The logical view states *darśana* as the intuition of the universal and *jñāna* as the knowledge of the particular. The scriptural view highlights *darśana* as the intuition of the self and *jñāna* as the cognition of the object. *Darśana* intuits the formless universal nature of the conscious drive and *jñāna* knows the formed particular nature of the object. The occurrence of both leads to the comprehension of reality as it is. The discussion of the simultaneity and the successive occurrence of *jñāna* and *darśana* in the respective state of empirical and transcendental cognition render an impeccable penetration into the nature of the empirical and transcendental state of the soul. In the case of mundane souls, *jñāna* is preceded by *darśana*, and they occur in succession because *jñāna*-varnanīya karma and *darśana-varnanīya* karma obscures them and the process of cognition is a gradual suppression and annihilation of karmic veils. But in the case of liberated souls, *jñāna* and *darśana* happen simultaneously because all karmas are annihilated completely. The cognition in liberated state of existence is a sudden illumination and thus, the absolute manifestation of the self followed by the manifestation of non-self.[68] The intuition of the self (*darśana*) concurrently manifests in the knowledge of the object (*jñāna*). Due to the suppression and annihilation of karmic veils, the universal (*darśana*) and particular (*jñāna*) are manifested simultaneously. The status of *darśana* and *jñāna* in the state of liberation will be discussed in the forthcoming chapter. Succinctly, *darśana* and *jñāna* is identical nature of the self, from the transcendental point of view. But from an empirical

67 Cf. Brahmadeva commentary to *Dravyasaṅgraha*: 43, 44. Quoted in Nathmal Tatia, *Studies in Jain Philosophy*, p. 73.

68 Cf. TS: 1.31; DS: 44; AM: 101.

point of view, there is successive occurrence in empirical cognition and simultaneous occurrence in transcendental cognition.

3.2.1 *Darśana*

Darśana has four varieties:

1. *cakṣur-darśana* or indeterminate cognition through visual sense organ,
2. *acakṣur-darśana* or indeterminate cognition through non-visual sense organs,
3. *avadhi-darśana* indeterminate clairvoyant cognition and
4. *kevaladarśana* or indeterminate omniscient cognition.

3.2.2 *Jñāna*

Jñāna has five varieties:[69]

1. *Mati-Jñāna* or empirical cognition — It is the knowledge gained through senses and the mind. It is either a perception or dependent on perception.
2. *Śruta-Jñāna* or articulate cognition — It consists of truths revealed by authentic persons and refers to conceptualisation through language.
3. *Avadhi-Jñāna* or clairvoyant cognition — It is the peculiar aspects of the material body acquired through spiritual practices but out of the natural range of senses.

69 Cf. TS: 1.9-32. Among the five varieties of knowledge, the first three (*Mati-Jñāna,* Śruta-*Jñāna,* and *Avadhi-Jñāna*) may be cognised as either enlightened or deluded. The last two (*Manahaparyāya-Jñāna* and *Kevala-Jñāna*) are inherently enlightened. Hence, some of the Jain texts divide eight varieties of knowledge by adding the three deluded knowledge of the first three varieties. Cf. TS: 1.32.

4. *Manahaparyāya-Jñāna* or mind-reading cognition — It is the act of reading or seeing the objects of others mind acquired by ascetics at a high level of spirituality. It is telepathic knowledge.
5. *Kevala-Jñāna* or omniscient cognition — It is the aftermath of the complete annihilation and suppression of karmic influences over the self, and it refers to the knowledge of all substances in all their qualities and modes.

A valid knowledge must involve the determination of the object. It is the process of ascertainment. This cognition can only have pragmatic confirmation, which bolsters to discern the desirable and undesirable. Thus, cognition (*pramāṇa*), which is different from sensation (*darśana*) and knowledge (*jñāna*), is incapable of the manifestation of the object as it is. The combination of both has much psychological and epistemological importance. Jain tradition classifies *pramāṇa* (cognition) into two; *pratyakṣa* and *parokṣa*. *Pratyakṣa* is the direct and immediate cognition, and *parokṣa* is indirect and mediate cognition. Having adhered to the two-fold demarcation, *Tarka* tradition has a different interpretation from *Āgama* tradition. *Āgama* tradition acclaims the identity of the subject and instrument of cognition, and therefore, *pratyakṣa* is the direct and immediate knowledge, perceived by the soul (*avadhi*, *manaḥaparyāya* and *kevala*). It is independent of sense organs and mind. All sensory and mental knowledge is indirect and mediate cognition (*mati/ ābhinibodhika* and *śruta*). *Tarka* tradition lends emphasis to the nature of the relationship between the subject and object for the calibration. They interpret the immediacy of knowledge as the independency of the instrument of cognition. In this sense, it includes sensory perception as *pratyakṣa* because sensory perception does not depend on any other agency for the manifestation of an object. Succinctly, cognition is the *pramāṇa*, and it is of two kinds; *pratyakṣa* (perceptual) and *parokṣa* (non-perceptual). *Āgama* tradition considers sense perception as *parokṣa* and conceives recollection (*smṛti*), recognition (*pratyābhiñja*), inference (*anumāna*) and verbal testimony (āgama) are the sub-divisions of *parokṣa*. Except for sense perception, Tarka tradition accepts all other cognitions are *parokṣa* because they dependent on perception for the manifestation of the object.

3.3 Pratyakṣa

Pratyakṣa is the composite of two Sanskrit words *prati* and *akṣa*, which etymologically means 'before' and 'organ,' respectively. In common parlance, it denotes 'the object present before sense organs'. The sense perception is the natural and direct means of knowing external objects. Thus, it possesses the status of direct or immediate knowledge. Evidently, sense perception is not the only means for immediate and direct knowledge. Hence, perception cannot be confined to sense perception. As there are divergent conceptions of *pramāṇa* in Indian *darśana*, so there are different conceptions about *pratyakṣa*. Concerning the exact definition of *pratyakṣa*, there are three views: it is a sensation without any element of determination, it is a knowledge arising from the sense-object contact, and it is an immediate knowledge.[70] Jainism holds the third view that states perception is the immediate knowledge, and the immediacy of knowledge is independent of any other external agency.

3.3.1 Pratyakṣa as the Immediate Knowledge

The Buddhist considers the object of perception is a unique individual (*svalkṣaṇa*), and the process of cognition is

70 Cf. D.M Datta, *The Six Ways of Knowing* (New Delhi: Motilal Banarsidass, 2017), p. 31. (Hereafter. D.M Datta, *The Six Ways of Knowing*).

mere sensing without any element of ideation (*kalpana*) in it. They define it as, "*Pratyakṣaṁ kalpanāpoḍhamabhrāntam*"[71] Their theory of perception is constructed on the theory of momentariness. For the object is momentary, the conceptual knowledge denigrates the real object and so distorts the real knowledge. Thus, they define perception as true knowledge that free from any concept. According to Akalanka and Hemacandra,[72] this indeterminate perception cannot be the cause of action or not capable of practical consequences, and the action or successful volition (the condition of the valid knowledge defined by Buddhist themselves) is caused only by the conceptual or judgemental knowledge.

Perception through the sense-object contact is the most renowned and common epistemological position. *Nyāya-Vaiśeṣika*, *Sāṅkhya-Yoga* and Kumārila Bhaṭṭa admit the perception is the knowledge derived from the contact of sense organ with an object. *Nyāya* defines it as "*indriyārtha sannikarṣa janyamjñānam,*" which means 'perception as the knowledge derived from the contact of sense with an object.'[73] Bhaṭṭa *Mīmāṁsa* defines it as, "*satsaṁprayṁoge puruṣasyendriyāṇam buddhijanma tatpratyakṣam*" which states that 'the perceptual cognition is produced by the efficient contact of the sense with their objects'.[74] *Sāṅkhya* sounds the same as "*prativiṣayādāyavasāyo dṛṣṭam,*" which claims

71 Dharamakirti, *Nyāybindu* (Banares: Chowkhamba Sanskrit Series, 1954), p. 13, quoted in Satish Chandra Chatterjee, *The Nyāya Theory of Knowledge*, p. 131.

72 *Nyāyaviniścayavivaraṇa*: 1.158. Cf. Vadiraja, *Nyāyaviniścayavivaraṇa: the Commentary on Akalanka's Nyāyaviniścaya* (Kashi: Bharatiya Jnana Pitha, 1949). (Hereafter, NVV); PM 1.1. 8. 27.

73 NS: 1.1.4.

74 *Mīmāṁsasūtra*: 1.1.4, Cf. Jamini, *Mīmāṃsa Sūtra* translated and edited by M. L Sandal (Delhi: Motilal Banarsidass, 1985). (Hereafter, MS).

'perception is definite cognition of a particular object through the contact of a sense organ.'[75] The *Yoga* system also defines perception in terms of sensory stimulation.[76] Gangeśa, the father of modern *Nyāya*, analyses and redefines the traditional *Nyāya* definition of perception. He claims that holding the sense-object contact as the necessary and unconditional instrument of perception is logically indefensible. It is too wide because it applies to inference and memory as forms of knowledge in which there is sense-object contact (mind as internal sense). It is too narrow because it excludes God's Omniscience, which is the direct perception of all truth and reality. To define perception in terms of sensory stimulation is a vicious circle. The sense organ is known from perception, and perception is known from the function of senses. Thus, to define perception by senses or sensory stimulation is to explain the *obscurum per obscuris*.[77] Therefore, modern *Nyāya* defines perception as "*pratyakṣasya sākṣātkāritvaṁ lakṣaṇam*", which means 'perception as the immediate knowledge with the character of immediacy (*sākṣātkāritvaṁ*)'.[78]

Prabhākara, Advaita Vedānta and Jaina define perception in terms of immediate knowledge. They are at one with modern *Nyāya* in recognising this truth about the essential nature of perception as immediacy. Prabhākara brings forth the definition of perception as "*sākṣātpratītiḥ pratyakṣam*".[79] For the Prabhākara School, 'it is the immediate knowledge

---

75 SK: 5.

76 YS: 1.7

77 Satish Chandra Chatterjee, *The Nyāya Theory of Knowledge*, pp. 138-139.

78 *Tattvacintāmaṇi*: 1. Cf. Gaṅgeśa, *Tattvacintāmaṇi*, translated and explained by V. P. Bhatta (Michigan: Eastern Book Linkers, 2005). (Hereafter, TC).

79 *Prakaraṇapañcikā*: p.51, quoted in Govardhan P. Bhatt, *The Basic Ways of Knowing*, p.154.

that we may have of the subject and object of knowledge and of knowledge itself'. Advaita Vedāntins also acclaims 'the immediacy of knowledge does not rest on its being caused by sense organs.'[80] Perception is immediate knowledge. *Vedānta Paribhāsha* defines it as, "*Pramāna caitanyasya viṣayāvacchina caitanya bhedhah.*"[81] When there is the unity of the consciousness reflected in the means of knowledge (*pramāṇa caitanya*) with the consciousness limited by the object (*viṣayāvacchinna caitanya*), then it is called the immediate knowledge. Such immediate knowledge is the Self itself because there is pure immediacy of knowledge in the Self.[82] It should be made clear that an object is immediately known empirically only in that form, which *anthakaraṇa* assumes and not in any other form, and that takes place due to the function of sense organs. The connection of perception with sensory stimulation is more accidental than essential.[83] Therefore, in Advaita Vedānta, senses are not the condition of the perception; instead, the immediacy of cognition is the specific condition of the perception.

Jain philosophy also adheres to perception is the direct and immediate knowledge of the objects by the Self. Perceptual cognition, according to Jaina, is depending directly on the activity of the self-luminous and self-conscious Self and relying indirectly on the subsidiary external conditions, i.e., the object, senses and mind. Ācārya Kundakunda, in *Pravaccanasāra*, expunges the inevitability of senses in perception, by using the analogy of lamp and eye: 'if the vision-faculty of the human being has the power to remove the darkness, the lamp would have no role to play. Similarly, when the self itself is of the

80 VP: p. 12.
81 VP: p. 13.
82 Cf. VP: p. 8.
83 Cf. VP: pp. 12-13; 34.

nature of pure consciousness, the sensual perception has a constrained role to play.'[84] Mānikyanandi states that the clarity of knowledge depends on the removal of obstruction, i.e., the karmic matter, and it is beyond the capacity of the sense organs.[85] Ensued from the general Jaina epistemological and psychological understanding Jaina scholars would claim that the external object, physical conditions, sense organs and mind can never be the determining conditions of the perception.

Akalaṅka, Vidyānandi, Mānikyanandi, Hemacandrasūri, and Vādidevasūri recognise "immediacy and lucidity" as the defining attribute of perceptual cognition. Hemacandrasūri defines *pratyakṣa* as "*viśadaḥ pratyakṣam*".[86] He interprets the meaning and nuances of the phrase immediacy and lucidity in the following aphorism. It has two implications. "It consists in either its independence from the service of another organ or in the apprehension of its content as 'this'."[87] It means, firstly, that perceptual cognition as the organ of knowledge in the trajectory does not depend on any other means of knowledge (non-perceptual), unlike verbal testimony and inference, and therefore, it is distinct. Perception manifests the object without

---

84 PS: 1. 67.

timirharā jayi diṭṭhī jaṇassa dveṇa ṇtthi kādavvam
aha sokkham sayamādā visayā kim tattha kuvvamti.

85 Cf. PKM: p. 219.

86 PM: 1.1.13.

The Jaina logicians generally define perception as 'the clear knowledge'. Akalanka, Vidyānandi, Mānikyanandi, and Vādidevasūri resonate with Hemacandrasūri's definition and interpretation of perception, i.e., the clear knowledge. Cf. NKC: 1. 3; PKM: 2. 3; PNT: 2. 2.

87 PM: 1.1.14, "*pramāṇānatarānapekṣedaṁtaya pratibhāso vā vaiśadyam*".

Vādidevasūri interprets clarity almost the same as Hemacandrasūri. He says, "Clearness consists in revealing the details in a greater degree than that done by any other means of knowledge."(*anumānādy* ādhikyena *viśeṣa-prakāśanam spaṣṭatvam*). Cf. PNT: 2.3.

the mediation or assistance of any other knowledge. Whatever is not clear is not perception, for example, the inference. Secondly, its object is manifested as 'this' and therefore, it is clear apprehension of the particular existent. Hence, perception is a clear knowledge, which does not need any other knowledge in order to manifest its object. To sum up, the definition of perception based on the defining attribute can be encapsulated as 'the clear and distinct cognition of an object'. Akalaṅka's descriptive definition of perception scotches all the ambiguity: "Perception is the knowledge, which is self-revealing and reveals the object as substance and as mode, as universal and as particular and which is determinate or conceptual and is essentially clear."[88] Therefore, *pratyakṣa* is the knowledge that has the immediacy and lucidity, and parokṣa is the knowledge that is devoid of immediacy and lucidity.

3.3.2 Classification of Perceptual Cognition

Ācārya Umāsvāmi and Ācārya Kundakunda portray the *Āgamic* classification of *pratyakṣa* as the direct and immediate perception of the Self. Hence, all knowledge that depends upon the sources other than the Self is *parokṣa* for *Āgamic* classification. *Tarka* (logical) classification of *pratyakṣa*, inclined by the development of logical theories of *pramāna* in the medieval Indian system, classifies *pratyakṣa* as sensory

---

88 NVV: 1.3.

"pratyakṣa lakṣaṇaṁ prāhuḥ spaṣṭaṁ sākāramañjaśā dravya-paryāya sāmānya-viśeṣāthātmavedanam."

Perception is conceptual in the sense that it has the power to manifest the object through the concepts. It is not the pure sensation of unique individuals as the Buddhist holds. It may be noted here that Jainas regard all knowledge as non-conceptual or *nirākāra* as against the Buddhist who regard knowledge as *sākāra*. But, here when Akalanka defines perception as sākāra, he means it *savikapaka* or the conceptual perception. (Cf. NVV: p. 86; Cf. Pushpa Bothra, *The Jaina Theory of Perception*, 3-5, 33).

perception and transcendental perception. The early imprints of the inclusion of empirical perception in the scope of *pratyakṣa* can be seen in *Nyāyavatāra* of Siddhasena: "such knowledge that takes cognizance of objects, not beyond the range the senses, is *pratyakṣa*."[89] Akalaṅka, Vidyānandi, Mānikyanandi, Vādidevasūri, and Hemacandrasūri instil the logical division of *pramāna* to formulate the theories of *pratyakṣa*. The logical classification is depended on the clarity and lucidity of apprehension. Thus, the direct apprehension of an object independent of other agencies includes the empirical perception under the scope *pratyakṣa*. *Pratyakṣa* is the *pram*āṇa that cognises the object directly and clearly. It determines the object as it is for the percipient. Hemacandrasūri's two alternative interpretations for the word *akṣa* is a clear indication of the possibilities of interpreting perception in two ways; the soul-perception and sense-perception. According to him, the Self or Soul is *akṣa* in the transcendental point of view, and the sense organ is *akṣa* in the empirical point of view.[90] The empirical perception is clear and distinct knowledge because it does not depend on any other instruments of knowledge for the manifestation of objects and thus, it possesses the defining attribute of perception, i.e., the immediacy and lucidity. The perception through the senses is called *sāṁvyvahārika pratyakṣa*, and the perception through the total self-manifestation of the Self is called *mukhya pratyakṣa*. The instrument of the *sāṁvyvahārika pratyakṣa* is senses and mind; whereas, the instrument of *mukhya pratyakṣa* is the Self, and the source of both *pratyakṣa* is the Self itself. *Mukhya pratyakṣa* is the cognitive activity through and by the conscious Self, without the mediation of sense and mind. It means the subject and instrument of *mukhya pratyakṣa* is the Self alone. Being the perception sans the function of sense organs, it is called as the supersensuous (*atīndriya jñāna*) or

89 NV: 4.

90 Cf. PM: 1.1.10. no. 31.

extrasensory perception (*yogi-pratyakṣa*). The word '*Mukhya*' means superior, and so it is called superior knowledge.

3.4 Sāmvyvahārika Pratyakṣa

Sāṁvyvahārika pratyakṣa is, according to *Tattvārtha Sūtra*, "*tad indriyā-nindriyanimittam*".[91] It is the knowledge attained through the sense organ and mind. It has three varieties of compositions; knowledge through the instrumentality of senses alone, of the mind alone and of the joint activity the sense and mind. For Hemacandrasūri, the authentic definitive empirical perception "is conditioned by senses and mind and is of the nature of determinate perception, speculation, perceptual judgement, and retention."[92] The phrase 'conditioned by' is employed to interpret the limitedness of the empirical perception with regard to the absolute clear perception of the Self. Akalaṅka and Māṇikyanandi also clearly state that this empirical perception is limited.[93] The cognitive activity conditioned by the senses implies a direct and active role of senses in it, even though the mind and Self have their own role in the process of cognition. The Self is by nature conscious and can know everything without any external assistance. But, its power of knowing is obscured by karmic influences. In the case of empirical perception, the senses and the mind along with other external and internal causes obstruct direct involvement of the conscious Self.

3.5 The Psychology of Sāmvyvahārika Pratyakṣa

The physical and psychological components of *sāṁvyvahārika pratyakṣa* or the empirical perception accrue the psychology

91 TS: 1.14.

92 PM: 1.1.20. *indriyamanonimitto avagrahehāvāyadhāraṇātma sāṁvyavahārikam*.

93 Cf. NVV: p.105; PKM : p. 229.

of it. Thus, the psychology of sāṁvyvahārika *pratyakṣa* must include physical and psychic elements. Perception is a cognitive process, which encompasses an array of epistemic evens. According to Jaina epistemology, the cognitive process commences with indeterminate intuitions and develops through speculations, perceptual judgement, and ends up in retention. The interpretive analysis of the cognitive process in sāṁvyvahārika *pratyakṣa* depicts the ancillary and conventional role of senses and mind in the genesis of self-generated and self-evolved cognition.

3.5.1 Four Stages of Empirical Perception

The consciousness is the causal state of all cognition. Cognition is the manifestation of consciousness. Jainism, especially the *agamic* classification of cognition, considers this self as the *akṣa* that knows all objects distinctly and clearly in space and time. Pūjyapada in *Sarvārtha Siddhi* refers to the soul as "*akṣṇoti vyāpṇoti jānāti iti akṣa* ātmā."[94] It reiterates that the soul is the agent of cognition. Therefore, the empirical perception is not possible without the conscious activity (*upayoga*) of the self. It attends to the object of knowledge. As the sun illumines and the earth remained in its own place, without having direct contact with the object, the Self illumines itself and the object.[95] As cognition is impossible without *upayoga*, the Jainas stresses that empirical perception arises only when the self actually operates towards senses and mind.[96] It suggests that the sense organ and mind is to be regarded as the ancillary or limited instrument of cognition. Hemachandrasūri concludes the discussion of the first lecture of the first book by defining self as "*sva parābhasīparinābyātma*

94 *Sarvārtha Siddhi*. 1.12. Cf. Pūjyapada, *Sarvārtha Siddhi*, translated by S. A. Jaina (Calcutta: Vira Sasana Sangha, 1960).

95 Cf. Indira Chandra Sastri, *Jaina Epistemology*, p. 174.

96 Cf. PNT: 1.2 no. 15.

pramāta", 'which means that the self is which reveals its own self as well as another and is liable to change'.[97] It corroborates the position of the self as the agent and enjoyer of the empirical perception.

Sāṁvyvahārika pratyakṣa is procured by the contact of the sense organ and mind with the object. This contact prevails in the process of perception. The process contains four stages; *avagraha*, *īhā*, *avāya*, and *dhāraṇā*. These four stages happen one after another but are not absolutely different from each other.[98] *Avagraha* is the initial stage of perception. It is the stage where the sense organs come into contact with the object without determining any of its special qualities. According to Ācārya Umāsvāmi, it is the stage 'of mere sensing of objects or grasping of their generic character.'[99] It is pigeonholed

---

97 PM: 1.1.42.152.

98 Cf. PM: 1.1.20; PNT: 2.7.

99 Cf. TS: 1.15; 18.

Umasvāmi calibrates the contact of the sense organ and mind with the object. All sense organ, except the organ of the eye, comprehends the object with their direct physical contact (*prāpyakāri*). The sense organ of the eye and mind comprehend their object without physical contact with the object (*aprāpyakāri*). (Cf. TS: 1.19; PNT: 2.5).

Some other Jaina scholars like Pūjyapāda, Devānandi, Akalaṅka, Vidyānandi and Hemacandrasūri define *avagraha* as determinate perception. It arises after *darśana* or the state of the mere sensation of the object. Hemacandra endorses *avagraha* happens, on account of sense-object contact, only when *darśana* transforms itself into the determinate perception (PM: 1.1.26). Vādidevasūri comments that *avagraha* is the very next stage to *darśana*. His commentary explains the sophisticated difference between *darśana* and *avagraha* in perception like this; "*Darśana* gives the impression is that 'something is'. When one has *avagraha,* one comes to understand not simply that 'something is' but to some extent 'what that something is': a man, a beast or some other object."(PNT: 2.7, p. 108). Therefore, there are two different views about *avagraha* among Jainas: *avagraha* as indeterminate perception and *avagraha* as determinate perception.

as the indeterminate perception or inarticulate sensation. *Īhā* is the intellectual enquiry about the specific nature of the indeterminate object. The state of doubt in perception remains in between the quick successive stages of *avagraha* and *īhā*. With a view of eradicating doubt, this mental state reflects upon the properties of the object. It identifies the special features of the object. It includes speculation, thought, reasoning, and examination. *Avāya* is the stage of determinate cognition with a definitive identification of the object of *īhā*. It is the state of perceptual judgement. *Dhāraṇā* is the retention of the identification of the object. It galvanises impression (*saṁskāra*) in the mind, which is experienced as the memory of the object apprehended in previous stages. It is the condition of memory.[100]

Ācārya Umāsvāmi reiterates that the object perceived in *Avagraha* persists in all the subsequent three stages.[101] There are identity and difference in the cognitive stages. Vādidevasūri explains it like this: "Though these are in some aspects one and the same, yet they are to be distinguished owing to the peculiarity in modifications. As they are perceived to be separate from one another owing to their not arising simultaneously; and as each of them reveals a new aspect of things; and as they come up one after the other; they are to be distinguished."[102] The subject of psychological processes of perception is the knowing self, and hence, they are non-different. Owing to the successive appearance of four stages and corresponding aspects of an object, they are different. Thus, Jainas asserts

100 Cf. PM: 1.1.29.

101 Cf. TS: 1.17.

102 PNT: 2. 12, 13.

kathaṃcid abhede'pi pariṇāma-viśeṣād eṣāṃ vyapadeśs bhedaḥ asāmastyenāpy utpadyamānatvenāsaṃkīrṇa-svabhāvatayānubhūyamānatvād apūrvāpūrva-vastu paryaya-prakāśakatvāt kramabhāvitvāc caite vyatiricyante.

that the four stages of the psychology of perception are neither completely different nor completely non-different.

3.5.2 Senses

Indian systems have recorded different and definite views of the senses. They conceive sense organs as the physical end-organs or sense-orifices (*Buddhism*), the unique capacity of the physical organ (*Mimāmsa*), the modification of subtle all-pervading material principle (*Sāmkhya*), an altogether different substance, which has its locus in the physical organs, and the subtle and material substance, which are composed of the same substance, the quality of which is sensed by it.[103] Jaina has quite a distinct view regarding the constitution and function of the senses.

The instrumental causes of the act of empirical perception are the constituent conditions of empirical perception. It produces a clear and distinct knowledge of the object to which with contact. The sense organs are "the conditions of specific cognitions."[104] Having asserted instrumentality of the senses in the process of cognition, Pt. Sukhlaji commented and defined senses as "that through the instrumentality of which one can attain cognition."[105] According to Jainism, the embodied state of the soul experiences the object of the knowledge through the

---

103 Cf. D. M Datta, *The Six Ways of Knowing*, p. 34.

104 PM: 1.1.21. no. 79.

"*jñānaviśeṣahetūnāmeveheāndriyatvenādhikṛtattvāt.*".

The reason for the assertion of the statement is because of the controversy regarding the inclusion of motor organs as a sense organ. According to Jainism, the realm of tactual sense organ extends to all motor organs because they are reducible to muscular movement due to the nervous stimulation and response. Cf. Vidyanandi, *Tattvarthaslokavartika*: p. 326, quoted in T. G. Kalghatgi, *Some Problems in Jain Psychology*, p. 51.

105 Pt Sukhlaji's Commentary on *Tattvārtasūtra*, p. 88.

instrumentality of senses. There are five organs of perception; the organ of touch, the organ of taste, the organ of sight, the organ of smell, and the organ of hearing. Accordingly, there are five types of sensory experiences and five types of perceptual objects. The objects are possessed of qualities such as touch, taste, odour, coloured shape, and sound. Hemacandrasūri defines senses as "the capacity of apprehending respective qualities" as its characteristic.[106] Each of the sense organs has its own characteristic capacity of experiencing their own qualities. Thus, a sense organ is the composite of physical and psychical elements. Indeed, they are the outer and inner structure of the sense organ. Jaina apprehends it as the physical (*drvyendriya*) and psychical (*bhāvendriya*) structure of the sense organ, respectively.

Of these, *drvyendriya* is caused "by the manifestation of the corresponding nāma-karma", and *bhāvendriya* is brought into being "by the subsidence and destruction of the obscuring karma and obstructive karma frustrating the relevant capacity."[107] *Drvyendriya* is 'the clusters of matter (*pudgala*) possessed of a particular form and definite shape (*niyathākārām*)', and *bhāvendriya* is 'the modes of the soul possessed of the nature of consciousness (*upayoga*).'[108] The material component confers and designs a definite form and physical appearance of the sense organ. *Nama-karma* becomes the material cause of the physical substance. The particular and definite shape of the sense organ possesses two composite parts; *nirvṛtti* and *upakaraṇa*. *Nirvṛtti* is the actual outer physical sense organ, and *upakaraṇa* is the external and

---

106 PM: 1.1. 21. no. 75.

107 PM: 1.1. 21. no. 77.

108 TS: 2.15; Cf. P.M 1.1. 22-23.

draveyendriyaṁ niyathākārāḥ pudgalāḥ
bhavendriyaṁ labdyupayogai.

internal capacity of the physical sense organ to produce the manifestation of the object. *Bhāvendriya* is dual in nature; *labdhi* and *upayoga*. *Labdhi* or attainment is the manifestation of the specific sense activity. The act of manifestation belongs to the competency of the conscious self. The self can engage the physical sense for the apprehension of the object. The suppression and annihilation of karmic influences generate and enhance the capacity of the self. *Upayoga* is the psychic force that determines the specific sensory experience. It is the attention and modification of the self.[109] Thus, *upayoga* is the conscious activity of the self. If there is no *labdhi*, a sense organ cannot apprehend its object, and if there is no *upayoga* towards the object, the object cannot be apprehended.[110] It means that the physical sense organ (*drvyendriya*) connects with the object only when it is appropriated by the psychic sense organ (*bhāvendriya*). Therefore, both aspects of the sense are necessary for the occurrence of perception. Umāsvāmi commented on the concept of sense in *Svapajña Bhāṣya*; 'a sense, as a physical organ (*nirvṛtti*), is the necessary condition of a sense as the capacity to perceive (*upakaraṇa*), and as a sentient application (*labdhi*). However, a sense as the sentient potential (*upayoga*) lies at the root of the other aspects of a sense.'[111] Thus, the sense organ is the material substance, which is conducive to engage in the manifestation of the self through the conscious activity for the apprehension of the relevant object.

3.5.3 Mind

The mind is the conventional concept of psychology and metaphysics as well. Obviously, the metaphysical

---

109 Cf. TS: 2.15-19; PM: 1.1. 22-23.

110 Cf. Pushpa Bothra, *The Jaina Theory of Perception*, p. 55.

111 Umasvati, *Svapajña Bhāṣya* quoted in Nathmal Tatia, *Commentary on Tattvārtha Sūtra* p. 44.

understanding enhances the psychological significance of the mind in the cognitive process. Indian systems generally accept the irrevocable place of the mind in cognition. *Sāṅkhya*, *Nyāya-Vaiśeṣika*, Prabhākara, Bhaṭṭa, and *Bhāmitī* school of *Advaita Vedānta* agree on the mind as the internal organ of perception. *Vivaraṇa* school of *Advaita Vedānta* squashes the organ status of the mind. *Nyāya-Vaiśeṣika* accepts the mind as the unconscious substance, and the internal sense organ "that is the instrument of the direct awareness of pleasure and pain etc."[112] The *Sāṅkhya* considers it to be the unconscious product of *ahaṅkāra* and cognised through the reflection of intelligent principle *Puruṣa*. It is called the organ because "it is the deliberating principle (*saṅkalpakam*), and possesses properties common to the sense organs (*sādharmyāt*)."[113] *Vedānta Paribhāsha* totally rejects the perception that the mind is the organ. For them, the mind (indecisive stage of mind) is one of the functions (*vṛtti*) of *antḥakaraṇa* along with *buddhi* (decisive stage of Mind), *ahaṅkāra* (ego-sense) and *citta* (recollection of impressions). Thus, the mind is to be understood as *antḥakaraṇa* in *Vedānta* view. The perception of internal qualities such as pleasure and pain does not require any internal sense (like mind) because these qualities are the modifications of *antḥakaraṇa*.[114] All the Indian systems unanimously agree that the mind is unconscious and non-luminous in its existence.

Jaina doctrines accept the instrumental function of the mind. However, it is not a sense. Therefore, Jaina declares the mind as "*anindriya*."[115] The prefix '*an*' is, however, not interpreted in a negative sense. Positively, it indicates that

112 *Tarkasaṁgraha*. 18. *sukhādyāupalabdhisādhanam indriyam manaḥ*.

113 SK: 27.

114 Cf. VP: pp. 10-11.

115 TS: 2.22.

'something higher than sense organs.' The mind is not the conscious self. As a means of cognition, it is an instrument. But, the function of the mind is not specific like that of the other sense organs. It appears as the common element in the sense apprehension of objects but, it has to depend on the sense organs for cognising the external objects. Thus, Jaina calls the mind as quasi-organ[116] *Pramānamimāṃsā* renders a positive definition of the mind: "*sarvārthagrahaṇaṁ manaḥ.*"[117] It states that 'the mind is the organ of apprehension of all objects of all the senses.' It obviously implies the higher status of the mind over the sense organs, which is specifically determined to be the organ of apprehension of the particular object. The mind is not confined to any of the physical qualities. Hence, the content and function of the mind is not identical with the sense organ; whereas, the inclusion of the phrase "organ of apprehension" affirms the instrumental character of the mind.

Like the sense organ, the instrumental character of the mind assumes two aspects; *dravya manas* and *bhāva manas.*[118] *Dravya manas* represent the unconscious and material composition of the mind. It is the physical aspect of the mind.

---

116 Cf. Indira Chandra Sastri, *Jaina Epistemology*, p. 248; Pt Sukhlaji's Commentary on *Tattvārtasūtra*, p. 93.

117 PM: 1.1.24.

118 When we understand the five sensed soul as the possessor of the mind, it is not claiming the complete absence of the mind in the lower sensed souls. *Bhāva manas* is possessed by all the sensed souls, without exception. The concern of the complete absence and classification of the soul is based on the possession of *dravya manas* only. Because the appropriate function of *bhava manas* requires the necessary help of the corresponding *dravya manas*. On account of that, the lower sensed souls can also move towards what is desirable and stand away from undesirable. But this use of the mind is just for the maintenance of the body and not meant for reflection and knowledge. *Saṃjña represents* here the specific type of behaviour is of the form of reflection over the merits and demerits of things.

Bhāva manas is the psychical attention of the mind. It is the attainment of the capacity to apprehend the objects owing to the suppression and annihilation of karmic obscurities. Hemacandra in *Pramānamimāṃsā* explains the logic behind the cognitive function of the mind (*bhāva manas*): "This function of the mind is the attainment consisting in the subsidence and destruction of the relevant obscuring karma and the specific activation of the self apt to apprehend its object."[119]

External sense organs become the instrument to the perceptible objects. The mind is the instrument to cognise the perceptible as well as non-perceptible objects. The object of sensuous and non-sensuous cognition comes under the scope of the object of the mind. It reflects over the objects, which are not even cognised by sense organs. Hence, Jains observes that "the articulate knowledge or the scriptural knowledge (*śruta*) is the domain of the mind."[120] The scriptural knowledge is the object of the mind. It doesn't mean that the mind is absent in all the sense intuition. The 'sense organs play a major role in sense perception, and the mind exerts influence in its generation'. Endowed with a particular kind of purity of the Self, the mental cognition 'occurs in mind.'[121] Like Vedānta, Jainism considers the object of internal perception, such as pleasure, is directly revealed to the Self. *Vedanīya Karman* directly obfuscates the soul and appears to be pain and pleasure, according to Jainism. In another way, they are the qualities of the soul mixed with

---

119 PM: 1.1.24.no. 90.

120 TS: 2.22. 1.20.

121 PM: 1. 1. 20. no. 72.

At the same time, empirical knowledge arises from the sense alone, the mind alone or the two acting together. Lower sensed souls and even some five sensed souls whose knowledge are through senses only. In the human being, one can easily recognise cognition with both mind and sense and even with the mind alone.

the karmic matter. The internal perception of mindless-animal and the Arhat (who do not apply the mind to any psychic activity) approbate the perception even in the absence of the mind.[122]

This instrumental character of the mind asserts the sole agent-hood of the Self in the cognitive process. Therefore, the mind is not a cognising agent but a limited instrument of cognition because it lacks consciousness and self-luminosity. The mind is not substance but the substantive matter, which has the function of the attainment and conscious activity. These natures are almost similar to the sense organs, but the mind is not the sense organ. It is a quasi-sense organ. It is the instrument to cognise sensuous and non- sensuous objects. Still, the sphere and scope of mind are limited in relation to the Self.

3.6 Yogi-Pratyakṣa

The Self (*dravya*) is identical to the consciousness (*guṇa*), but the karmic veils obscure the pristine nature of the conscious Self. In the empirical perception, these obscurities are suppressed partially, and it is limited cognition. The gradual suppression of karmic veils divulges the higher cognition that unleashed from the rein of the sense organ and mind. The culmination of the progression consummates in pure cognition. It results in the illumination of the self and object. Only a self-illuminated Self can illuminate the object and consequently expunges the veil of ignorance. The removal of the veil of ignorance directly implies the cessation of karmic influences. The sense organ and mind fall short of this function. Therefore, they have no role in the realm of pure perception (*pratyakṣa*). In the strict sense, the clear and distinct knowledge (*pratyakṣa*) arises only in the Self. Thus, the content and nature of perception definitely

122 Cf. Indira Chandra Sastri, *Jaina Epistemology*, p. 250.

presume the existence of extrasensory perception. Since this cognition is devoid of the function of a sense organ or the above function of sense organs, it has been called *atīndriya pratyakṣa*. The authentic and definitive perceptual cognition, which is characterised by immediacy and lucidity, is known as *yogi pratyakṣa*. Therefore, in Jainism, *yogi-pratyakṣa* is *pratyakṣa*.

Ācārya Umāsvāti and Ācārya Kundakunda understand it as 'the instances of innate knowledge' and 'pure cognition beyond senses'.[123] Siddhasena Divākarka and Hemacandrasūri define it as 'the cognition that occurs in the gradual illumination of the self-illuminative Self and without the intervention of sense organs and mind, which acquires through meditation and practice.'[124] Akalaṅka and Vādidevasūri define it as 'the perception that arises in the Self without any intermediation of senses and mind.'[125] Māṇikyanandi yields an elaborative definition; "*Mukhya* is that clear, non-sensuous and infinite knowledge of which all veils are removed by special conditions".[126] The special conditions are the mental and bodily disciplines. Hence, *yogi-pratyakṣa* is the total and direct illumination of the conscious Self when ignorance is removed by the regular practice of mental and bodily discipline. This manifestation of the Self is always accompanied by some supernatural or supernormal powers. From the above discussions, one shall sum up the major features of the *yogi-pratyakṣa* in Jainism as;

123 Cf. TS: 1.12; PS: 1.13.

124 Cf. NV: 1. 27; PM: 1.1.15.

125 Cf. Akalaṅka, *Akalaṅkagranthatrayī*: p.2. *mukhyam atīndriyam jñānam*, quoted in Pushpa Bothra, *The Jaina Theory of Perception*, p. Cf. PNT: 2. 18. *pāramārthikaṁ punarutpattāvātmamātrāpekṣam.*

126 PKM: p. 241. *sāmagrīviśeṣaviśleṣitākhilvaraṇamatīndriyīṁ aśeṣato mukhyaṁ.*

1. Self-manifestation of the innate nature of the conscious Self.
2. Cognizant of the object with its modes.
3. Independent of the service of the ancillary instruments such as sense organs and mind.
4. Emerging on the gradual cessation of the karmic obscurities.
5. The existence of varieties of *yogi pratyakṣa*.
6. The definite consummation in perfect knowledge.
7. Acquisition of perfection through a disciplined life.

Owing to the variation of the degrees of that cessation of the obscurities, *yogi-pratyakṣa* has three varieties.[127] They are *Avadhi-Jñāna* (visual intuition), *Manaḥaparyāya-Jñāna* (intuition of the modes of other minds), and *Kevala-Jñāna* (pure cognition). Of these, *Kevala-Jñāna* enjoys a unique status because all the other two varieties of knowledge are accompanied by ignorance. *Kevala-Jñāna* is perfectly innate and emerges due to the total elimination of knowledge covering karma. The other two varieties of *yogi-pratyakṣa* depend on the degree of suppression and annihilation of the karmic influences.

3.7. The Psychology of Yogi-Pratyakṣa

The Self is the subject and instrument of *yogi-pratyakṣa*. Vādidevasūri says, "The subject of all forms of valid cognition is the Self."[128] Knowledge is the natural property of the soul. That which does not originate from a thing can nevertheless illumine that thing, as in the case of the lamp. The knowledge, which originates in the Self, can illumine itself and the object, just as the lamp illumines itself and the pot. Obstruction

---

127 Cf. PM: 1.1.18.

128 PNT: 7. 55. *pramāta pratyakṣādi-prasiddha* ātmā

is something external. *Yogi-pratyakṣa* can be obtained by eliminating these external obstructions. The removal of karma entails the illumination of fourfold infinities or perfections (*ananta darśana, ananta jñāna, ananta sukha* and *ananta vīrya*). In this state, the Pure Self exists in the auspicious body with infinite apprehension (*darśana*), comprehension (*jñāna*), happiness (*sukha*), and power (*vīrya*).[129] The nature and extent of the knowledge of the Self depend on the nature and extent of the karmic obscuring veil. Complete annihilation of the veils of karma is the prerequisite of perfect knowledge and omniscience. In the strict sense, all the varieties of knowledge other than omniscience are somehow being affected by the karmic influences due to the constant rise of knowledge covering karma.[130] Therefore, there were two components in the psychology of *yogi pratyakṣa*; the gradual illumination of the self and the gradual removal of the veil of karma.

3.7.1 The Self-illumination of the Self

The self-luminous and self-conscious Self is the contentious discussion in Indian philosophy. The supernatural perception or transcendental perception is based on the assumption of the self-luminous and self-conscious Self. There are differences of opinions about the cognition of the Self. *Nyāya-Vaiśeṣika* holds the Self, which is known by an act of inference from its qualities. Later, *Nyāya* admits yogic intuition as the means of cognition of Self. *Sāṅkhya* infers the existence of the Self through its reflection in Buddhi or intellect, the first evolute of *Prakṛti*. *Yoga* maintains that the Self is the object of higher intuition. Bhaṭṭa *Mīmāṁsa* holds that the Self is the object of internal perception and it is self-revealing. Prabhākara considers the Self as the unilluminated but allows self-illumination of cognition. For Prabhakāra School, the Self is the substratum of

129 Cf. DS: 50.

130 Cf. TS: 13-14.

consciousness and cognition but it is something unconscious. *Advaita Vedānta* clearly states that the Self, which is known by the immediate and intuitive consciousness.

According to Jainas, the Self is self-luminous and self-conscious. Vādidevasūri affirms it by saying that "the certain knowledge of the Self consists in the clear illumination of the self, just as that of the outside thing, in that of the outside thing."[131] He continues to say that, in the cognition, "I know the young elephant along with myself," it is not the cognition of the elephant that reveals the Self and the elephant, as Prabhākara holds. But it is the Self which reveals itself through itself, the elephant, and the cognition of the elephant.[132] Jadunath Sinha observes, "For, whatever is revealed in our experience is cognized, and whatever is cognized is an object of consciousness. Thus, it is self-contradictory to suppose that the Self and its cognition are not objects of perception, though they are directly revealed in our experience."[133]In the cognition of the elephant, the cognisor, "I" or the self (*pramāta*), the instrument "myself" (*pramāṇa*), and the result "knowing" (*pramiti*) are as much objects of perception as the cognized object, the elephant (*prameya*). At the same time, they retain the respective character as the subject, object, instrument, and the result of cognition. Persuaded by the misconception that to be perceived is to an object, Prabhākara has squashed the perceptibility of the Self. One cannot deny the cognition of the cognizing subject because cognition and the cognizing Self are directly revealed in our experience.

---

131 PNT: 1.16.

Svasya vyavasāyaḥ svābhimukhyena prakāśanaṃ
bāhyasyeva tad ābhimukhyena,
karikalabhakam aham ātmanā *jānāmi*.

132 Cf. PNT: 1.16.

133 Jadunath Sinha, *Indian Psychology: Perception*, p. 244.

Siddhsena Divākarka contends the inevitability of self-luminous Self in the function of the cognition of the Self. He says, "The Self is the knower, doer, and enjoyer, illumines Itself and others, undergoes changes of condition, is realised only in self-consciousness."[134] Hemacandrasūri establishes the self-luminous nature of the soul on the ground of three arguments in *Pramāṇa-Mīmāṃsā*. He reiterates the indubious existence of the Self, the knower status and author status of the Self through these three arguments. He argues:

> Firstly, the Self is of a self luminous nature, because its being is not susceptible to doubt. That which is not of self-luminous nature cannot but be susceptible to doubt, for example, a jar [...]. Nobody is known to doubt that 'Do I exist or not [...]. Secondly, the Self is of luminous nature, because it is the knower. Whatever is not of self-luminous nature, such as a jar for example, is not a knower. Thirdly, that which is the author of an act cannot be the object of such an act [...]. The Self is the author of the act of knowing and hence cannot be its object.[135]

The clear and distinct cognition of the Self consists in the clear illumination of the Self. How does this self-illumination work? The cognition does not generate its self-consciousness in a specific time, but the cognition is generated along with the nature of self-consciousness. That is to say, "the knowledge does not engage in the act of revealing itself, but the knowing process is self-conscious by nature."[136] In empirical cognition, the self-illumination of cognition is limited due to the influence of karmic veils; whereas, with the removal of karmic obscurities, the self-illumination is absolute and clear in *yogi-pratyakṣa*.

134 NV: 31.

135 PM: 1.1.15. no. 49.

136 PNT: 1.17, p. 67.

Therefore, Hemacandrasūri defines *yogi-pratyakṣa* as "*tat sarvarthāvaranavileya cetanasya svarūpāvibāvo mukhyaṁ kevalam*", which means 'the full manifestation of the innate nature of a conscious self, emerging on the total cessation of all obstructive veils, is called 'that' *yogi-pratyakṣa*'.[137] Owing to the cessation of all obscurities, everything is perceptible directly and clearly. The illuminated self of *yogi* "does not seize or release; does not evolve into the object of knowledge; the object of knowledge does not transform to the self; but without exception, one sees and knows all objects of knowledge around."[138] Amṛtacandra Sūri explains the psychology of cognition in *yogi-pratyakṣa* as follows:

> This Self, according to its innate nature, of no seizing, no releasing, no evolution into anything else, evolves owing to its characteristic nature of absolute knowledge, which is its own principle (*tattva*). And thus, sanding forth like a genuine jewel of motionless and radiant light, it possesses an everywhere glittering efficacy of vision and knowledge; so then It becomes by Itself, in Itself, aware of the Self in its entirety without remainder. To explain otherwise, by simultaneous, intuitive perception of the multitude of all things, wavering of notion is excluded, and there is cessation of all supposed acts such as grasping and releasing. In this way, the Self by first evolving into all distinguishable appearances and then again not evolving into any appearance, sees and knows everything without exception everywhere whilst remaining in isolation.[139]

---

137 PM: 1.1.15.

138 PS: 1. 32.

geṇahadi ṇeva ṇa sumcadi ṇa param pariṇmadi kevalī bhagavam
pecchadi samatado so jāṇdi savvam ṇiravasesam.

139 Amṛtacandra Sūri commentary to *Pravaccanasāra:* 1. 32.

The gradual unfolding of consciousness of the Self to higher and higher states is resulting in the progressive widening of knowledge, till the Self becomes perfect, and knowledge becomes co-extensive with reality. This is the state of omniscience of the Self, i.e., the perfect *yogi-pratyakṣa*. The resonance of the upward movement of consciousness replicates reflects in the different states of supernatural perception. "The manifested effect conditions the nature of the manifesting agent, and similarly, the manifesting agent determines the nature of effects."[140] This is the evident principle of causality in Jainas. There is an invariable relationship between the nature of the supernatural perception and the nature of the subject of supernatural perception.

The total illumination of the Self illuminates or manifests all the substances and their modes clearly and distinctly. It is direct and perfect knowledge. Siddhasena Divākarka in *Nyāyavatāra* defines *yogi-pratyakṣa*: "That which is characterised as free from all obstructions and shines as the absolute is called transcendental perception; it uninterruptedly illumines the nature of all objects." [141]The radiance of the perfect manifestation is vividly explained by Ācārya Kundakunda in *Pravaccanasāra*; "the full manifestation of the Self perceives directly those not present modes, which yet to originate, and which had originated in the past, not existing in the present, of a substance".[142] Ācārya Umāsvāmi sounds the same as 'the subject matter of direct perception is all the substances with all their modifications.'[143] The cognition of the self-illuminated Self is identical with the cognition of the whole reality. 'Knowledge of the Knower is also the knowledge

140 SS: 311. *kammaṁ paḍucca kattā kattāraṁ taha paḍucca kammāṇi*

141 NV: 27.

142 PS: 1.37-39.

143 TS: 1.29. *sarvadravya paryāyeṣu kevalsya*.

of the known,' and only one who knows the real Self can know the non-self.[144] 'It comprehends all objects of knowledge directly and simultaneously, and this all-compassing and indestructible knowledge are beyond sensory knowledge of the world.'[145] This does not come under the scope of empirical perception. Hence, Vādidevasūri comments the genesis of *yogi-pratyakṣa* 'is totally dependent on the soul alone.'[146]

3.7.2 Psychic States of the Soul: Interaction between Karma and Soul

Jainas impeccably holds the sovereignty of the Self over karmic matter. However, they reiterate the real interaction between the Self and karmic matter. Karma obliterates the clear and distinct cognition of the Self. It makes different psychic states (*bhāva*) of the Self. Ācārya Kundakunda in *Samayasāra* encapsulates the interaction between the Self and karma and the successive psychic states of the soul:

> The psychic states corresponding to wrong belief, wrong knowledge, non-discipline, and psycho-physical activity are the causes of karma such as *jñānāvarṇiya*. On account of the psychic states relating to pure perception etc., the karmic conditions are absent. This absence of conditions in one who has discriminative knowledge causes the blocking up of psychic inflow (*bhāvāsrava*). If the psychic inflow is blocked up, the blocking of karmic inflow (*dravyāsrava*) necessarily follows. When there is no inflow of material karmas, the inflow of *nokarmic* material is also stopped. When there is no inflow of *nokarmic* body-building materials the process

144 Cf. SS: 15; 202.

145 Cf. PS: 1.15, 21. 22.

146 PNT: 2.18. *Pāramārthikaṃ punar-utpattau* ātmamātrāpekṣam.

of body-building will completely disappear which means the cessation of *saṁsāra*.[147]

The karmic material is the *modus operandi* for the psychic and physical changes in the Self. Owing to the gradual suppression and annihilation of the karmic influences, there are impermanent physical and psychic states of the Self. Correspondingly, the active Self engages in a suitable responsive reaction. It is the cognitive activity of the Self. Thus, the self-evolving Self procures modifications or changes in response to the operation of karma.

The gradual progression ends up in the annihilation of karma and the concurrent realisation of the true nature of the Self. The Self, at each state, is the possessor of knowledge. Thus, the origination of each verity of knowledge, whether empirical or supernatural, is due to the gradual destruction and abatement of karma.[148] On the destruction of the *Ghatī* (inimical) karmas, the self-conscious Self attains absolute manifestation of the Self and other objects. Then, the Self attains supreme effulgence. The possessor of this knowledge obtains liberation from karma. It is the state of pure, discriminative and clear knowledge. It is the paramount state of cognition, which is identical to the soul. Thus, the stoppage of karmic flow into the Self is the necessary postulate for the manifestation of the supernatural perception.

According to the degree of interaction between karma and Self, they are five states (*bhāvas*) of the Self. The soul is the substance, which is permanent in the midst of modifications. These modifications, such as cognition, pain and pleasure, etc., are characterised by some states or conditions. "It is these different conditions possibly characterising a mode that

147 SS: 190-192.

148 Cf. PNT: 2. 14; SS: 314-316; 203; 293.

is called *bhāvas*."[149] These states are "due to the suppression of the deluding karma, elimination of the eight types of karma, partial suppression and partial elimination of the four destructive karmas, the rising of the eight types of karma and the last state constitute the innate nature of the soul."[150] The last state is "the nature of the self manifests in the form of pure *upayoga*, and he does not cause any kind of impure psychic states."[151] All these states of the soul are not found together simultaneously in all the souls. Among these, the first four states of the soul are due to direct interaction with karma, and the last one is about the essential nature of the soul.

3.7.2.1 *Audāyika*

This state of soul is due to the rising (*udaya*) or the manifestation of eight types of karma. It is the state of bondage and ignorance. The modes characterised by this condition is accidental. It generates four types of passions (*kāṣyā*) such as anger, deceit, greed, and conceit as well as deludes the world view (*mithyādarśana*). It is the cause of undisciplined self, and it sprouts six colourings (*laṣyā*) such as black, blue, grey, red, yellow and white. It results in the four transmigration realms (*gati*) which are the respective habitats of infernal beings, sub-humans (plants and animals), men and gods and three sexual feelings (*veda*) such as feminine, masculine, and neuter.

3.7.2.2 *Aupaśamika*

It is the state of Self due to the suppression of the deluding karma (*mohaṇīya karma*). The two varieties of deluding

---

149 Pt. Sukhlalji, *Commentary on Tattvārtha Sūtra*, p. 74.

150 TS: 2.1 *aupaśamikar ksyāikau bhāvau miśraś ca jīvasya svatattvam audayika pārināmikau ca*; Cf. SS: 190-192.

151 SS : 183.

edaṁ tu avivarīdaṁ ṇāṇaṁ jaiyā du hodi jīvassa
taiyā ṇa kiṁci kuvvadi bhāvaṁ uvaogasuddhappā.

karma (view deluding karma (*darśana mohaṇīya karma*) and conduct deluding karma (*cāritra mohaṇīya karma*) are being temporally suppressed, which results in enlightened world view and enlightened conduct. Since both are achieved by temporary suppression, they are very short-lived.

3.7.2.3 *Ksāyopaśamika*

It is the state of Self due to the partial suppression and partial elimination of the destructive karma. Thus, it depends on the annihilation (*ksāya*), mitigation (*upaśama*) and activity (*udaya*) conditions of karma. This state of the Self is characterised by 'four kinds of knowledge (empirical, articulate, clairvoyant and mind-reading), three kinds of deluded knowledge (deluded empirical, deluded articulate and deluded clairvoyant), three kinds of intuition (visual, non-visual and clairvoyant), and the five kinds of potential (beneficence, gain, satisfaction, comfort and power) along with enlightened world view and enlightened conduct.'[152]

3.7.2.4 *Ksyāika*

It is the state of Self due to the total elimination of karma, particularly four destructive karmas. After the elimination of karmas, the Self shines forth in its pure nature. It is the level of determinate cognition. The pure nature of Self is presented as the enlightened world view (*samyak darśana*), enlightened conduct (*cāritra*), omniscience (*jñāna*), perfect intuition (*darśanopayoga*), beneficence (*dāna*), gain (*lābha*), satisfaction (*bhoga*), comfort (*upabhoga*) and power (*virya*).[153] This discriminative knowledge distinguishes between the Self and karma that arises in the Self. Here, the nature of Self manifests in the form of pure consciousness. Further, the Self is no more subjected to any modification in future.[154]

---

152 Cf. TS: 2.5.

153 Cf. TS: 2.4.

154 Cf. SS: 182-183.

3.7.2.5 *Pārināmika*

This state of the Self is about the natural and original of the Self. It is not the result of any karmic influences or process but the illumination of the innate nature of the Self. It is *pārināmika bhavā* of the Self. These constituent *bhavās* are '*Jīvatva*,' '*bhavyatva*', and '*abhayatva*'.[155] *Jīvatva* means that being attended with the essential attribute or quality of the Self, i.e., 'Sentience' (*upayoga*). *Bhavyatva* denotes the capacity of the Self of 'being worthy of liberation', and *abhayatva* represents the nature of the Self, which deprived of liberation or 'being unworthy of liberation'. Since *Jīvatva* has intruded in both *bhavyatva*, and *abhayatva*, the omniscience exists in potential form in both. The omniscience in potentiality becomes explicit in the former and remains as the eternal potentiality in the latter. Hence, it says, "the soul is never bereft of sentience, however feeble and indistinct this may be in undeveloped organisms."[156]

The five types of psychic states of the Self constitute the nature of the Self. A non-soul is absent of these states of existence. The soul-hood is entrenched into these states of the Self. However, the bound and liberated Self must be featured by one of these states. Obviously, all five types cannot be seen simultaneously in the embodied soul at the same time. *Pārināmika and Ksyāika* ingrains in the liberated souls. Thus, these are the psychic states of the supernatural soul. In the case of worldly souls, some possess three, some possess four, some possess of five, and none of them is possessed of just two states.[157]

---

155 Cf. TS: 2.7, 2.8 "*Upayogo lakṣaṇam*". There are characteristics of the Self other than these innate modes, such as existence etc., which are common to the non-soul and the soul where as these three innate states are unique to the soul.

156 *Tattvārtha Sūtra*: *That Which Is*, trans. By Nathmal Tatia, p. 39.

157 Cf. Pt. Sukhlaji, Commentary on *Tattvārtha Sūtra* of Vācaka

3.8 Conclusion

This chapter explores the epistemological and psychological foundations of yogi-pratyakṣa, providing an interpretive analysis of *pramāṇa*, *pratyakṣa*, and *yogi-pratyakṣa* to reveal the underlying epistemological and logical presuppositions of Jainism. These concepts also form the core principles of Jaina psychology. Stating the self-illumination of the Self and the manifestation of the object as the defining attributes of *pramāṇa*, Jaina has explixcitly denied the *pramāṇa* status of sense organ, sense-object contact, and object. Instead, Jainism upholds cognition (*jñāna*) as the true pramāṇa. According to Jaina doctrine, cognition is the conscious activity of the Self, with the Self and this conscious activity being intrinsically identical. This identity, however, is obscured by karmic influences. Through the suppression and eventual annihilation of these karmic veils, the Self achieves a state of clear and distinct perception. Consequently, *pratyakṣa* is defined as the immediate and lucid cognition of the Self, independent of the limitations imposed by sense organs and the mind. In Jainism, the Self serves as both the subject and instrument of *pratyakṣa*. Thus, in Jainism, the nature of perception is extrasensory. The study of cognition (*jñāna*), empirical perception (*sāṁvyavahārika pratyakṣa*), and transcendental perception (*yogi-pratyakṣa*) supports the notion of a perfect and pure perception of the Self. The limpid perspicacity of cognitive process enhances the epistemological validity and psychological significance of *yogi-pratyakṣa*. As cognitive activity is a gradual progression, transcendental perception is characterized by progressive stages. The forthcoming chapter will further explore these various degrees of *yogi-pratyakṣa*.

Umāsvāti, p. 75-76.

CHAPTER 4

Yogi-Pratyakṣa in Jain Philosophy

The interpretive understanding of the metaphysical, psychological and epistemological backup of *yogi-pratyakṣa* divulges the meaning and scope of *yogi-pratyakṣa* in Jain philosophy. Recent studies in parapsychology focus on three primary areas of experiential inquiry: informational cognition, mind-matter relations, and survival research. These areas correspond to the Jain conceptions of *yogi-pratyakṣa*, manifesting as *Avadhi* (clairvoyance), *Manaḥparyaya* (telepathy), and *Kevalajñāna* (omniscience). This chapter offers an analytical and interpretive examination of *yogi-pratyakṣa*, building upon the discussions from previous chapters. It delves into the unique nature and function of *yogi-pratyakṣa* within Jain philosophy, beginning with an analysis of related terms and common concepts in Indian philosophy. The chapter proceeds by detailing the Jain understanding of *yogi-pratyakṣa* and its various manifestations, ultimately highlighting its epistemological validity and soteriological significance. By elucidating the nature and function of *yogi-pratyakṣa*, the chapter aims to substantiate its role within Jain thought and its broader implications for understanding cognition and spiritual liberation.

4.1 Related Terms

Indian philosophy and tradition are conversant to the doctrine of supra-cosmic powers and the possibility of instantaneous knowledge. Several concepts within this tradition bear resemblance to *yogi-pratyakṣa*, each addressing the nature, scope, and conditions of extrasensory perception in nuanced ways. However, *yogi-pratyakṣa* represents a distinct and comprehensive framework within Jain thought. While it shares foundational elements with broader Indian philosophical ideas, *yogi-pratyakṣa* is uniquely articulated within Jainism. A detailed examination of related terms and concepts reveals the specific features that set Jain yogi-pratyakṣa apart from other interpretations of extrasensory perception in Indian philosophy. This discursive study highlights the distinctive nature of the Jain understanding of *yogi-pratyakṣa*, clarifying its unique contributions and perspectives within the broader philosophical landscape.

4.1.1 Ārṣajñāna

Ārṣajñāna refers to the intuitive knowledge possessed by the authors of the *Śāstras*, who are born with this innate understanding. The extent of this knowledge is shaped by their past virtuous karma. *Ārṣajñāna* enables the apprehension of all objects, transcending both time and space, and includes comprehension of *dharma* and other super-sensible entities. This intuitive knowledge encompasses both sensory and non-sensory objects. The development of *Ārṣajñāna* is supported by practices such as austerities, meditation, and moral achievements, which enhance the supernatural abilities of its possessor. Unlike ordinary perception, which relies on external sense organs, *Ārṣajñāna* is accessed through the mind's direct connection with the Self and specific *dharma*. Thus, *Ārṣajñāna* represents a form of intuitive perceptual knowledge that bypasses the external senses. Instead, it is a cognitive process where the mind plays a crucial role, allowing for the perception of both normal and extraordinary objects without the involvement of the external sense organs.

4.1.2 Siddha Darśana

Siddha Darśana is the perception of occultists. Different from *Ārṣajñāna*, *Siddha Darśana* falls short of the perception of supersensible objects because the external sense organs are the instruments of occult perception. Yogic practices, meditation, moral accomplishments and austerities are neither causal nor instrumental factors for this perception. They perceive subtle, hidden, and remote sensible objects through external senses with occult powers. These objects are not perceptible for external senses in their normal conditions. It is the perception through the external sense organs sharpened by the application of certain unguents or ointments or intoxicative medicines.[1] This external application over sense organs generates occult powers. To the consideration of genesis, it is purely sensuous. External sense organs are the causal factor for this supernormal perception, but it is not confined to the scope of ordinary sense perception.

4.1.3 Prāibhajñāna

Prātibhajñāna is intuitive knowledge. It is an intrinsic quality. External factors have little importance here. Patāñjali

---

1 Cf. PDS: 556; Indira Chandra Shastri, *Jaina Epistemology*, pp. 326-327. Robert E. Svabodha, in his book *Aghora: At the Left Hand of God*, describes the purpose of intoxicants. The intoxicant medicines or ointments deteriorate the body and the mind is partially unleashed from the captivity of the body. He says, "Your mind works so fast that your body can't keep up with it, and it becomes flaccid, loose. The less the mind self identifies with the body the better for your Sadhana, but worse for your body; your physical health will give way to improved mental health." Cf. Robert E. Svabodha, *Aghora: At the Left Hand of God*, p. 179.

refers to *prātibha* as the supernatural knowledge and later, Vyāsa comments and names it as *t*ārka in *Yogabhāṣya*.[2] Perfecting one's own intellect stirs up intuitive knowledge. It has two varieties: the higher or permanent intuition and the lower or occasional intuition. Higher intuition is equivalent to ārṣa*jñāna*, which is the intuition of Seers. The perfection of *prātibha* is the intuitive knowledge of the object irrespective of time and space. Comprehensiveness and simultaneous revelation of the mind or intellect are the distinctive features of it. Lower intuition is the flash or ephemeral intuition of ordinary people. *Prātibha* is that a direct perceptual cognition of a future object produced by the mind. Since it is not known by any other means of knowledge except through intuition, it is a valid cognition. It is not a doubtful cognition because of the absence of contradictory factors. It is not erroneous cognition because the cognition is produced by an object, which has real existence in the future. But the future object is non-existent to the present place. It implies that the object is not non-existent, but non-existence is in its relation to the present place. The object of intuitive cognition "is reproduced in memory owing to a certain cause, and the reproduction of the object in memory is the cause of its presentation in consciousness. The intuition of the object, therefore, is the effect of its reproduction in memory."[3] Apparently, the mind or intellect functions as the instrument for *Prātibhajñāna*. The mind intuitively and immediately perceives a future object without the assistance of the external sense organs.

4.2 Yogi-Pratyakṣa in Indian Philosophy

An enquiry into the similar idea of *yogi-pratyakṣa* (extrasensory perception) in Indian philosophical traditions reckons the distinction of the Jaina view. Except for the early

2 Cf. YS: 3. 54; 3.33. *Yogabhāṣya*: P.308.

3 Jadunath Sinha, *Indian Psychology: Perception*, p. 345.

Nyāya-Vaiśeṣikas, *Cārvāka*, and *Mīmāṃsā*, all the Indian philosophical systems unanimously acknowledge the existence and function of the extrasensory perception. The *Cārvāka* excoriate extrasensory perception in order to safeguard their epistemology. For them, all perception is the only means of knowledge. The *Mīmāṃsa* adamantly holds that the past, the future, the distant and the subtle can only be conceived and known by the injunctions of the Vedas. Due to the stringent adherence towards the contact of sense organ and object as the conditions of *pramāṇa*, the early *Nyāya-Vaiśeṣika* raise doubt on the validity of super-sensual cognitions.

The *Vedānta* systems accept yogic powers and perception. The realisation of Brahman through *Śravaṇa*, *Manana*, and *Nididhyāsana* is the aim of *Vedāntic* systems. *Aparokṣānubhūti*, an Advaita *prakaraṇagrantha* (introductory book), explains about the ground of supernatural powers attained by practice and meditation. 'A person who meditates upon a thing with great assiduity and firm conviction becomes that very thing.' 'The perfection of such meditation is by the thought of Brahman by which one attains perfection.' 'It is the perfection of cognition or perception called *Samādhi*.'[4] Another Advaita *prakaraṇagrantha*, Ātmabodha, says, "The perfect *yogi* of realisation and enlightenment sees, through his 'eye of wisdom' (*jñāna-cakṣu*), the entire universe in his own Self and regards everything else as his own Self and nothing else."[5] It clearly

4 Cf. *Aparokṣānubhūti*: 124; 126; 129; 140. Cf. Śaṅkarācārya, *Aparokṣanubhūti*, translated and edited by Swami Vimuktananda (Almora: Advaita Ashrama, 1938). (Hereafter, *Aparokṣanubhūti*).

5 Ātmabodha: 47.

samyagvijñanavānyogī svātmanyevākhilaṁ jagat
ekaṁ ca sarvamātmānaīkṣate jñānacakṣuṣā.

Cf. Śaṅkarācārya, Ātmabodha, translated and commented by Swami Chinmayananda (Mumbai: Central Chinmaya Mission Trust, 2012[3]). (Hereafter, Ātmabodha).

reiterates the yogic-perception (the eye of wisdom) of the entire universe in Self. The yogin perceives 'all that is perceived as *Ātman*.'[6] *Viśiṣtadvaita Vedānta* accepts *yogi-pratyakṣa* as it is caused by special potency and acquired by yogic practice or by the grace of God as in the case of intuitive knowledge of sages.[7]

Buddha tradition remarkably contributes much to the study of *yogi-pratyakṣa.* Dharmakirti defines yogic knowledge as 'that which acquired by the merits of meditation on transcendental reality.'[8] The commentary reckons three stages of *yogi-pratyakṣa.* In the first stage (*bhāvanāprakarṣa*), the object begins to be cogent. In the second stage (*prakarṣaparyantāvasthā*), the transcendent reality is conceived as if it is covered with a translucent sheath. In the third stage (*yogi-pratyakṣa*), impeccable perception of the object as in the perception of a *āmalaka* fruit on one's palm.[9] It is the state of perfect extrasensory perception. In contrast to most of the Indian thought systems, the Buddhist concept of highest perception is indeterminate intuition free from all mental constructions and determinations. Aniruddha in *Abhidhammatthasaṁgaho* divides consciousness into two: subliminal consciousness (below the stage of consciousness) and supraliminal consciousness (above the stage of consciousness). The supraliminal consciousness is again divided into two: normal consciousness and supra-normal consciousness. The

---

6 Ātmabodha: 48. ātmaivedaṁ *jagatsarvamātmanḥ.*

7 *Nyāya Pariśuddi*: p. 95. Referred in S.M. Srinivasa Chari, *Fundamentals of Viśiṣtadvaita Vedānta* (New Delhi: Motilal Banarsidass, 1998, reprint). p. 83.

> *yogī-pratyakṣam prakṛṣtādṛṣta-viśesjam...*
> *sa ca adṛṣta-viśeṣaḥ yogābhyāsa-tapaścaryādibhiḥ jāyate.*
> *bhagava-prasāda-labda-yogī-pratyakṣam divyam.*

8 *Nyāyabindu*: p. 14. *bhūtārthabhāvanāprakarṣaparyantjaṁ yogijñānaṁ ceti.*

9 *Nyāyabindu*: p. 15.

supra-normal consciousness is the state of *yogi-pratyakṣa*, and the highest stage of supra-normal consciousness is called transcendental consciousness (*lokottara citta*).[10]

Of other systems, later *Nyāya-Vaiśeṣika* (post-fifth century) and *Sāṅkhya-Yoga* systems have accounted for their remarkable teachings and cogent presentations.[11] The interpretive understanding of *Nyāya-Vaiśeṣika*, *Yoga*, and Jain systems enriches the psychological, spiritual, epistemological and practical implications of extrasensory perception in Indian tradition.

4.2.1 Nyāya-Vaiśeṣika

Nyāya-Vaiśeṣika defines valid knowledge as the right apprehension of the object as it is. In other words, valid knowledge must correspond to the object. There are four valid means of knowledge: perception, inference, verbal testimony, and comparison. The modern schools of *Nyāya* expose the limitation of the stringent definition of perception in terms of sense-object contact (*indriyārthasannikarṣa*).[12] They would comment that, on the one side, the old definition abrogates

---

10 Cf. Jadunath Sinha, *Indian Psychology: Perception*, pp. 355-361; Indira Chandra Shastri, *Jaina Epistemology*, pp. 334-338.

11 There are some other reasons by which the research is confined to Nyāya-Vaiśeṣikas and Yoga systems. Firstly, they are realistic philosophers; secondly, the wordings in classifications of extrasensory perception are rather identical; thirdly, the epistemological, psychological and practical implications are well pronounced in them; fourthly, the immediate influence of Vaiśeṣika system (atomism and spiritual materialism) and Yogic practices of the Yoga system is well conspicuous in Jainas doctrines; fifthly, the recent development of comparative studies between western cognitive psychology as well as parapsychology and Yoga psychology and parapsychology.

12 The traditional definition of Nyaya is that "non-erroneous cognition which is produced by the contact of the sense organs with the objects (*indriyārthasannikarṣa*)". Cf. NS: 1.1.4.

the inclusion of extrasensory perception and divine perception under the scope of perception. On another side, it validates inference and memory, where the mind functions as the internal sense organ, as forms of perception. Recuperated from the defects of traditional definitions, the modern schools of *Nyāya* define perception in terms of immediacy (*sākṣātkāritvaṁ*). Perception is the valid presentational knowledge which is immediately known by the knower or the subject.[13] The immediacy is characterised as that which is not brought about by the instrumentality of any previous knowledge. Thus, "perception is the knowledge that is not derived through the instrumentality of other knowledge."[14] It brings both yogic perception and divine perception under the scope of perception. Hence, Jayanta Bhaṭṭa defines *yogi-pratyakṣa* as "the perception of subtle, hidden, remote, past and future objects."[15] He extends the scope of *yogi-pratyakṣa* even to the perception of super-sensible dharma.[16]

For the modern schools of *Nyāya*, *indriya* (sense organ) is "the locus of contact between mind and an object, when the contact is the cause of the knowledge other than memory."[17] Viśvanātha, in *Bhāṣā-Pariccheda*, rightly interprets the meaning of 'contact' (*sannikarṣa*) or 'operation' (*vyāpāra*).[18] In perception, this contact obtains the nature of the medium dimension. It becomes an extraordinary cause

---

13 Cf. TC: 1. P. 552. *Pratyakṣasya sākṣātkāritvaṁ lakṣaṇam*

14 TC: 1. P. 552. *Jñānākaraṃkam jñānamiti tu vayam.*

15 *Nyāyamañjarī*: p.103. *darśanasya ca paro atiśayaḥ sūkṣma vyavahita viprakṛṣṭa bhūta bhaviṣyadādi viṣayatva percm.*

16 *Nyāyamañjarī*: p.107-108.

17 TC: 1. P. 550. *Indriyatvam ca smṛtyajanaka jñāna hetu manas saṃyogāśrayśatvam.*

18 Cf. *Bhāṣa Paricceda*: 58-63. *Bhāṣa Pariccheda*, Visvanātha-Nyāya-Pancānana, translated and edited by Swami Madhavanand (Uttarakhand: Advaita Ashrama, 1940, 6th impression). (Hereafter, BP).

(*asādhāraṇa kāraṇa*) by the relation of inherence (*saṁvaya*) and conjunction (*saṁyoga*). The extraordinariness of *indriya* lies in its capacity of having an 'operation' (*vyāpāra*). The operation is the connection between the organ and the object (*viṣaya indriya saṁbandhaḥ*). It has two dimensions: ordinary operation and extraordinary operation. The subliminal perception (*laukika pratyakṣa*) arises from the ordinary operation of the sense organ with the object. In extrasensory perception (*alaukika pratyakṣa*), the sense organ conceives objects through the extraordinary operation. It animates an extra-ordinary contact between the sense organ, mind and object. Viśvanātha defines it as 'the supernormal connection of the mind due to concentration or *yoga*.'[19] This supernormal connection or the extraordinary operation of sense organs, mind and object behaves as the psychology of *yogi- pratyakṣa* in *Nyāya* philosophy.

The extraordinary contact is of three kinds: *sāmānyalakṣaṇa sannikarṣa*, *jñānalakṣaṇa sannikarṣa*, and *yogaja sannikarṣa*.[20] *Sāmānyalakṣaṇa sannikarṣa* is the extraordinary operation or contact (between *indriya* and *viṣaya*) through the knowledge of the common or universal feature; for instance, the perception of universal cowness in a perceptible cow. *Jñānalakṣaṇa sannikarṣa* is the extraordinary operation or contact based on knowledge with regard to that particular object. It is called the operation through the knowledge of association in which past knowledge is associated with the present perception of the object; for instance, the perception of fragrant rose, where fragrance is associated with the rose even though the fragrance is not the object of the perception. Above mentioned two extrasensory operations and its resultant knowledge are not held under the circumference

19 BP: 65.

20 Cf. BP: 63-66.

of *yogi-pratyakṣa*. Therefore, the research confines its study on the third supernormal connection (*yogaja sannikarṣa*) in which knowledge is on account of concentration (*yoga*). The connection is not a direct, intrinsic, and luminous function of the self. Instead, it is the operation of the Self with other constituent elements of the perception through meditation and concentration.

Nyāya-Vaiśeṣika accepts the hierarchy of extrasensory perception. According to the Nyāya-*Vaiśeṣika* system, there are two classes of *yogi-pratyakṣa*: *yukta* and *viyukta pratyakṣa*. *Yukta pratyakṣa* is the result of the perfect concentration of yogin. *Viyukta pratyakṣa* is the perception of yogin who is striving for. In *yukta pratyakṣa*, the self is in connection with the mind only; whereas, in *viyukta pratyakṣa*, the self is in connection with other factors such as the mind, sense organ and object. The first one totally is alienated from the connection of senses; whereas, the second one is prompted with the function of senses. But objects of *viyukta pratyakṣa* are not perceptible mere through senses alone.[21] Resonance to the general structure of *Nyāya-Vaiśeṣika* stream of thought, Praśastapāda in *Padārthadharmasaṅgraha* reiterates the division of *yogi-pratyakṣa*. He comments on the nature and scope of the extrasensory perception like this:

> Yogin who are in ecstatic conditions [*yukta*] appear precisely true cognitions of the real forms of such things as their own self as well as the selves of others,

---

21 Cf. Piotr Balcerowicz (2016), "Extrasensory Perception in Jainism". pp. 7-8.

Piotr Balcerowicz (2016) extracts the teachings of extrasensory perception in *Vaiśeṣika-sūtra* (9.13-17). He comments that this classical exposition in *Vaiśeṣika-sūtra* is the later addition to it because the notion of extrasensory perception is totally absent in the early *Nyāya-Vaiśeṣika* texts. (Cf. Piotr Balcerowicz (2016), "Extrasensory Perception in Jainism". pp. 5-8)

ākaśa, space, time, air, mind, qualities, actions, generalities and individualities inhering in these and inherence; and the cognitions of those thought about by the mind aided by properties or faculties born of yoga. In the case of yogins out of the ecstatic conditions [*viyukta*], direct sensuous knowledge appears with regard to subtle, hidden, and distant objects, by means of the mind through fourfold contact [the self, mind, sense-organ, and object], by the force of faculties born of yoga.[22]

Having impeccably demarcated the scope of two kinds of extrasensory perception, Praśastapāda ratifies the inclusion of moral accomplishments and practices along with the meditation in the nature and constitution of the extrasensory perception. Following the classical demarcation of the extrasensory perception, Viśvanātha also classifies *yogi-pratyakṣa* into two: *yukta* and *yujñāna*. *Yukta* is a yogin who has attained perfection of concentration; whereas, *yujñāna* is a yogin who is striving for perfection in concentration. Thereupon, there are two resulting virtues; the constant and spontaneous knowledge of everything in the universe and the knowledge, which is aided by meditations, respectively.[23]

Śrīdhara, an adherent of *Vaiśeṣika* School and a commentator of Praśastapāda's *Padārthadharmasaṅgraha*, embarks an interpretive understanding of extrasensory perception.[24] The commentary consolidates the teachings of other systems, even without adulterating the originality

22 PDS: 6,10. P. 392.

23 Cf. BP: 65; 66.

24 Cf. *Nyāyakandali*, pp. 411-417. Cf. Srīdhara, *Nyāyakandali*, translated and edited by Mahāmahopādhyāya Gaṅgādhara Śāstri Tailaṅga (Banares: E. J Lazarus & com., 1916). (Hereafter, *Nyāyakandali*).

of *Nyāya-Vaiśeṣika* thought system. Depended on the constituents of the formation of knowledge, there are two types of extrasensory perceptions: yogic (ecstatic) and non-yogic (non-ecstatic). Yoga means *Samādhi*, which is roughly translated as ecstasy. Yogic perception is again divided into two: *samprajñāta* (conscious ecstasy) and *asamprajñāta* (unconscious or supra-conscious ecstasy). In *samprajñāta samādhi*, the mind concentrated upon self with a motive of attainment of knowledge and liberation; whereas, in *asamprajñāta samādhi*, the mind is simply engrossed in the self without having distractions, even without the thought of liberation. Non-ecstatic condition for the extrasensory perception consists of the four-fold contact and in the accumulation of moral and spiritual excellence through yogic practices. It is the state when the mind is not in the state of complete engrossment in the self.

4.2.2 Sāṅkhya-Yoga

Sāṅkhya claims the real existence of the object. According to the *Sāṅkhya* theory of causation (*satkāryavada*), the effect pre-exists in the cause. The creation of various objects at various times is the manifestation of the implicit causes due to the vibration of energy (*rajas*) acting in different formations of mass (*tamas*), energy (*rajas*) and essence (*sattva*).[25] It means that the present form of the object is not a new creation but a manifestation of already existing causes. It substantiates different dimensions of the existence of an object. It states that the perceiving object is the sub-latent object in the past and the potential object for the future. Thus, so-called future objects exist as latent or potential, and the so-called past objects exist as sub-latent. Based on the theory of causation and theory of evolution of worldly objects, Vijñānabhikṣu and Anirudhha point out that a yogin can come into contact with the past and

25 Cf. Indra Chandra Shastri, *Jain Epistemology*, p. 328.

future that exist in the present as sub-latent and potential by virtue of certain peculiar powers (*atiśaya*), produced by practice and meditation.[26] The peculiar power is the ramifications of the complete subjugation of the *tamas guṇa* and manifestation of *sattva guṇa* of the mind. It implies that the mind (*buddhi*) is the ultimate cause of *yogi-pratyakṣa*, which connects with prakṛti, the uncaused cause of all existence.

Patañjali in *Yogasūtra* discusses the different means of acquiring extrasensory perception and supernatural powers (*Siddhi*); by birth (*janma*), through herbs (*auṣadhi*), incantations (*mantra*), austerities (*tapas*) and concentration (*samādhi*).[27] But he reiterates the superiority of the extrasensory perception through concentration (*samādhi*) because "those obtained by concentration are without any subliminal imprints."[28] The yogic concentration yields a higher status in the *Yoga* system. Vyāsa extracts two reasons for this; firstly, they are not derived from the latent impression of previous actions or previous birth, nor accumulate new impressions and secondly, the voluntary exercise of these powers at each

---

26 Cf. Aniruddha, *Sāṅkhyasūtra Vṛtti*: 1. 90; *Sāṅkhya Pravaccana Bhāṣya*: 1. 91, quoted in Indra Chandra Shastri, *Jain Epistemology*, pp. 328-329.

27 Cf. YS: 4.1. *janmauṣadhimantra tapasamādhijāḥ siddhayaḥ*.

The supernatural powers acquired through the austerity (*tapas*) and sacred chanting (*mantra*) are not even considered *yogi-pratyakṣa*. According to *Yoga*, Virtues are not the direct cause of *siddhi* because these virtues "are derivatives and a derivative cannot induce changes in the primal substance. It has to happen naturally by itself once the obstacles hindering its ingress are eliminated (*Bhāṣvatī*: P. 604). Therefore *Yogasūtra* says, *yogi-pratyakṣa* "takes places through the filling in of their innate nature."(Cf. YS: 4.2. *jātyantarapariṇāmaḥ prakṛtiāpūrāt*.). The role of austerity, virtues or sacred chanting is the instrumental and not direct cause. (Cf. YS: 4.3).

28 Cf. YS: 4.6 *tatra dhyānajam-anāśayam*.

stage of yogic concentration.[29] Therefore, yogic concentration is the purport of *yogi-pratyakṣa* in *Yogasūtra*.

The *Yoga* system is a methodical effort to ensconce the mind or *Anthakaraṇa* (intellect) in Pure Consciousness. More than metaphysical and epistemological theorising, therefore, it propels practical methods. The *Yoga* system envisages liberation by the practice of concentration and detachment. The restlessness and attachment are due to the modification of the mind. Thus, the substantial objective of *Yoga* is that the cessation or annihilation of the modification of the mind (*citta-vṛtti nirodhaḥ*).[30] The mind is the composite of *sattva*, *rajas*, and *tamas guṇas*. The interaction of three *guṇas* galvanises modifications of the mind. The preponderance of *sattva guṇa* spurs up the excellency of the mind. The fullest expression of *sattva guṇa* earmarks the tranquil state of mind. It is the pinnacle of wisdom and known as the state of discriminative enlightenment. It demarcates between the mind as the unconscious evolute and *Puruṣa* as the pure conscious substratum. Possession of discriminative knowledge facilitates supernatural powers and knowledge. According to *Yoga*, it is the state of *Samprajñāta Samādi* where the single-minded concentration on the object of concentration prevails. It perfects in supra-conscious concentration (*Asamprajñāta Samādi*) where the consciousness of object concentration ceases to exist.

Samprajñāta Samādi of mind is the result of the cessation of modifications of mind by the practice of concentration. *Yogasūtra* defines it as 'the state of concentration that is reached

29 Cf. Vyasa Commentary on YS: 4.6. p. 354.

30 Cf. YS: 1. 2. Mind or *citta* encompasses three internal organs-*Buddhi* or intellect, *Ahaṅkāra* or ego, and *Manas* or mind. The totality of the internal organ is also called *antaḥkaraṇa*. In a general sense, it may also denote as *Buddhi*.

with the help of *Vitarka*, *Vicāra*, *Ānanda* and *Asmitā*.'[31] Each stage calibrates the nature of the object on which the mind is concentrated upon. The nature of the object is featured as *Grahītā* (the cognisor), *Grahaṇa* (the instrument of cognition), and *Grāhya* (the object cognised). *Vitarka* based *samādhi* set any of the sixteen gross principles as the object of concentration (Five *Bhū*tas, Five Organ of Perception, Five Organ of Action, and Mind-part of *Citta* where volition originates). *Vicāra* based *samādhi* directed towards subtle entities (Five *Tanmātras*, *Ahaṅkāra*, and *Mahat* or *Buddhi*). According to the nature of engrossment, yogins classify *vitarka* and *vicāra* into two forms. *Vitarka* contains *savitarka* and *nirvitarka* forms, and *vicāra* possesses *savicāra* and *nirvicāra* forms. *Savitarka* and *savicāra* is the state of concentration on gross and subtle forms of objects, respectively that has endowed with the help of words and their meaning. *Nirvitarka* and nirvichāra is the state of concentration on the gross and subtle forms of objects bereft of words and their meanings. They are the pure state of mind "devoid of its own nature of reflective consciousness, and the object on which it is contemplating remains illuminated."[32] Ānanda is the mode of concentration on the internal sense of bliss perfused one's organs. This concentration is based neither on words nor on any subtle or gross objects. It is the practice of *Sānanda-samāadi*. *Asmitā* is the mode of concentration on 'Pure I'.[33] The yogin realises himself/herself as the knower

31 YS: 1. 17. *Vitarkavicārānadāsmitārūpānugamāt Samprajñāt.*

32 YS: 1. 43. *Svarūpaśūnyevārthamātranirbhāsā nirvitarkā.*

33 The pure 'I' sense is not *Puruṣa*. It is the cogniser, the subject of cognition, i.e. *Buddhi* or *Mahat*. *Buddhi* is the knower. *Puruṣa* is the Seer. (Cf. YS: 2.20). The knower can be the knower only when it knows, and not when it does not. Therefore, the object of *Buddhi* can be known and unknown to *Buddhi*. The Seer is always Seer of Himself and therefore, the object of *Puruṣa* is always known. *Buddhi* is revealed with the help of *Puruṣa*. *Puruṣa* is never an object of concentration. It performs as the reflector of *buddhi*. Being a witness

of that bliss and penetrates into the nexus of his/her 'I' sense. Succinctly, *Vitarka* and *vichāra* states concentrate on *Grāhya*, *Ānanda* concentrate on *Grahaṇa*, and *Asmitā* concentrate on *Grahītā*.[34]

The logistics of practice and detachment in the form of accessories or limbs of *Yoga* (*aṣṭāṅgayoga*) catalyse the flattening of distractive modifications and nurturing of concentration. It evolves through the rigorous physical and psychic practices (*yama*, *niyama*, *āsana*, *prānayāma*, and *pratyāhara*) and develops through the engrossment or intense concentration (*Saṁyama- Dhāraṇā*, *Dhyāna*, and *Samādi*), which consummates in the arrested state of mind, i.e., the fixity of the mind. The common nature of the engrossment is that the mind is being engrossed in the object of concentration (gross, subtle, feeling-bliss, and 'Pure I') and is possessed of its nature. The proximity of the faculty of knowing and the knowable is so intense and close because "the objects of concentration shins forth in mind devoid of thought of even the self."[35] The engrossment on these objects brings mastery over them. The mastery empowers one to leverage the activities of respective elements (*Tattvas- Grāhya*, *Grahaṇa*, and *Grahītā*) at one's will.[36] It nurtures and enhances supernatural powers

---

for the modifications of *buddhi*, *Puruṣa* is the cause that sustains *buddhi*. When *buddhi* merges into its causal state, it will not affect *Puruṣa* consciousness because Buddhi is witnessed by *Puruṣa* by virtue of the intrinsic power of activity. It is a state of being in itself. *Puruṣa* by himself cannot be the object of concentration, but the pseudo-*Puruṣa* or Pure 'I' sense can be the object of concentration. The 'I' is regarding itself as the Seer and is the subject of deep and intense concentration (Cf. YS: 3. 35; YB: p. 179-185, 310-312).

34 Cf. YB: p. 44.

35 YS: 3. 3. *tadevārthamātranirbhāsam svarūpaśūnyamiva samādhiḥ.*

36 Cf. YS: 3.44. *sthūlasvarūpasūkṣmānvayārthavattva saṁyamātbhūtajayaḥ.* (mastery over *Grāhya*)

and knowledge. The supernormal knowledge of the *Tattvas* denotes both supernormal knowledge of the cosmic world and the subtle world.

By mastering the concentration on *Tattvas*, *Yogasūtra* says, "the light of knowledge dawns".[37] It is the knowledge, of the past, present and future of the object (*atītānāgata jñānam*); knowledge of the previous birth (*pūrvajāti jñānam*); knowledge of the form of the expressions of all beings (*sarvabhūtaruta jñānam*); knowledge of other minds (*paracitta jñānam*); knowledge of the distant and oblivious object or subtle objects (*sūkṣmāvyāvahitaviprakṛṣṭa jñānam*); knowledge of cosmic regions (*bhuvana jñānaṁ*). It stimulates the supernatural powers, such as the invisibility of the body, prediction of death, extra-ordinary physical and spiritual strength, control over the activities of cosmic and heavenly bodies and as many.

The above discussed supernatural knowledge and powers are derived voluntarily. However, "when the knowledge related to *Puruṣa* is acquired, these faculties are developed involuntarily."[38] *Buddhi* apparently possesses the knowledge, but it is inherently unconscious. Pure consciousness is the nature of *Puruṣa*. Thus, through the categories of cognition, one cannot attain self-realisation. *Puruṣa* is revealed by incessant concentration and meditation (*Saṁyama*) and

---

YS: 3.47. *grahaṇasvarūpāsmitāvayārthavattvasaṁyamātindriyajayaḥ*. (mastery over *Grahaṇa*)

YS: 3. 48. *tato manojavitvaṁ vikaraṇabhāvaḥ pradhānajayaśca*. (mastery over *Grahītā*)

37 YS: 3. 5. *tajjayāt prajñālokaḥ*.

Yogasūtra elaborately explains about the supernatural knowledge gained through concentration. The third chapter of *Yogasūtra* (*Vibhūti pada*) is particularly dedicated to the discussion of supernatural knowledge and powers. Cf. YS: 3. 16-42.

38 Swami Hariharananda Aranya, annotation to YS: 3.6, p. 312.

not by intellectual conception. Derived knowledge from this *Saṁyama* is the highest knowledge relating to *Puruṣa*. *Yogasūtra* states: "From the knowledge [relating to] of *Puruṣa* arises prescience (*prātibha*), supernormal power of hearing (*śrāvaṇa*), supernormal power of touch (*vedana*), supernormal power of sight (*ādarśa*), supernormal power of taste (*āsvāda*) and supernormal power of smell (*vārtā*)."[39] Acquiring these powers and knowledge, a Yogin has endowed with the capacity of all-knowing and supremacy over all beings. This supernormal power of omniscience is the afferent of discriminative enlightenment. But, *Yogasūtra* poignantly warns one from the complacency and contentment of the mind in the attainment of the supernatural powers. Therefore, it says, "these powers are impediments to *Samādhi* but are accomplishments in a normal fluctuating state of mind"[40] Extrication from the supernatural knowledge leads one to the perfect state of liberation. [41] Abiding in the state where the mind ceases to be operative, i.e., beyond all supernatural powers and knowledge, is the liberation where the self remains in itself. It is the state of *Asamprajñāta Samādi*. Since the self is a pure conscious entity and *buddhi* is only the apparent source of consciousness, the cognition that evolved from *buddhi*, whether natural or supernatural, lacks purity and perfection. Therefore, the supernatural powers and knowledge that attained with the help of *buddhi* are not paraphernalia of liberation. But they are the convoys in the trajectory of liberation.

4.3 Yogi-Pratyakṣa in Jainism

Different interpretations of *yogi-pratyakṣa* loom out of the different standpoints (*naya*). Following the traditional Jaina hermeneutics (*naya*), *yogi-pratyakṣa* has three prevalent

---

39 YS: 3. 36. *prātibhaśrāvaṇavedanādarśāsvādavārtā jāyanthe.*

40 YS: 3.37. *te samādhāvupasargā vyutthāne siddhayaḥ.*

41 Cf. YS: 3. 50. *tadvairāgyādapi doṣavījakṣaye kaivalyam*

interpretations; metaphysical, pragmatic and etymological interpretations. These interpretations ensure the right understanding of *yogi-pratyakṣa*. Metaphysical interpretation (*naigama*, *saṃgraha*, and *vyavahāra nayas*) highlights the constitutional and existential factors of *yogi-pratyakṣa*. Pragmatic interpretation (*ṛjusūtra*) favours a successful volition and purpose of *yogi-pratyakṣa*. Etymological interpretation (*śabda*, *samabhirūḍha*, and *evambhūta*) derives from the analysis of the root meaning of *yogi-pratyakṣa*. Jaina interpretation assimilates all these interpretive dimensions (as we have seen in previous chapters) in its understanding of *yogi-pratyakṣa*. Thus, Jaina states that *yogi-pratyakṣa* is the perception (*pratyakṣa*) of the self-evolving Self. The self-evolving Self validates the constitutional and functional role of the Self in *yogi-pratyakṣa* and cognitive as well as the practical value of *yogi-pratyakṣa*.

Jaina delineates *yogi-pratyakṣa* as *mukhya-pratyakṣa or pāramārthika pratyakṣa*. It is the direct perception of the Self without the instrumentality of any agents. The Self is the subject as well as the instrument of *yogi-pratyakṣa*. Hence, Jainas dismays the possibility of sense organs or contact of sense organs and mind as the instrument of *yogi-pratyakṣa*. Different from *ārṣajñāna*, *siddha darśana*, and *prātibha jñāna*, the acquisition of spiritual powers or occult powers through the practice of austerity, meditation and intoxicant ointments cannot generate *yogi-pratyakṣa*. They may animate the operation of sense organs. However, the sense organs are the inherently limited and unconscious instrument and hence, unable to perceive all aspects of an object, according to Jaina doctrine. Jaina includes all sense depended-cognitions into *mati* and *śruta jñāna*. *Yogi-pratyakṣa* in Jainism is the total independence from the sense organs and mind. Jainas would agree that the spiritual and ethical practices, such as fasting, following virtues and vows, austerities and contemplation, have certainly engaged in the process of the accumulation of *yogi-pratyakṣa*. But they are not the defining attribute of the *yogi-pratyakṣa*. Ācārya Samantabhadra and Ācārya Kundakunda reiterate that the supernatural powers, the mastery over the natural and supernatural beings, physical excellence, virtuous life and moral excellence are not the immediate causes of *yogi-pratyakṣa*. Instead, the destruction cum annihilation of karma and self-luminosity of the Self are the immediate causes of *yogi-pratyakṣa*.[42] Thus, *yogi-pratyakṣa* functions in the removal of ignorance (*karma*) and the illumination of the Self. Rejection of the operation of sense organs and mind in the psychology of *yogi-pratyakṣa* perturbs *Nyāya-Vaiśeṣika* in a pejorative position.

Yogi-pratyakṣa is not the mental reconstruction of past images or memory, as some of the critics would say.[43] The mind, an atomic quasi-sense organ, precludes from entering into operation or contact with all the objects of the world simultaneously. In fact, the *Nyāya-Vaiśeṣika* also spurns the possibility of simultaneous cognitions on account of the atomic nature of the mind. The theory of obfuscation of *tamas* over the mind in *Sāṅkhya-Yoga* is more or less the same the theory of

---

42 Cf. AM: 1.1-4; PS: 1. 69; 75-76; 79.

The performance and observances of the physical, moral, and spiritual excellence with a motif of sensual pleasures rage up karmic passions and activities which exacerbate impurities. The happiness caused by such competency and excellence endanger the self's trajectory towards pure –cognition.

doṣāvaraṇayorhānir niḥśessāśtyatiśāyanāt
kvachid yathā svahetubhyo bahirantar-malakṣayaḥ. (AM: 1.4)

43 Piotr Balcerowicz summarises Kumārila Bhaṭṭa's (*Mīmāṃsā-śloka-vārttika*) and Parthsasārathi Miśra's (*Nyāya-ratnākara*) criticism over *yogi-pratyakṣa*. They consider *yogi-pratyakṣa* as a kind of memory, which does not have any cognitive value. Cf. Piotr Balcerowicz, "Extrasensory Perception (*yogi-pratyakṣa*) in Jainism and Its Refutations," p.5.

obfuscation of *avaraṇa* over the Self in Jainas. Jaina difference from *Sāṅkhya-Yoga* lays in the metaphysical considerations. *Sāṅkhya-Yoga* holds the conception of unmoved but conscious Self (*puruṣa*). Hence, the Self is bereft of qualities and changes. *Prakṛiti* is the cause of change and evolution. Mind or *anthakarṇa* is the evolution of *prakṛiti*, which is apparently conscious due to the reflection of *puruṣa*. But this unconscious mind does not have an active role in the Jainas concept of *yogi-pratyakṣa*. For Jaina, *yogi-pratyakṣa* is the function of the self-evolving conscious Self. Therefore, the different gradations of extrasensory perception are the gradual unfolding of the Self. It confers cognitive value for each stage of *yogi-pratyakṣa*. But in *Sāṅkhya-Yoga*, all cognitions, whether sensory or extrasensory, are the modification of unconscious *anthakarṇa*. Therefore, *Yoga* promulgates the method to suppress the modification of *anthakarṇa* or *citta*. Since the lower degrees of *yogi-pratyakṣa* are the modification of *citta*, they have to be subdued. There is indeed an impeccable resemblance in the ladder of spiritual development between *Yoga* (*aṣṭāṅgayoga*) and Jainas system (*guṇasthāna*). A comparative study of *aṣṭāṅgayoga* of *Yoga* and *guṇasthāna* of Jaina is a matter of intellectual pursuit in its own. Still, different from *Sāṅkhya-Yoga* systems, Jaina approbates different degrees of *yogi-pratyakṣa* as the perception of the Self. Hence, the cognitive activity of *yogi-pratyakṣa* is not to be suppressed; instead, it has to be perfected. The perception of the Self occurs in the progressive manifestation of the pristine nature of the Self (*cetanasya svarūpāvibharvao*) after the gradual suppression of karmic veils (*āvaraṇa*).

Recaptured from the systematic investigation of the previous chapter, the self-luminous and self-conscious nature of Self is irreproachable and irrevocable epistemological and metaphysical postulates in Jainism. The Self is inherently capable of apprehending or manifesting the Self and objects. The apprehension of all objects with all their qualities and modes irrespective of time and space is natural to the Self. Different from *Nyāya-Vaiśeṣika*, Jaina logically corroborates the inherent capacity of the Self to apprehend all things vividly without the assistance of any other extraneous conditions and the existence of pure and perfect cognition in the state of liberation. Therefore, the omniscience, the apex of *yogi-pratyakṣa*, is tantamount to the liberation in Jainism. The opacity of the inherent capacity of the Self is due to the curb of karmic obscurities. However, the inherent nature (pure consciousness) of the Self is never totally blotted out due to these obscurities, as gold is, however much is heated, never loses its intrinsic nature.[44] The nature and scope of knowledge (*jñāna*) rely on the nature and density of corresponding karmic veils (*jñānāvarṇa*). It entails that the degree of subsidence and annihilation of karmic veils correspondingly features with the degrees of extrasensory perception.

The different degrees of *yogi-pratyakṣa* and its perfection in the omniscience are the remarkable and significant features of the Jaina concept of *yogi-pratyakṣa*. *Yogi-pratyakṣa* can be the partial (*deśa/vikala-pratyakṣa*) and the complete perception (*sarva/sakala-pratyakṣa*) of the Self. It embarks with the suppression and annihilation of corresponding karmic obscurities. Varied in the degrees of subsidence and extinction of karmic veils, it can be partial and complete. The partial *yogi-pratyakṣa* is of two kinds: *Avadhi* (clairvoyance) and *Manaḥparyaya* (telepathy). The perfect *yogi-pratyakṣa* is *kevalajñāna* (omniscience), which is characterised by the complete cessation of all karmic obscurities and the full manifestation of the Self. Nathmal Tatia makes a sensible and remarkable comment here; "The Jainas conceive infinity as

---

44 Cf. SS: 184.

jaha kaṇayamaggitaviyaṁ pi kaṇayabhāvaṁ ṇa taṁ pariccayadi
taha kammodayatavido ṇo jahadi ṇāṇī du ṇāṇittaṁ.

having infinite gradation, and as such, there is no absurdity in this conception."[45] This section deals with the partial (*deśa/vikala-pratyakṣa*), and the subsequent chapter discusses the complete perception (*sarva/sakala-pratyakṣa*).

4.3.1 Avadhi

Avadhi is the clairvoyant cognition. Etymologically, it means 'limit'. It is limited knowledge because its scope is confined to objects 'having the definite form (*rūpiṣv*)' and 'having the limited extension'.[46] At the same time, it is conceived by the Self. It perceives material objects, which are not the object for normal sense-object contact. The annihilation and suppression of karmic obscurities are the inevitable conditions for *avadhijñāna*. Echoed from the general trends of Jainas doctrines, Vādidevasūri defines *avadhijñāna* as, "the knowledge which arises when its enveloping hindrance subsides in a particular way, which is connoted with some dispositions (*bhāvapratyaya*) and in others acquired by means of righteousness (*guṇapratyaya*), and which has for its objects things having a form (*rūpin*)."[47] The types and scope of *avadhijñāna* reveal the nature and function of *avadhijñāna*.

4.3.1.1 Two Types of Avadhi

Avadhijñāna appears with appropriate partial elimination and partial suppression of knowledge covering karma (*kṣayapaśama*). Therefore, *kṣayapaśama* is the common ground in all the degrees and varieties of *avadhijñāna*. Jaina classifies *avadhijñāna* into two: *bhavapratyaya* (in-born

45 Nathmal Tatia, *Studies in Jain Philosophy*, p.63

46 Cf. TS: 1. 28. PM: 1.1.18.

47 PNT: 2.21.

avadhijñānāvaraṇavilaya viśeṣasamudbhavaṁ
bhavguṇapratyayaṃ rūpidravyagocaram avadhijñānam.

clairvoyance) and *guṇapratyaya* (acquired clairvoyance).[48] *Bhavapratyaya* entitles the souls who are born with the requisite partial elimination and partial suppression of karmic veils. The heavenly and infernal beings are the possessor of clairvoyance by birth. As the birds are capable of flying and fishes are capable of swimming by their birth, *avadhijñāna* is natural to them. The destruction and subsidence of karmic veils ingrains in the constitution of *bhavapratyaya*, yet the *nimitta kāraṇa* is the birth of the beings that possess it.[49] The *guṇapratyaya* evolves from the partial suppression and partial elimination of knowledge covering karma, which is enhanced by the practice and meditation. The practice implies meritorious requirements such as ethical vows, and meditation denotes concentrated contemplation. Only the sub-human and human beings are capable of possessing it.[50] It does not invariably appear in all sub-human and human beings. Instead, it features only those who have engaged in ethical life enriched by the right knowledge and faith. There are six subtypes of *guṇapratyaya*;[51]

1. *Anānugāmika*—It is constrained and reserved to the particular place alone.
2. *Ānugāmika*—It accompanies and is not confined to a particular place but will not last a lifetime.

48 Cf. TS: 1. 21, 22, 23.

49 Cf. Pushpa Bothra, *The Jaina Theory of Perception*, p.108.

50 The extrasensory knowledge of animals and birds are an unfathomable doctrine in philosophy and science as well. There are some anecdotes and references in myths, epics and stories. But, in general, they are not given any philosophical importance. Perversely, Jainas corroborates the extrasensory knowledge of animals and birds. Cf. Indra Chandra Shastri, Jaina Epistemology, p. 340.

51 Cf. TS: 1. 23.

3. *Hīyamāna*—It gradually contracts in range. It is the state which encompasses more objects at the time of genesis but deteriorated gradually.
4. *Vardhamāna*—It gradually expands its range. It initiates with the cognition of a relatively small area of objects. Incrementally, with the assistance of ethical and spiritual exertion, it enters into the cognition of the wider area of objects.
5. *Anavasthita*—With the contraction and expansion range, it fluctuates repeatedly
6. *Avasthita*—It has risen in a being, continues till death or into the next life and sometimes even until omniscience achieved.

Regarding the spatial extension of the object cognised in *avadhi*, Akalaṅka demarcates three kinds of *avadhijñāna*.[52] They are *deśavadhi*, *paramāvadhi* and *sarvāvadhi*. All three are conditioned by psychic qualities. In addition to that, *deśavadhi* is conditioned by birth, as in the case of heavenly and hellish beings. *Deśavadhi* and *paramāvadhi* are three of grades; *jaghanya* (the minimum stage), *utkṛṣṭa* (the maximum stage), and *ajaghanyotkṛṣṭa* (the middle stage). *Sarvāvadhi* is one without gradation. *Sarvāvadhi* perceives innumerable unit of space in addition to those already covered by *paramāvadhi*. *Deśavadhi* is possible to human and sub-human souls; whereas, *paramāvadhi* and *sarvāvadhi* is reserved exclusively for the human being, those who have a high degree of spiritual and moral excellence.

4.3.1.2 The Scope of Avadhi

The scope of *avadhijñāna* embarks with the point where the Self commences to function independently and extends

52 Cf. *Tattvartha Rajavartika*: pp. 56-57, quoted in Indra Chandra Shastri, *Jaina Epistemology*, pp. 348-349.

up to the frontier of omniscience. *Avadhijñāna* intuits the substance, which has form or shape (*rūpin*). The formless categories, such as *jīva*, *dharma*, *adharma*, ākāśa, and *kāla*, are not the object of its cognition. The domain of *avadhijñāna* is confined to matter. On account of the meritorious accomplishments, the scope and durability are gauged. It penetrates into and conceives material objects irrespective of different time (*kāla*) and space (*ākāśa*). Time and space imply the existence of material objects at a particular time and space. It comprehends only formed objects, which contents of the space and time. The highest grade of clairvoyance emerges with the comprehension of all the atoms of a space point. Concerning modes, it cannot know all. It possibly knows all modes of atoms only at the dawn of omniscience. [53] To encapsulate, *avadhijñāna* perceives all objects, which have form and shape (*rūpa*), but *avadhijñāna* cannot comprehend all their modes.

At this juncture, the clear idea of the Jaina conception of the relative subtlety of time, space, matter and modes calibrates the scope of clairvoyant perception. The absolute subtlety is not the object of clairvoyant comprehension since they are formless. Nathamal Tatia eloquently explains the nature and scope of the relative subtlety:

> Of the time, space, atom, and mode, the succeeding one is subtler than the preceding one. It implies that with the increase of the capacity for penetration into time, there is necessarily an increase in the capacity for extending over space, and comprehending more of matter and modes; but an extension in space does not necessarily involve more penetration into time nor does comprehension of more matter and modes

53 Cf. Nathmal Tatia, *Studies in Jain Philosophy*, pp.63-64.

involve necessary spatial extension and temporal penetration.[54]

These four factors (time, space, atom, and mode) excel one after the other in minuteness. So with one unit of time, there are innumerable units of space. With one unit of space, there is an infinite unit of atoms, and with one unit of the atom, there are an incomprehensible amount of modes.[55] It suggests that the cognition of material object in a particular time and space necessarily engage in the various degrees of perception. The perception of an object in a particular time never entails the perception of spatial, substantial, and mode factors of an object. It demands a higher potency to conceive them. The higher degree of perception presupposes the higher degree of quality of the Self by mitigation and suppression of karmic veils and practice of discipline and meditation.

4.3.2 Manaḥparyāya

Manaḥparyāya literally means the modes (*paryāya*) of mind (*mana*). *Manaḥparyāyajñāna* is 'the cognition of the modes of mind.'[56] Conventionally, it can be translated as mind-reading or thought reading. In the realm of modern psychology, it amounts to telepathy and mentalism. The mind is an incumbent material substance as the instrument of apprehension of all objects of all senses. The previous chapter has described the substantial (*dravya*) and functional (*bhāva*) aspect of the mind. The mind as a particular material substance (*dravya*) is the composite of a cluster of atoms (*manovargaṇās*). The attainment (*labdhi*) aspect of the mind (*bhāva*) consists

54 Having completed a thorough study based on *Nandisūtra* (16) and *Viśeṣāvaśyaka Bhāṣya* (611-631), Nathmal Tatia encapsulates the main teachings of the relative subtlety of time, space, matter and mode. Cf. Nathmal Tatia, *Studies in Jain Philosophy*, p. 64.

55 Cf. Indra Chandra Shastri, *Jaina Epistemology*, pp. 344-348.

56 PM: 1.1.18.

of the annihilation of relevant karmic veils and the special activation of the Self (*upayoga*), which appropriate to conceive its object. The mind engages in the thinking process. It assumes different shapes corresponding to the different objects that are thought of. These shapes are the modes of a mind. The modes of mind are the changes in the states of mind. These changes entail acts of thought. Thus, every act of thought replicates in the modes of mind. *Manaḥparyāya* is the direct experience of such modes of thought activating in the other individual minds. The direct experience is as always stands for the perception of the Self without the instrumentality of the mind. The cognition which directly apprehends the states of mind of others is *manaḥparyāyajñāna*. Assimilating Jainas teaching of the mind and the perception, Vadidevasūri defines *manaḥparyāya*: "Telepathy, which has for its object the mental substance and its modes, arises from the subsidence of its peculiar cover (i.e., obstacles which suppress it), the subsidence being due to self-control and purity."[57] It has explained about the object, condition, and means of *manaḥparyāyajñāna*. The object of *manaḥparyāya* is the mind substance and its states or modes; the condition is the subsidence and annihilation of karmic veils; the means of attainment is practical and spiritual disciplines.

4.3.2.1 Two Types of Manaḥparyāya

Jainas suggests two verities of *manaḥparyāya*: *ṛjumati* and *vipulamati*. The demarcation is based on "the purity and infallibility."[58] *Ṛjumati* is less pure and ephemeral in comparison with *vipulamati*, which is pure, lucid and everlasting, i.e., lasts up to the dawn of omniscience. The former

57 PNT: 2.22.

saṃyama viśuddhi nibandhanād viśiṣṭāvaraṇa vicchedāj jātam
mano dravya paryāyālambanaṃ manaḥparyāya jñānam.

58 TS: 1.25. *viśuddhy apratipātābhyāṃ tadviśeṣaḥ.*

is conversant to a few general modes of the mind; whereas, the latter vividly address the divergent and complex modes of the mind. Hence, the latter had a lucid and direct penetration into the minds of others. The upward stage spiritual development is nursed by *vipulamati*; whereas, *ṛjumati* is subjected to the oscillation that may plunge again into degradation. The former is infallible in this sense, and the latter is confined to an ephemeral existence. It reckons that *vipulamati* lasts until one attains omniscience.

4.3.2.2 The Scope of Manaḥparyāya

The understanding of the subject and object of *manaḥparyāyajñāna* calibrate the scope of it. The *saṁjñi* (possession of the mind) soul is the subject of *manaḥparyāyajñāna*. They (*saṁjñi* soul) have the faculty of apprehension of all objects of all organs. With the practice of the physical and mental discipline, those souls catalyse their power of thought-reading. It establishes clearly that only the self-disciplined human beings have the competency to inherit telepathic knowledge (*manaḥparyāyajñāna*). Consequently, the hellish or heavenly being precludes from this kind of direct perception. Having summarised the conditions mentioned in *Avaśykaniryukti* and *Nandisūra* for the possession of *manaḥparyāyajñāna*, T. G. Kalghatgi presents them in *Some problems of Jaina Psychology*. "They are:

(i) The human beings in the *karmabhūmi* must have fully developed sense organs and a fully developed personality. They must be *paryāpta*.

(ii) They must possess the right attitude (*samyagdṛṣṭi*). As a consequence, they must be free from passion.

(iii) They must be self-controlled, and they must be possessed of *ṛddhi*, i.e., extraordinary powers."[59]

---

59 T. G. Kalghatgi, *Some Problems of Jaina Psychology*, p. 139. He summarises the teachings of *Avaśykaniryukti* (76) and *Nandisūra* (39-44).

Therefore, *manaḥparyāyajñāna* is inherited by human beings those who have a penchant for physical and mental discipline. The disciplined life correspondingly expedites the mitigation and extinction of karmic influences, whereupon one attains the direct perception of others minds and their states of operation.

Pūjypāda Devanandi in *Sarvārthasiddhi* enumerates the four causal factors of *manaḥparyāya*:

(i) *kṣayopaśama* of *viryāntarāya*,

(ii) *kṣayopaśama* of *manaḥaparyāyajñānāvaraṇa*,

(iii) *aṅgopāṅga nāma-karman*,

(iv) the contact with other minds.[60]

Viryāntarāya subjugates the natural and supra-natural powers of the soul. The subsidence of this suppression (*kṣayopaśama*) is the general cause of cognition. The extinction of the karmic veil over the cognition of mind substance (*manaḥaparyāyajñānāvaraṇa*) is the second cause. The perfection of the constitution of the body and its parts (*aṅgopāṅga nāma-karma*) is a necessary prerequisite for the perfection of mind substance which nurtures the cognition of thoughts. The fourth causal factor is the physical mind.

About the nature of *manaḥparyāya,* there is consensus among Jainas, which features for the direct perception of mental states of others. Regarding the cognition of the object of *manaḥparyāyajñāna*, there are two prevalent views in the Jainas traditional philosophy. The division is with regard to the possibility of cognition of objects in *manaḥparyāya*. Jinabhadra and Hemacandrasūri propose the first view, and Pūjypāda Devanandi and Akalaṅka stand for the second view. Jinabhadra holds the direct perception of the states of

60 Cf. *Sarvārthasiddhi*: 1.23.

mind, but the external objects of states of mind are cognised indirectly through inference.[61] The external objects are the contents of the states of mind. The objects under conception may be material or immaterial. The immaterial objects are not the object of perception, according to Jinabhadra.[62] Therefore, he asserts that the function of *manaḥparyāya* is the perception of the states of the mind that is engaged in thinking of the external objects. Ensued from this stream of thought, Hemacandrasūri reckons that *manaḥparyāya* is the direct perception of the mental states, and cognition of external object of thought is inferential and indirect. He would say that cognition in *manaḥparyāya* evolves from the direct perception of states of mind, which are not possible without objects.[63] Thus, cognition of external objects of different states of mind of others is inferential knowledge.

On another hand, Pūjypāda Devanandi and Akalaṅka hold that the mental states and their external objects are the objects of direct cognition in *manaḥparyāya*. According to Jainas tradition, *manaḥparyāya* is the direct (clear and distinct) perception of the mind substance and its modes. The directness necessarily implies direct apprehension of the object by the Self and independent of any external agency. Therefore, the inclusion of inference in the process of *manaḥparyāyajñāna* jeopardise its existential status as direct perception. Pūjypāda in *Sarvārtha-siddhi* acclaims 'that coginiton in *manaḥparyāya* is totally due to the subsidence and annihilation of the respective karmic veils and direct perception of the states of mind by the Self.'[64] It is not through the apprehension done by the mind

61 Cf. *Viśeṣāvśyakabhāṣya*: 814, quoted in T. G. Kalghatgi, *Some Problems of Jaina Psychology*, p. 139.

62 Cf. Indra Chandra Shastri, Jaina Epistemology, 351.

63 PM: 1.1.18. *Yadbāhyacintanīyārthajñānaṁ tat* ānumānikameva.

64 Cf. *Sarvārtha-siddhi*: 1.9.

because "the mind is the only inactive background and does not make any contribution in such cognition. It is exclusively due to the potency of destruction-cum-subsidence, although it is designated by means of the *manas* of oneself or of another (on account of its association with it)."[65] Therefore, it is not *mati-jñāna*, and so, empirical perception, inference and verbal testimony have no decisive role in the cognitive process of *manaḥparyāya*. Unleashed from the activity of sense organ and mind, *manaḥparyāyajñāna* conceive the object clearly and distinctly (*pratyakṣa*).

4.3.3 Difference between Avadhi and Manaḥparyāya

Avadhi is the direct perception of the material substance and its modes. *Manaḥparyāya* is the direct perception of the fine modes of the mind. The understanding of the difference between *avadhi* and *manaḥparyāya* has a significant cognitive value in Jainism. The iconoclastic views challenge the validity and constitution of *manaḥparyāya* as a separate category of cognition.[66] According to them, the scope *avadhi* encompasses all the material substance, including the mind as a material substance. Therefore, they suspend the validity of *manaḥparyāya* as a separate means of knowledge. They regard *manaḥparyāya* as a specific type of *avadhi*. According to them, sub-human beings (possessed of two or more sense organs) also inherit the mind through the attraction and repulsion and advocate the theory that they also avail telepathic knowledge. The orthodox views confine the scope of *manaḥparyāya* to the self-disciplined human beings alone and clearly assert the difference between *avadhi* and *manaḥparyāya* in the process of cognition.

Ācārya Umāsvāti and Hemacandrasūri reiterate the cognitive value and importance of *avadhi* and *manaḥparyāya*

65 Nathmal Tatia, *Studies in Jain Philosophy*, p. 66.

66 Cf. Nathmal Tatia, *Studies in Jain Philosophy*, P. 69.

in their state of constitution and function. The distinguishing features of both expose their unique status in cognitive activity. According to them, 'the difference between the two consists in the difference of purity (*viśuddhi*), scope (*kṣetra*), subject (*svāmin*) and object (*viṣaya*).'[67] Lucidity and immediacy are the distinctive features of perceptual cognition, and therefore, the purity of perception has cognitive value in the progression of cognition. The lucidity of perception is conditioned by the suppression cum annihilation of karmic obscurities. *Avadhi* and *manaḥparyāya* are perceptual cognitions and conditioned by karmic veils. Of these two, *manaḥparyāya* is more lucid than *avadhi*. Thus, the self of *manaḥparyāya* must be in a purer state than *avadhi*. The person who inherits *avadhi* perceives the material clusters, and the person who possesses *manaḥparyāya* conceives the finer and subtler matter, i.e., the mind, with its modes. The perception of the subtlety and finer modes of the mind demand much purer perception. The ground of lucidity lays in not a lesser or greater extent of the sphere of objects but the knowledge of a lesser or greater number of subtle features of the objects concerned. In this regard, *manaḥparyāya* enjoys a higher status of purity than *avadhi*. Hemacandrasūri says, "owing to the variation of the degrees of the cessation of obscurities veils, transcendent intuition admits of two varieties: visual intuition of limited extension and intuition of the modes of other minds."[68] The lucidity (*viśuddhi*) distinguishes them in the cognitive process. The apprehension of lucidity consummates in pure (extrasensory) perception and pure cognition. The commentary to *Tattvārthasūtra* summarises the discussion about the differences between them like this: "In short, clairvoyance is extensive but shallow, whereas mind-reading is more limited but deep."[69]

---

67 Cf. TS: 1.26. *Viśuddhikṣetrasvāmiviṣayebhyaḥ avadimanaḥparyāyayoḥ* PM: 1.1.19. *Viśuddhikṣetrasvāmi viṣayebhyaḥbhedath*

68 PM: 1.1. 18. *tathārathbye avadimanaḥparyāyaḥ ca.*

69 *Tattvārthasūtra*: *That Which Is*, p. 21.

The difference based on the lucidity of perception is pivotal to understand other differences between them. The objects (*viṣaya*) of *manaḥparyāya* are limited and much concentrated to the mind substance and states of mind, whereupon it enhances conversancy with the mind and its modes. Hence, better than the wide extensity of *avadhi*, *manaḥparyāya* entails clarity and distinctness in perception. *Avadhi* perceives all clusters of matter, which has shape and form but not all their modes. On the other side, *manaḥparyāya* perceives the infinitesimal or finer parts of the material clusters. The lucidity is acquired by practice and discipline. According to the gradation of the soul, human beings possessed of five sense organs and mind gets an edge to achieve the pure perception other than sub-human beings. Even among human beings, only those who have fully developed sense organs and who have mastered over passions, ignorance, and activities by the practice of self-discipline are entitled to achieve *manaḥparyāya*. In this regard, the authentic possessor (*svāmin*) of *manaḥparyāya* is 'a spiritually advanced ascetic'. *Avadhi* is possible even for the sub-human beings, human beings, denizens of hell and heaven and any of the realms of existence (fully or partially self-restrained or completely devoid of self-restraint). The scope (*kṣetra*) of *avadhi* extends up to all the inhabited worlds, and the subjects of *avadhi* are the inmates of these inhabited worlds; whereas, the scope (*kṣetra*) of *manaḥparyāya* is confined to the sphere inhabited by human beings and the subjects of *manaḥparyāya* are the self-disciplined, virtuous, and morally accomplished human beings. Thus, *manaḥparyāya* is the exclusive capacity of self-disciplined human beings alone.

4.4 Conclusion

In Indian philosophical systems, *yogi-pratyakṣa* is often treated in a descriptive and speculative manner. While this is true across many traditions, Jainism presents a distinctive approach. In Jain thought, *yogi-pratyakṣa* is rooted in the self-luminous nature of the Self and its inherent ability to manifest objects. Unlike other Indian systems, Jainism posits that *yogi-pratyakṣa* represents the direct perception of the Self, independent of the sense organs and mind. According to Jain philosophy, the practice of meditation, discipline, and moral achievements create the conditions necessary for *yogi-pratyakṣa*. The fundamental cause of *yogi-pratyakṣa*, however, is the gradual emergence of the self-luminous and self-conscious Self and the simultaneous dissolution of karmic veils. The varying degrees of *yogi-pratyakṣa* are validated through the progressive refinement of conscious activity, which is influenced by factors such as purity (*viśuddhi*), scope (*kṣetra*), subject (*svāmin*), and object (*viṣaya*). In Jainism, *Avadhi* and *Manaḥparyaya* represent the lower degrees of *yogi-pratyakṣa*. *Avadhi* pertains to the clear perception of material substances, while *Manaḥparyaya* involves the distinct cognition of mental states. Both are considered valid forms of *pratyakṣa pramāṇa*, or direct knowledge, within the Jaina framework. *Avadhi* and *Manaḥparyaya* are viewed as sequential cognitive stages achieved by a disciplined practitioner, ultimately leading to the culmination of cognitive actuality, or omniscience (*kevalajñāna*). The significance of *Avadhi* and *Manaḥparyaya* as intermediary stages in the journey towards ultimate knowledge is crucial for their soteriological value. The nature, conditions, and scope of omniscience will be explored in detail in the subsequent chapter.

CHAPTER 5

Kevalajñāna: The Paramount of Yogi-Pratyakṣa

Owing to the degrees of the annihilation of karma and the illumination of the Self, *yogi-pratyakṣa* has different progressing variation. The pinnacle of this process is achieved through perfect self-illumination and the complete eradication of karmic obscurations, culminating in omniscience (*kevalajñāna*). Once all karmic obscurities (*āvaraṇas*) are dissolved, the Self experiences a state of clear and distinct perception. This pure perception, intrinsic to the Self, is regarded as the embodiment of liberation in Jainism. Omniscience, or pure perception, is thus tantamount to liberation. This chapter delves into the nature and function of *kevalajñāna*, examining its epistemological and soteriological foundations. It begins with an analysis of various definitions of *kevalajñāna* and related concepts. The discussion then explores the epistemological, psychological, and soteriological significance of *kevalajñāna* within Jaina doctrine, including an examination of *guṇastāna* (stages of spiritual development), *arhatahood* (attainment of arhatship), and *siddhahood* (attainment of final liberation). The objective of this chapter is to provide a logical elucidation of the perfect state of *yogi-pratyakṣa* and to place *kevalajñāna* within Jaina epistemology and soteriology.

5.1 Īśvarajñāna and Kevalajñāna

The omniscience of God (*Īśvarajñāna*) is an ethical and religious postulate. To become the moral governor of the universe, the knowledge of the entirety, irrespective of time and space (*sarvajñāna*), is the necessary prerequisite. Again, to ratify the authenticity and validity of the scriptures (*Śāstras*), God's omniscience is an inevitable postulate. The *Yoga* system eschews the concept of creator, protector and destroyer God, but it reiterates the omniscience of God on the ground of the "Teacher of the teachers".[1] God, as the supreme teacher, yields the knowledge to the teachers of the system, and they later assimilate and codifiy this knowledge in the form of scripture (*Śāstras*). *Yoga* advocates the possibility of super-sensuous knowledge in any being. It is not equally flourished or developed in all. The degree and density of it have veered in living beings accordingly. Thus, the gradation exists in cognitive faculty. It is in the state of progression. The augment of the cognitive faculty will ultimately reach the acme of perfection, where further progress would be none. The particular being who has unparallel and excessive super-sensuous knowledge is Īśvara (God). *Yogasūtra* says, "He is unmatched and the seed of omniscience".[2] The living beings may inherit the apex of super-sensuous knowledge, but the state of the omniscient God is unmatched. He is 'Special Puruṣa'. Vyāsa enumerates this phrase like this; "There are many persons who have a special power. Īśvara is one such, but His special feature is that no one has as much power as He has, nor can anybody else's power exceed His; that is why He is called Īśvara."[3] He attains perfection naturally in the form of omniscience and omnipotence. Over abounding of luminous *sattva guṇa* of

1 YS: 1. 26. *sa eṣaḥ pūrveṣāmapi gurūḥ kālenānavacchedāt*.

2 YS: 1. 25. *tatra nirathiśayam sarvavjñabījam*.

3 Vyāsa commentary to YS: 1. 24, p. 59.

buddhi predominates fully and completely in Him by nature. Thus, He is eternally omniscient and always liberated, and so, He is different from human omniscience and all the souls in bondage and liberation.

Nyāya calibrates the self into two categories: the common soul (*Jivātman*) and the Supreme Soul (*Paramātman*). *Paramātman* is God. The distinctive feature of God (Īśvara), according to *Nyāya*, is the omniscience (*sarvajñaḥ*) and oneness (*ekam*).[4] According to the teachings of *Nyāyamanjari*, divine knowledge is the eternal and essential feature of the Supreme Soul. The creation of the universe is initiated by the divine will, which is inseparable from divine knowledge.[5] Annaṁbhaṭṭa further explains it with logical arguments. The immediate apprehension, the desire and the activity are the necessary prerequisites in order to be a causal agent. A finite soul is inefficient to have an immediate apprehension of the earth atom. Therefore, "the Supreme Soul, who is the causal agent in the production of all binaries (*dvaynuka*), has an immediate apprehension of all the atoms of all the elements. A Soul that can apprehend atoms in their totality may quite reasonably be described as omniscient."[6] In the wake of the absence of latent impressions and ensued cognitions, the divine knowledge cognises all objects of the universe by a single all-embracing intuition. It is not successive or simultaneous cognition, but it is of 'the nature of creative intuition'.[7]

Jainas doctrine squashes the existence of such omnipotent and omniscient or creator God. According to Jainas, there

4 Cf. *Tarkasangraha*: 17. *tatreśvaraḥ sarvajñaḥ paramātmā eka eva*.

5 Cf. *Nyāyamanjari*: pp. 200-201, referred in Jadunatha Sinha, *Indian Psychology: Perception*, p. 369.

6 *Tarkasaṁgragha Dīpikā*, Pp. 94-95.

7 Cf. Jadunatha Sinha, *Indian Psychology: Perception*, p. 370.

are four conditions of existence. They are: hellish (*Nāraka*), sub-human (*tiryanca*), human (*manuṣya*) and heavenly (*deva*). The divine beings or the dwellers of heaven may have possession of plenty of supernatural powers, including extrasensory perception. The heavenly acquisitions of knowledge by birth and the external physical excellence as well as spiritual competency of the divine souls are totally different from *kevalajñāna*. The perception acquired through the extinction of karma and illumination of the self is defined as *kevalajñāna*.[8] According to Jaina, heavenly beings inherit the perception but are subject to impurities. They indulge in the extra-ordinary states and experiences but they only cater their sensual gratification through such indulgence and thus, hamstrung by karmic impurities.[9] Therefore, the complete annihilation of impurities ensures a higher status for the *kevalajñāni* than divine beings.

5.2 Kevalajñāna

Kaivalya and *Kevalajñāna* amounts to the state of liberation. The Sanskrit term '*Kevala*' denotes 'alone, one, sole, mere, unmingled, isolated, and exclusively one's own (not common with others). *Kaivalya*, being in the same genre, commonly represents the state of absolute unity, perfect isolation, abstraction, detachment from all connection, and single-absolute existence of the Soul. *Kaivalya Upaniṣad* delineates *kaivalya* like this: "The experience (*jñānam*) of absolute oneness which destroys the endless experience of change and multiplicity (*saṁsārārṇavanāśanam*). Therefore, having experienced this, one attains the fruit of liberation (*kaivalyaṁ*

---

8 Cf. AM: 1.6

doṣāvaraṇayorhānir niḥśesṣāśtyatiśāyanāt
kvachid yathā svahetubhyo bahirantar-malakṣayaḥ.

9 Cf. PS: 1.73-74.

phalamaśunate); indeed, one attains *kaivalya*."[10] *Kevalajñāna* is the composite of two Sanskrit words; *kevala* and *jñāna*. In the philosophical realm, *kevalajñāna* reckons 'the highest, perfect, simple and pure single knowledge'.

In the *Sāṅkhya* system, *kaivalya* indicates the existence of *puruṣa* as 'single and solitary witness' (*asaya-puruṣasya sākṣitvam siddham kaivalyam*), and it is the state of final beatitude and the state of emancipation (*kaivalyārtham*).[11] It yields the discrimination between *puruṣa* and *prakṛti*, which results in the absolute and permanent extrication from all sorts of modifications and sufferings. The *Yoga* system animates the attainment of *viveka-khyāti* (the discriminative enlightenment between *puruṣa* and *prakṛti*) through practice and concentration. *Yogasūtra* of Patañjali mentions that 'the inclination towards *viveka-khyāti* naturally gravitates towards *kaivalya* (the state of liberation).'[12] According to *Yogasūtra*, '*kaivalya* is the state of permanent cessation of all the activities, state of unmingled with Buddhi, and state of the perfect isolation of *Puruṣa* for all time. In other words, it is its aloofness from everything else. There the Self remains (*puruṣa*) in itself, and absolute consciousness retains in its own self.'[13]

Advaita Vedānta endorses *kaivalya* as the absorption in the Absolute Brahman. It is the state of sole existence of Brahman. *Vedāntasāra* states: "The soul absorbed in the Supreme Brahman. The soul is identified with the Absolute Brahman, Supreme Isolation, and embodiment of Bliss, in which there

10 *Kaivalya Upaniṣad*. 2.2. Cf. *Kaivalaya Upaniṣad*, translated by Swami Chinmayananda (Mumbai: Central Chinmaya Mission Trust, 2015).

11 Cf. *Sāṅkhyakārika*: 17, 19, 21.

12 Cf. YS: 4. 26.

13 Cf. YS: 4.26; 34.

is not even the appearance of duality."[14] *Advaita Vedānta Prakaraṇagranthas* (introductory books), *Tattvabodha* and Ātmabodha, acclaim *kaivalya* awareness like this: 'I am not these multiplicities of identities, but I am unattached, and of the nature of *Saccidānanda* (Existence-Consciousness-Bliss), effulgent (*prakāśasvarūpaḥ*), the indweller of all (*sarvāntaryāmī*) and the formless awareness (*cidākāśrūpaḥ*) and I am Brahman alone (*brahmaivāhamasmiti*).'[15] In The Buddhist system, *kevala* has been used in two senses: 'oneness' and 'perfectness'.[16] According to the above-mentioned systems, *Kaivalya* or *kevala* is different from the state of omniscience. At the same time, most of them accept omniscience as the independent supernatural power, which attains in the trajectory towards liberation. *Sāṅkhya*, *Yoga* and *Advaita Vedānta* systems demarcate the state of *Kaivalya*, which is indifferent towards omniscience. For these three systems, *Kaivalya* is the state of liberation where cognition is absent. *Nyāya-Vaiśeṣika* also accepts omniscience as the apex of *yogi-pratyakṣa* and the omniscience of God. However, *Nyāya-Vaiśeṣika* considers liberation as a state free from all cognitive activity.

Except to Jainas, none of the Indian systems associates *kaivalya* (liberation) with *kevalajñāna* (omniscience). In Jainism, *kevalajñāna* is the cognitive actuality and the perfection of the cognitive process. For Jainas, the *kevalajñāna*

---

14 *Vedāntasāra*: 226. Cf. Sadānanda, *Vedānta-sāra*, translated by Swami Nikhilananda, (Kolkata: Advaita Ashram, 2010).

15 Cf. *Tattvabodha:* pp. 110-111; Ātmabodha: 31-38; 57. Cf. Śaṅkarācārya. Ātmabodha, translated and commented by Swami Chinmayananda (Mumbai: Central Chinmaya Mission Trust, 2012[3]); Śaṅkarācārya. *Tattvabodha*, translated and commented by Swami Chinmayananda (Mumbai: Central Chinmaya Mission Trust, 2016).

16 Cf. *Saṁyuttanikāya*: 153, quoted in Indra Candra Shastri, *Jain Epistemology*, p. 366.

(omniscience) is *mokṣa* (liberation). In the Jaina dogmatic and philosophical literature, *kevalajñāna* denotes the 'perfect knowledge that exists alone'.[17] The supreme aloneness (*kevala*) signifies the sole activity of the Self as the subject and instrument in the genesis of *kevalajñāna* and the single operation of cognition in *kevalajñāna* independent of any other means or conditions of knowledge.[18] *Kevalajñāna* exists alone because it evolves from the complete annihilation (*kṣayopaśama*) of knowledge-covering karma (*jñānāvaraṇīya karma*) and the illumination of the Self. There are no more conditions (*kṣayopaśama*) for different cognition.

The doctrine of omniscience has philosophical and religious importance in Jainism.[19] According to Jainas, the path

---

17 Cf. Jibin Paul, "The Concept of Isolation in Indian Thought System," in *Philosophy Today*, Vol, 1, No. 1. (2020).

18 Cf. TS: 1.31; *Viśeṣāvaśyakabhāsya* G. 823, quoted in Indra Chandra Shastri, *Jaina Epistemology*, p. 366.

19 Ram Jee Singh in his book, *The Jaina Concept of Omniscience*, mentions seven reasons for the importance of omniscience in Jainas doctrine and life. 'Firstly, after the rejection of both God and Veda, there is an utmost need for a reliable source of its scripture and dogma. Hence, the source of scripture should be the omniscient (*Tirthankara*) who possesses infinite and eternal knowledge. Secondly, the efficacy of rites and ritual is replaced by the path of knowledge, faith, and conduct. Knowledge is the nexus of the path, which leads to omniscience. Thirdly, Jainism is the religion and philosophy, which idealise self-help in the trajectory of liberation. In this, omniscience is a reliable ideal for a human being. Fourthly, the nature of the soul is knowledge and therefore, the zenith of knowledge is the realisation of the original nature of the soul. It is the natural state of the soul. Fifthly, the attainment of omniscience once means that it is an eternal inheritance. It becomes the ground of the immortality of the soul. Sixthly, liberation is, according to Jainas, freedom from karma and subsequently, the state of infinite knowledge. Seventhly, the dominant systems of Indian philosophy, which prompted omniscience, heavily influence Jainas in its spiritual aspiration and search for reality. (Cf. Ram Jee Singh, *The Jaina Concept of Omniscience*, pp. 47-49)

of liberation is natural to human beings. It is attained by virtue of conduct, characterised by the right faith and right knowledge. The conduct (*dharma*) is the disposition to be ensconced in its own nature (*svabhāva*) of the Self. The disposition is the state of equanimity (*sāmaya*), and the equanimity of the Self is the state that devoid of ignorance and delusion. The Self is the substance that exists (*sat*) with the quality and mode, and therefore, the nature (*svabhava*) of the self consists of the modification (*pariṇāma*). There are auspicious as well as inauspicious modifications of the Self. The equanimity of the self is the pure and auspicious modification (*śubhapariṇāma*) of the self; whereas, the delusion and ignorance is the impure and inauspicious modification (*aśubhapariṇāma*) of the Self. The existence of the self in pure modification is endowed with the quality (*guṇa*) of pure consciousness (*śuddhaupayoga*). The pure consciousness reveals in the form of cognition. The pure and auspicious modification of the Self attains the perfection of knowledge and happiness, which is beyond the sense. The pure modification is identical to pure cognition. It has two simultaneous effects; the illumination of the pure Self with its modifications and the extinction of impure modification owing to the karmic influences. It perfects in omniscience (*kevalajñāna*).

5.3 Defining Kevalajñāna in Jain Philosophy

Jaina philosophical tradition has attempted to define *kevala*. There are three prevalent definitions in Jaina texts: *jñānayaka* and *jñāna* and knowable *jñeya* definitions, which are ensued from the metaphysical and epistemological credentials of Jainism. Positively, the state of *kevala* is defined as the state where 'the Self attains pure modification, which is identical to the pure nature, knows all objects of the three worlds and three times. It is all-knowing, and such a Self is called *svayambhū*.'[20] It is the definition of *kevala* from the perspective of the Knower (*jñānayaka*). The *svayambhū* nature renders the self-dependency of the Self for cognition. It means that the Self cognises the knowable object without mediation and dependency of any other agencies, such as the mind and senses. It is a unique and self-identical nature of the Knower, which is neither identical with *apramatta* nor *prammatta* beings.[21] According to Hemacandrasūri, "*kevala* is the full manifestation of the innate nature of a conscious Self (*cetanasya savarūpāvirbhāvo*)."[22] Hence, Ācārya Umāsvāti demarcates the distinct nature of omniscience as "*pratyakṣam*" (perception).[23] The power of perception (*pratyakṣam*) is the innate nature of the Self, and the state of *kevala* is the perfect and complete illumination of the innate nature of the Self.

To substantiate *jñāna* definition of *kevala*, Jaina acclaims the identity between the Self and consciousness. The Self comes into contact with the object through the faculty of cognition. According to Jainism, the faculty of cognition functions through knowledge (*jñāna*) and perception (*darśana*). These faculties are identical with the Self at the transcendental level but different in the empirical level. In the case of empirical cognition, *jñāna* is preceded by *darśana*, and they occur in succession because *jñāna-varnanīya* karma and *darśana-varnanīya* karma obscures them. But in the case of *kevala*, *jñāna* and *darśana* happen simultaneously because all karmas are completely annihilated. Ācārya Umāsvāti squarely

---

20 PS: 1. 16.

taha so laddhasahāvo savvaṇhū savvamogapadimahido
bhūdo sayamevādā havadi syambu thi ṇiddiṭṭo.

21 Cf. SS: 6.

ṇavi hodi appmatto ṇa pamatto jāṇgo du jo bhāvo
evaṁ bhaṇaṁti suddhā ṇādā jo so du so ceva.

22 PM: 1.1.15.

23 Cf. TS: 1.12.

enumerates it in the discussion of the liberation: "The *kevala* arises when deluding karma (*mohanīyāvaraṇa*) is eliminated (*kṣaya*) and, as a result, knowledge-covering (*jñānāvaraṇa*), intuition covering (*darśanāvaraṇa*) and obstructive karma (*antarāyāvaraṇa*) are eliminated."[24] Ācārya Kundakunda defines *kevalajñāna*: "The state of destruction of *ghātī* karmas where self-dependent Self attains infinite knowledge and indestructible happiness. It is beyond the experience of senses and experience through the supreme lustre (*teja*) of the Self's own nature (*svabhāva*)." [25] The destruction of *karma* necessarily implies the state of cognition independent of the senses. The opacity of knowledge and different means of knowledge is due to the influence of *karma*. Therefore, the removal of *karma* has concurrently resulted in the perfect cognition, i.e., *kevalajñāna*.

Jñeya definition of *kevalajñāna* is from the perspective of an object of knowledge (knowable object). As one see above, cognition, in the *kevala* state of existence, is a sudden illumination. Thus, the absolute manifestation of the Self entails the manifestation of non-self (*artha*-object).[26] The intuition of the Self (*darśana*) concurrently manifests the object (*jñāna*). Such a revelation of innate nature of the Self extinct all the conditions (āvaraṇa) of knowing, and results in the perception (*pratyakṣa*) of all the knowable objects (*j*ñeya). An object of knowledge has different modes of existence: the existence based on time (the past, present and future), the existence based on modes (the origination, annihilation and permanence), and the existence based on the status (the

---

24 TS: 10.1. *mohaksayāi jñāna darśanaāvaraṇa antarāyakṣayāc ca kevalam.*

25 PS: 1. 19.

pakkhīṇghādikammo aṇamtavaravīrio ahiytejo
jado adimdio so ṇaṇam sokkham ca pariṇamadi.

26 Cf. TS: 1.31; DS: 44; AM: 101. PM: 1.1.15.

substance, quality and mode). A complete cognition of an object of knowledge means the cognition of all these expressions or modes of an object of knowledge. It frames definition of *kevalajñāna*: "The knowledge which knows objects those are without space points, with space points, with form, without form, the modes of the future that are yet to originate, and the modes of the past that have vanished, is a perfect knowledge, i.e., beyond five senses."[27] From the domain of knowledge or the object of knowledge, Ācārya Umāsvāti defines the *kevala*: "*sarvadravyaparyāyeṣu kevalasya*."[28] It suggests that omniscience is 'the direct perception of all the substances and their innumerable modes.'

Ācārya Kundakunda defines *kevala* as, "the direct and simultaneous cognition of all the substance and their modes by the Self without the assistance of the senses."[29] Vādidevasūri's definition of *kevalajñāna* sounds the same sense: "The complete is pure knowledge consisting in a direct cognition of all substances and their modes, which arises when owing to a peculiar group of conditions all the (knowledge) covering hindrances are annihilated."[30] The direct and simultaneous cognition independent of sense organs and mind is the perfect single cognition, i.e., *kevalajñāna*. Indra Chandra Shastri, in

---

27 PS: 1.41.

apadesasm sapadesam muttamamuttam ca pajjayamajādam
palayam gadam ca jāṇdi tam ṇāṇmadimdiyam bhaṇiyam.

28 TS: 1. 30.

29 PS: 1.21-22.

pariṇamado khalu ṇaṇam pachchakkhā savvadavvapajjāyā
so ṇeva te vijāṇadi uggahapuvvāhim kiriyāhim.
ṇātthi parokkham kimci vi samamta savvakkhaguṇsamiddhassa
akkhtīdassa sada sayameva hi ṇāṇjādassa.

30 PNT: 2. 23.

sakalaṃ tu sāmagrīviśeṣataḥ samudhbhūta samastāvaraṇakṣayāpekṣaṃ
nikhiladravaparyāya sākṣātkārisvarūpaṃ kevalajñānam.

Jaina Epistemology, scrutinises the meaning of the nature of *kevalajñāna*:

> It is infinite, because it has finite modes as its object. It is eernal, because it functions incessantly. The other types of cognition do not illumine the object constantly. They do so, only when it is desired and the attention is paid. In the case of *kevalajñāna* the attention is permanent. It is not recurrent. All the objects are always under-cognition. Further, *kevalajñāna* is imperishable. Once appeared it never vanishes. It has one degree only. There is no gradation in it; because, it appears when the soul is completely purified. It is the sate of perfection. Degrees are possible in imperfect state only.[31]

Thus, for Jainas, *kevala* is the infinite, eternal, permanent, imperishable and solitary state of perfect cognition. These definitions highlight the cognitive value and epistemological competency of *kevalajñāna*.

5.4 Three Epistemological Problems in Kevalajñāna

The above-discussed definitions of *kevalajñāna* extract three epistemological problems; the cognition of the Self, cognition of all the modification of the substances, and occurance of direct and simultaneous cognition. The previous chapters have already dealt with the first problem in detail, and the second and third problems have their references in them. Refrained from the redundant explanations of the first problem, this section concentrates on the second and third problem. *Kevalajñāna* experiences its own nature. The attainment of its own nature means "the pure cognition about the origination of its own nature (*svabhāva*) that is without

31 Indra Chandra Shastri, *Jaina Epistemology*, p. 366.

destruction and destruction of the impure state that is without origination (*utpāda*)."[32] 'That is without destruction' is the essential and eternal quality (*guṇa*) of *Jīva* (the Self). 'That is without origination' is the beginningless association of karmic influence and its concurrent states of the Self. The own nature of the Self is the existence with its essential qualities and its pure modifications. The quintessential quality of the Self is knowledge, besides other qualities.[33] The nature of all objects is knowable because they are coextensive with the knowledge. Significantly, the knowledge is coextensive with the Self. The indissoluble relationship between the Self, knowledge and the objects of knowledge unleashes the self-cognition to cognise the objects directly and simultaneously. Ācārya Kundakunda reiterates it like this: "The Self is coextensive with knowledge. Lord Jina has expounded that knowledge is coextensive with the objects of knowledge. All the objects of the universe and beyond are the objects of knowledge. Therefore, knowledge is all-pervasive; it knows everything."[34] Therefore, the self-

---

32 PS: 1.17.

bañgavihīṇo ya bhavo sambhavaparivajjido viṇāso hi
vijjadi tasyeva purṇo ṭhidisambhavaṇāsasamavāyo.

33 Cf. PS: 1. 27.

ṇāṇam appa tthi madam vaṭṭdi ṇāṇam viṇā ṇa appāṇam
tamhā ṇāṇam appā appā ṇāṇam va aṇṇam va.

34 Cf. PS: 1.24.

ādā *ṇāṇpmāṇam ṇāṇam ṇeyappamāṇamuddhiṭṭham*
ṇeyam loyāloyam tamhā tu savvgayam.

The indissoluble relationship among the knower (*jñāyaka*), Knowledge (*jñāna*) and objects of knowledge (*jñeya*) is not an identity (*tādātmya*) relationship. They are not becoming one. The knower cognizes all objects of knowledge without mutual identification or transformation. The soul has self-illumination. Both the knower and known remains in their own status of existence, without mutation and losing their own nature (*svabhāva*). Since the soul is all-pervasive, the knowledge of the object has been known to the knower without

cognition of the Self in relation to *kevalajñāna* corroborates all-pervasiveness of knowledge and the perception of all objects of knowledge.

Jayarāśi Bhaṭṭa, in *Tattvopaplava-siṃha*, has challenged the perception of past and future objects. He says, "The perception of the yogins cannot be produced by the perceived object, because past and future objects cannot produce anything. Or, if they could produce, they would lose their status of past and future objects."[35] Jaina repudiates, what is the nature of the object of cognition? An object of knowledge is the substance (*dravya*), which is possessed of qualities (*guṇa*), and modes (*paryāya*). The existence (*sat*) is its nature. Existence consists of change and permanence (origination, destruction and permanence). Change is due to the modifications (*paryāya*) in substance (*dravyaparyāya*) and qualities (*guṇaparayāya*), and it extends over three times (past, present, and future) and infinite space. It is poignant truth that the ordinary human

---

entering into that. (Cf. PS: 1. 28-29; 32). The pure Self and its pure cognition know the object of knowledge without being subjected to transformation, without being become the owner of these objects and without being originated in the form of these objects. (Cf. PS: 1. 52). Ācārya Kundakunda enumerates it with the analogy of the immersing of the sapphire in milk. The sapphire immerses in the milk. Due to its special potency, the blue lustre imparts to the whole of milk. Similarly, due to the special potency of the *kevalajñāna*, the knowledge imparts to the whole object of knowledge. (Cf. PS: 1. 30). The sprawling actually indicates all-pervasiveness of the Self.

35 *Tattvopaplava-siṃha*: p. 168, 1-3, *tathā yogi-pratyakṣasya pratīyamānârtha-janyatā na sambavati vyatītânāgatayor ajanakatvāt. janakatve vâtītânāgatā hīyate.*

Cf. Sukhlalji Sanghavi and Rasiklal C. Parikh (ed.), *Tattvopaplavasimha of Shri Jayarasi Bhatta* (Varanasi: Baudhha Bharati, 1987), quoted in Piotr Bacereowicz, "Extrasensory perception (*yogi-pratyakṣa*) in Jainism and Its Refutations" in Christopher Key Chapple (ed.), *Yoga in Jainism,* Routledge Advances in Jaina Studies (Oxon–New York: Routledge, 2016), p. 111.

being cannot cognise the complexity or the innumerable aspects of an object of knowledge (*anekānta*) with the assistance of senses. At the same time, one cannot simply snub cognition of human being. However, the cognition of the human being is partial and limited. The partial apprehension of human being is constrained to seven modes of predication (*Syādvāda*).[36] The Jainas doctrines hold on the admittance of the partial apprehension (*syād*) in the process of cognition (*prāmaṇa*). Hence, the human being has a partial viewpoint (*naya*) towards the apprehension of the object of knowledge.

The seven modes of predication concurrently emerge into the seven forms of the judgement of the object of knowledge (*Sapta-bhaṅga-naya*).[37] "The knowledge of realities and *pramāṇa* at once illuminates every object. The knowledge

---

36 The seven modes of predications (*Syādvāda*) are accordingly; (1) *Syād-asti* (it is) (2) *Syād-nāsti* (it is not) (3) *Syād-avaktavya* (it is indescribable) (4) *Syād-asti-nāsti* (it is, and it is not) (5) *Syād-asti-avaktavya* (it is, and it is indescribable) (6) *Syād-nāsti-avaktavya* (it is not and it is indescribable) (7) *Syād-asti-nāsti- avaktavya* (it is and it is not and is indescribable).

37 Siddhasena Divākara says, "a thing is conceived from one particular point of view is the object of *naya*." (Cf. NV: 29. *ekadeśaviśiṣtaḥ artho nayasya viṣayo mathaḥ*). Āchārya Samantabhadra perceives an object of knowledge as "the substance which is the collection of three times brought by *naya* and *upanaya*." (Cf. AM: 10. 107. *ayopanayaikāntānāṁ trikālānāṁ samuchchayaḥ*). The seven varied forms of judgments or expressions (*Sapta-bhaṅga-naya*) are accordingly; (1) as being, with reference to itself (2) as not being, with reference to another (3) as indescribable, simultaneously with reference to itself and another (4) as successively being and not being, with reference to itself and another (5) as being and indescribable, with regard to reference to itself, and simultaneity with reference to itself and reference to another (6) as not being and indescribable, with regard to reference to another, and simultaneity with reference to itself and another (7) as being, not being, and being indescribable with regard to reference to itself, a reference to another and simultaneity with reference to itself and reference to another.

which derived gradually is purified by *naya* of *syādvāda*"[38] Thus, the doctrine of *Syādvāda* and *Sapta-bhaṅga-naya* estimate the innumerable aspects or the complexity of an object of knowledge and the limitations of human apprehension and expressions. Significantly, the doctrine of the Self (*jīva*) and not-self (*ajīva*) validates the nature of the Self as the knower and the nature of the non-self as knowable. It approbates the existence of an omniscient one who can only apprehend such a complex object in its entirety. Thus, Sidhhasena Divākara propels that "since things have many characters, they are the objects of all-sided knowledge, omniscience."[39] The relative existence of every object of the universe entails that the perfect knowledge of one is impossible without knowing all. Ācārāṅga expresses it in the form of the maxim: "*je egaṁ jāṇai se savvaṁ jāṇai, je savvaṁ jāṇai se egaṁ jāṇai*" which means "one who knows one knows all, and one who knows all knows one."[40] It naturally presupposes the existence of the omniscience as the highest form of cognition because "nothing remains unknown in omniscience."[41] Thus, according to Jainas, *kevalajñāna* is the knowledge of reality (the relative existence of the object), which is perfected through the knowledge of the entire universe. Succinctly, *kevalajñāna* is the self-born, direct, ubiquitous, stainless, and simultaneous knowledge of the Self and objects.

Ācārya Kundakunda, in *Pravaccanasāra*, initiates a prolific and impregnable discussion on the simultaneous and

---

38 AM: 10. 101.

tattvajñānaṁ pramāṇaṁ te yugapat sarvabhāsanam
kramabhāvi cha yaj-jñanaṁ syādvāda-naya-samṁskṛtam.

39 NV: 29. *anekāntātmakam vasthu gocaraḥ sarvsaṁvidam.*

40 Ācārāṅga *sūtra*: 1.3-4, quoted in Nathmal Tatia, *Studies in Jaina Philosophy*, p. 70.

41 The commentary to TS: 1.30. *na ca kevalajñana viṣayāt paraṁ kiñcit jñeyam asti.*

direct cognition in the state of *kevalajñāna*.[42] According to Jainas, the Self is the source of pure cognition. However, it is blurred and detained by the karmic condition, even though not completely. The sensory knowledge, according to Jainas, is procured by the destruction-cum-subsidence of knowledge obscuring karmas (*kṣayopaśama*). The resultant of this is that the limited and successive knowledge. Here, this cognition has functioned with the assistance of (intrinsically limited) senses and mind. Thus, sensory knowledge is indirect knowledge, and it has to go through the different stages of cognition. In *kevalajñāna*, there is the annihilation of knowledge obscuring karma (*kṣāyika*). The resultant of this is that the self-illumination of the self and pure and auspicious modification of the self, which is pure cognition. It is the direct, eternal, and simultaneous cognition of the infinitude of the object of knowledge. The *kevalajñāna* is direct knowledge or cognition by the Self, and so, it is devoid of stages of cognition.[43] Ācārya Kundakunda amalgamates all the (four) means of knowledge to one and the same state, i.e., the omniscience. The various kinds of knowledge refer to this unitary state of knowledge as to when the sunlight reappears completely then the clouds disappeared completely.[44] In the absence of gradation in cognition, *kevalajñāna* cognises the substances and their modes simultaneously in respect of their substance (*dravya*), place (*kṣetra*), time (*kāla*), and being (*bhāva*). The implications of direct and simultaneous cognition will be discussed further in detail, under the concept of the psychology of *kevalajñāna*.

---

42 Cf. PS: 1. 19-21; 47-52: 55.

43 Cf. TS: 1. 31. *ekādīni bhājyāni yugapad ekasmin* ācaturbhyaḥ.

44 Cf. SS: 204.

ābhiṇisudohimaṇakevalaṁ ca tam hodi ekkameva padaṁ
so eso paramaṭṭho jaṁ lahiduṁ jādi.

5.5 The Psychology of Kevalajñāna

The direct and simultaneous cognition of *kevalajñāna* delineates the psychology of *kevalajñāna*. There are three philosophical constitutes in the psychology of omniscience: *darśana* and *jñāna* as the conscious activity, the self-illumination of the Self, and mitigation and annihilation of karmic obscurities. There are three views regarding the relationship between *darśana* and *jñāna* in the state of omniscience. They are known as *Kramavāda* (Theory of succession of *darśana* and *jñāna*), *Sahavāda* (Theory of simultaneity), and *Abhedavāda* (Theory of Identity).[45] *Kramavāda* states that both *darśana* and *jñāna* are two different states of consciousness, and they occur alternatively in the state of omniscience. Two conscious activities cannot occur simultaneously. It must be known consecutively. *Sahavāda* advocates both *darśana* and *jñāna* occur simultaneously in omniscience. The omniscient comprehends all things at one and the same time. *Abhedavāda* propels *darśana* and *jñāna* are not two different things functioning at one and the same time, but just one thing functioning at the same time. They synchronise in omniscience, and they are identical in that level of omniscience.

Ācārya Umāsvāti and Pūjyapada Devanandi (commentator of *Tattvārthasūtra*) are the advocates of *sahavāda*. Since the object of cognition is possessed of universal form and a particular form, the conscious activity in the form of *kevaladarśana* and *kevalajñāna* has been attributed to the state of omniscience. 'The conscious activities (*darśana* and *jñāna*), manifesting themselves as *mati*, *śruta*, *avadhi*, and *manaḥparyāya*, occur alternatively in an empirical self. The conscious activity (*kevaladarśana* and *kevalajñāna*) occur

---

45 Cf. Ram Jee Singh, *The Jaina Concept of Omniscience*, pp. 61-67.

simultaneously in an omniscient self.'[46] Ācārya Kundakunda cogently states that '*darśana* and *jñāna* of an omniscient occur simultaneously, as the light and heat of the sun occurs simultaneously.'[47] *Dravyasangraha* also holds that the cognition in the liberated state of existence is a sudden illumination of every object as the sun appears in a cloudless sky.[48] Ācārya Samantabhadra, in *Āpta-Mīmāṁsā*, demarcates between the limited cognition and complete cognition. He comments that the complete cognition "at once illuminates every object".[49] Akalaṅka and Vidyānandi, in their respective commentaries on *Āpta-Mīmāṁsā*, reiterate the simultaneity of *darśana* and *jñāna* in omniscience.[50]

The alternative or successive occurrence of the conscious activity in omniscience is untenable. The annihilation of karmic veils and the manifestation of the Self and all objects validate the simultaneous occurrence of conscious activity in the omniscient soul. Once the problem of the occurrence of *darśana* and *jñāna* is settled, then mull over the mode of relationship between *darśana* and *jñāna* in the state of omniscience. Agreeing to the simultaneity occurrence,

---

46 Cf. TS: 1. 31. *ekādīnī bhājyāni yugapad ekasminn* ācaturbhyaḥ.

47 Cf. *Niyamasāra*: 159.

Jugavaṁ vaṭṭai nāṇaṁ kevala-ṇāṇissa daṁsaṇaṁ ca tahā
diṇayara-payāsa-tāpaṁ jaha vaṭṭai taha muṇeyavvaṁ.

48 Cf. DS: 44.

49 AM: 101. *tatvajñānaṁ pramānaṁ te yugapat sarvabhāsanam.*

50 *Aṣṭaśatī* (Akalaṅka commentary on Āpta-Mīmāṁsā 101) says, 'if the *jñāna* and *darśana* (of a *kevalin*) were to occur alternately in succession, his omniscience would be only a contingent occurrence.' The annihilation of karmic veils necessitates the simultaneous manifestation of universal and particular; *Aṣṭasahasrī* (Vidyānandi commentary on Āpta-Mīmāṁsā: 101) echoes Akalaṅka comments. 'The absolute perfection of the soul implies flattening of karmic veils which leads to the simultaneous revelation of universal and particular.' Cf. Nathmal Tatia, *Studies in Jain Philosophy*, p. 78.

Siddhasena Divākara impeccably states that the relationship between *kevaladarśana* and *kevalajñāna* is identical.[51] Because, after the simultaneous extinction of *darśanāvaraṇa* and *jñānāvaraṇa*, logically follows the dawn of *kevaladarśana* and *kevalajñāna*. Giving priority to one of them in the origination procreates disruption. Synchronous emergence of both while retaining the distinction is also equally untenable because, according to Jainas, two conscious activities cannot occur simultaneously. After the suppression of karmic veils, the persisting existence of distinction in the conscious activity entangles Jaina doctrine in the logical inconsistency. Therefore, the distinct appearance of *darśana* and *jñāna* in omniscience is impossible. Incidentally, the absolute distinction between *darśana* and *jñāna* (in successive and simultaneous occurrence) constrains the omniscient self from the comprehension of reality simultaneously. The philosophical and logical deliberations of Siddhasena Divakara can be encapsulated like this: '*darśana* and *jñāna* occur and perceive simultaneously in the omniscient self without distinction because one and same *upayoga* is responsible for both *darśana* and *jñāna*.'[52]

The successive occurrence of conscious activity (*darśana* and *jñāna*), in limited perception, is unanimously accepted by the three schools of thought. The divergence is about the occurrence of conscious activity in the state of omniscience. Cognition (*upayoga*) is the manifestation of the Self and non-self (object). Such cognition arises from the suppression and annihilation of karmic veils. The causal state of pure *upayoga* is 'the conscious drive,' which implies pure *darśana* and pure *jñāna* as functionaries. The effectual state of limited *upayoga*

51 Cf. *Sanmati-tarka-prakaraṇa*: 2. 3. Siddhasena Divakara, *Sanmati-tarka-prakaraṇa*, quoted by Nathmal Tatia, *Studies in Jain Philosophy*, p. 75.

52 *Sanmati-tarka-prakaraṇa*: 2. 19, 20, 25, 30,31, quoted by Nathmal Tatia, *Studies in Jain Philosophy*, p. 75.

is constrained (not completely) by opacity (āvaraṇa) of karma. All the means of knowledge (*pramāṇas*) are the result of either complete or partial suppression of the obfuscation. There is no complete or total suppression of karmic obscurities in the sensory and limited extrasensory perception, and there are possibilities of collective and inter-changeable combinations of different means of knowledge at that state of cognition.[53] But the perfect extrasensory perception (omniscience) is the perfect illumination of the Self (*dravya*) in its own right with its qualities (*guṇas*) and modes (*paryāya*) after total extinction of karmic obscurities. It is the existential (*sat*) and causal state of the Self (*dravya*). These qualities (*guṇaparyāyas*) are natural to the Self and not distinct from the Self but not identical to the Self. The conscious activity (*kevaldarśana* and *kevalajñāna*) in the causal state is to comprehend the universal (*dravya*) and particular aspect (*guṇaparyāyas*) of the Self. *Kevaldarśana* and *kevalajñāna* are one and identical but are said to be different not in the sense of origination and function but because of the object of the conscious activity, which is twofold universal (*dravya*) and particular (*guṇaparyāyas*). Succinctly, *darśana* and *jñāna* occur alternatively in the perception up to the state of omniscience; *kevaldarśana*

53 *Tattvārthasūtra* says (1. 31) "The soul can possibly possess from one to four types of cognition alternatively." (*ekādīnī bhājyāni yugapad ekasminn* ācaturbhyaḥ). There are four alternative combinations of cognitions; one type, two types, three types, and four types. These are the incomplete state of perfect perception. The co-existence of these conscious activities in one soul, at a time, is criticised by opponents because it is a clear contradiction to the general postulate of Jainas cognition, i.e. two conscious activities simultaneously. Jainas explains that the co-existence of conscious activities is in respect of potency and not in respect of the activity. It means that even when the existence of different conscious activities in a self, the active engagement in the form of having cognition is possible only for one of them at a time, and the rest remain just potencies. (Cf. Pt. Sukhlaji's Commentary on *Tattvārthasūtra*, Commentary to 1.31. pp. 51-53).

and *kevalajñāna* occur simultaneously in the paramount of extrasensory perception, i.e. the omniscience; and the identity and difference is the eternal relationship that permeates in *kevaldarśana* and *kevalajñāna*.

5.6 Guṇssthānas and Kevalajñāna

Omniscient self is not an abstract and impractical idea. There are definite ways for the realisation of omniscience. Therefore, the omniscient self is a reality. In Jainism, the stages of the spiritual development of the Self are known as *guṇasthānas*.[54] There are fourteen stages, according to Jainas. The consummation of *guṇasthānas* is the acquisition of the omniscience status of the Self. Again, the self-illumination and the extinction of the karmic bondage have been working in tandem in the conception of the stages of spiritual development (*guṇasthānas*). "The deluded world-view (*mithyādarśana*), non-abstinence (āvirati), laxity (*pramāda*), passions (*kaṣāya*) and the actions of the body, speech, and mind (*yoga*) are the

54 *Tattvārthasūtra* and some of the secondary texts yield discussion on *guṇasthānas*. *Tattvārthasūtra* (chapter nine) discussions are not a full-fledged or detailed study. In *Tattvārthasūtra*, the first three stages and eighth and ninth stage are eluded. The later commentaries of *Tattvārthasūtra* (*Sarvārthasiddhi* of Pūjyapāda Devanandi *Svopajña Bhāṣya* of Siddhasenagaṇi) render elaborative study *guṇasthānas*. *Samayasāra* of Ācārya Kundakunda (6; 68; 110-112) also mentions about *guṇasthānas*. He discussed *guṇasthānas* from the perspective of *Karta* (the agent) and *Karma* (actions). Thus, excluding the last stage (because of the absence of all karmic conditions) of *ayoga kevali* (omniscience without the activity), he treats thirteen stages of spiritual development. According to him, *guṇasthānas* are unconscious secondary conditions, which curb the activity of thought, word and deed. It implies that they are not immediate causal conditions producing karma. Some other references may be available from; T. G Kalghatgi, *Some Problems in Jaina Psychology*, pp. 150-167; Nathmal Tatia, *Studies in Jaina Philosophy*, pg. 261-293; Indra Chandra Sashtri, *Jaina Epistemology*, pp. 402-405; Walther Schubring, *The Doctrine of the Jainas*, pp. 319-320.

conditions of bondage."[55] Each stage of *guṇasthānas* exerts to eliminate conditions of bondage. Among the fourteen stages of *guṇasthānas*, the research lends significant importance to the penultimate (thirteenth) and ultimate stages (fourteenth).

The lowest stage is the state of the perversity of attitude towards reality (*mithyādṛṣṭi*). It is the state of spiritual inertia or the spiritual slumber with an oblivious consciousness. The second stage is a halting stage (*sāsvādana*), and it is not an upgraded stage of the first. The lurch of the self may end up in the fall from the higher stages of enlightenment. This stage is the container for the falling self before slumping into the first stage. The third stage is a combination of delusion and enlightenment (*samyak-mithyātva*). It is the transition stage from the deluded status of the self to the enlightened status. When the self extricates from the clutches of view-deluding karma, the self commences enjoying the first dawn of enlightenment in the fourth stage (*samyak-dṛṣṭi*). Even though it is ephemeral in nature, it leaves indelible impressions on the self. It is earmarked with a steady vision and enjoys the company of knowledge and will but lacks spiritual strength and abstinence. In other words, this stage of the self is bereft of moral and spiritual backup.

The empirical self must facilitate the moral and spiritual stimuli to occupy the higher stage. Along with the steady vision of the self, the practice of partial abstinence and self-restriction shape the fifth stage (*deśa-virata*) of spiritual development. The sixth stage (*sarva-virata*) emerges from complete self-restriction and abstinence. This stage features the attainment of certain supernatural powers in rudimentary form. Still, it is not a definite feature. However, some souls may attain it. With the self-restraint self, the spiritual inertia persists even at this stage. The seventh stage (*apramatta-virata*) nurtures freedom

---

55 TS: 8.1. *mithyādarśanāvirati pramāda kaṣāya yoga bandhahetuvaḥ.*

from the spiritual inertia (*apramatta*), which unleashes the potential energy of the self. With the attainment of special purification and energy, the eighth stage (*apūrva-karaṇa*) restricts the duration and intensity of the harmful karmas as well as galvanises the function of beneficial karmas. It is enriched with novel and unprecedented (*apūrva*) extrasensory experiences. The ninth stage (*anivṛtti-karaṇa*) has endowed with progressively purer experiences but is still abetted by the influence (*anivṛtti*) of passions. Thereafter, the tenth stage (*sūkṣma-sāmparāya*) is devoid of all the passions except the subtle (*sūkṣma*) greed. By suppressing (*upaśānta*) the remains of retaining subtle greed along with other passions, the eleventh stage (*upaśānta-kaṣāya*) entail the empirical self to the purer state, which extricates it from the origination of all kinds of passions. There is the only thin demarcation between the eleventh and the twelfth stage because the former is the apex of the ladder of subsidence of karma, and the latter is the apex of the ladder of annihilation (*kṣīṇa*) of karma. The twelfth stage (*kṣīṇa-moha*) is the stage of annihilated passions or the stage of complete self-restriction with eliminated passions. It is the peril of the destructive (*ghāti*) karmas, which leads to the subsequent stage of perfect intuition and perfect knowledge.

The thirteenth and the fourteenth stage are the states of omniscience. The former amounts to 'the omniscience with physical activity (*sayoga-kevalī*)', which is equivalent to *Jivanmukta* (liberation while living) in other systems. Except for the activity (*yoga*) of the body, the sense organ of speech and the mind, all the conditions of the bondage are dismayed in this state of omniscience. The life span of the embodied existence, which has been already destined due to āyuḥkarman, cannot be scotched prematurely.[56] But the physical activity is no more subjected to bondage because all the passions and

56 Cf. TS: 2.52.

delusions are absolutely purged.[57] Among the eight kinds of karma, "bondage (*bandha*) follows from ignorance (*ajñāna*) if there be infatuation (*moha*), but not from ignorance where infatuation has disappeared."[58] In this stage, therefore, the activities are extricated from the clutches of karmic bondage. Each stage of progression of the self obtains an excellent efficacy of purity and consciousness free from infatuations. Here, cognition is neither the activity of the mind or the sense organ. It is the direct and simultaneous perception of the Self.

Different from other Indian philosophical systems, Jaina holds that the influx of karma (*āśrava*) as the cause of the bondage and ignorance (*ajñāna*) as the ramification of karma. The commentary to *Tattvārthasūtra* mentions: "All categories of knowledge, other than omniscience, are accompanied by ignorance due to the constant rise of karma."[59] The doctrine of karma has taken precedence in Jainas epistemology. Therefore, liberation necessarily implies 'the omniscience with no activity' (*ayoga-kevalī*) because the annihilation of non-destructive karma concurrently quells the physical activity of the body, mind and sense of speech.[60] *Samayasāra* reiterates

57 Cf. TS: 10.2.

58 AM: 10. 98

ajñānānmohato bandho nājñānād vītamohataḥ
jñānastokāchcha mokṣaḥ syādmohān mohitonyathā.

59 The commentary to *Tattvārthasūtra*: 1.12. p. 14.

60 The elimination of both destructive and non-destructive karma is an inevitable prerequisite for liberation in its true sense (Cf. TS: 10.3). The trajectory of the soul from the omniscience with activity to the omniscience without activity is functioned through practice and mediation. The stoppage of one activity requires another activity as the instrument. After the close observation in the Jainas tradition and philosophical thought system, Nathmal Tatia enumerates this process of the stoppage of activity like this: "The gross activities of the body are used to stop the gross activities of speech and the mind. Then it uses the subtle activity of the body to stop the gross activity of the body as

the omniscience by sabotaging all the karmic activities by saying like this; "the real being who is of the nature of Knower is neither identical with *Apramatta* nor *Prammatta* beings. His nature as the knower is unique and self-identical."[61] Enhancement of the suspension of the activity facilitates through the practice of 'white meditation'.[62] At the last stages of the *guṇasthāna*, the object of meditation is limited to 'the subtle infallible physical activity and irreversible stillness of the Self.'[63] The omniscience enters into the state of suspension of all residual subtle activities of the body which is corollary disembodied liberation. It is the fourteenth stage, and that is the consummation of *guṇasthāna*, which is liberation.

Referring to the Jainas' philosophical texts, Nathamal Tatia demarcates three states of the Self in the process

---

well as the subtle activities of speech and mind. The soul then enters the third stage of white meditation, which is accompanied by subtle activities and has no fall. It now has to stop the subtle bodily activity through the activity itself, for there is none other than this. By means of this meditation, the soul contracts and fills the cavities created in the embodied state. Then it enters the fourth stage of white meditation, which stops even the residual subtle activity and has no reversion." (Nathmal Tatia, Appendix to *Tattvārthasūtra: That Which Is*, p. 281).

61 SS: 6.

ṇavi hodi appmatto ṇa pamatto jāṇgo du jo bhāvo
evaṁ bhaṇaṁti suddhā ṇādā jo so du so ceva

62 *Tattvārthasūtra* mentions the four types of meditation: mournful (ārta), wrathful (*raudra*), analytic (dharma) and white (*sūklāni*). The first two nourishes worldly life. Analytic mediation is practised by people who are complete self-restraint free of laxity. It is possible at the fourth to the seventh stage of spiritual development. At the higher level of meditation of the same is extended to the eleventh and twelfth stages of spiritual development (9. 27-38). The white meditation is possible in person at the stage of complete self-restraint with suppressed passions and at the stage of complete self-restraint with eliminated passions." (9.39).

63 Cf. TS: 9.41-47.

(*guṇasthānas*) of unfolding the potentiality of the Self: the exterior self (*bahirātman*), the interior self (*antarātman*), and the transcendental self (*param*ātman). He continues to say: "Considered from the point of view of *guṇasthāna*, the soul before it cuts the knot (*granthi*) and experiences the first dawn of the spiritual vision is the exterior self, and the soul after the vision and before the attainment of omniscience is the interior self. On the attainment of omniscience, the self becomes the transcendental self. To be a transcendental self, the soul has to be raised from the state of the interior as much as the exterior self. This process of uplift movement is *yoga*."[64] Therefore, the manifestation of the transcendental self and its resultant cognition is clear and distinct perception (*yogi-pratyakṣa*).

5.7 Arhatas and Siddhas

According to Jainas, omniscience arises when the four destructive karmas (*gathikarama*) are wearing off. But the complete annihilation of destructive karmas happens only when the other four non-destructive karmas are annihilated where the body terminates its earthly existence. In the true sense, this is the state of liberation that is free from all karma.[65] Therefore, there are two kinds of omniscient beings: 'the omniscience with the body' (*sayoga kevali*) and 'the omniscience without body' (*ayoga kevali*). These two kinds denote, in the religious realm of Jainism, as *Arhat* (variant: *Arihant*) and *Siddha*, respectively. The salutation to both is the part of the prescribed daily religious formula (*Namokāramantra*) for a faithful religious life.[66] *Namokāramantra* is the fundamental

---

64 *Samādhitantra*: 17, quoted in Nathmal Tatia, *Studies in Jain Philosophy*, pp. 281-282.

evaṁ tyaktvā bahirvācaṁ yajed antar aśeṣataḥ
eṣa yogaḥ samāsena pradhīpaḥ paramātmanaḥ.

65 Cf. TS: 10. 1-4.

66 Referred in the commentary to *Dravyasaṁgraha* 49, p. 75

prayer of Jaina devout. It is the prayer of salutation. The prayer indicates the gradual unfolding of the potentialities of the Self. In other words, it depicts the picture of gradation of supernatural perception, which culminates in omniscience. In this prayer, a Jain devout acknowledge and bow in front of five kinds of divine souls. Among them, *Arhats* and *Siddhas* are the penultimate and ultimate state of perfect knowledge. *Arhats* and *Siddhas* have no sensuous activities and no sensory-pleasure experiences. They enjoy all-knowledge and infinite bliss without the help of any senses.

Arhat is the living omniscient beings. *Dravyasaṁgraha* defines it as, "The pure soul existing in the auspicious body, possessed of infinite faith, happiness, knowledge and power, which has destroyed the four gathi karmas, is to be meditated on as an Arhat."[67] Even among the living omniscient being (*Arhat*) has a difference following the purport of their function. The omniscient *tirthaṅkaras* is different from the ordinary omniscient being in respect of the incumbency to preach and found a religious community. Nathmal Tatia briefs it out like this:

> The capacity to reveal and effectively preach the truth however, does not belong to all the enlightened and omniscient souls. It is only those rare souls, who have acquired the potency of the revealing the truth and

---

Namo Arihaṁtānaṁ Namo Sidhhānaṁ
Namo Āyariyānaṁ *Namo uvajjhāyānaṁ*
namo loya savvasāhunaṁ.

(The obeisance [bow] to *Arihant*, obeisance to *Siddhas*, obeisance to Āchāryas, obeisance to *Upādhyayas*, and obeisance *Sāddhu*) Nemicandra in *Dravyasaṁgraha* briefly elaborates on the nature of the five groups of people. Cf. DS: 50-54.

67 DS: 50.
naṭṭhacadughāikammo daṁsanasuha ṇāṇa vīrya maio
suhadehattho appā suddha ariho viciṁtijjo.

establishing a religious community by their moral and virtuous activities of the past life, that are capable of revealing the truth and preaching it to the world at large on their attainment of omniscience. Such souls become the *tithaṅkaras*, founders of religion, who are the embodiment of the best and the highest virtues that the human mind can conceive of, the fullest expression of the personalities of embodied existence.[68]

These souls have incarnated into the universe on special occasions. They have endowed with the supernatural power by birth and conception, and they acquire excellence in their powers through the adoption of ascetic vows, attainment of perfect knowledge, and final liberation.[69] The ordinary omniscient beings attained liberation by practising the discipline taught by *tirthaṅkaras*. But the commentaries to *Tattvārthasūtra* mention an exceptional group of omniscient souls who are enlightened in isolation, inspired by internal vocations, without the assistance of any diktats or disciplines taught by the eminent teachers or founders like *tirthaṅkaras*.[70]

Siddha is the disembodied omniscient being. *Dravyasaṁgraha* defines it as, "The soul which is bereft of the bodies produced by eight kinds of karma, which is the seer and knower of *loka* and *aloka*, and which stages at the summit of the universe."[71] Ācārya Umāsvāmi states the nature of *Siddha* in *Tattvārthasūtra*. According to him, elimination of all types of karma (*kṛtsnakarmakṣayo*), the perfection of knowledge

68 Nathmal Tatia, *Studies in Jaina Philosophy*, p. 268.

69 Cf. The commentary to Āpta-Mīmāṁsā: 1.p. 25.

70 Cf. The commentary to *Tattvārthasūtra*: 10. 7, pp. 257-258.

71 DS: 51.

naṭṭhaṭṭhakammadeho loyāloyasya jānao daṭṭhā
purisāyāro appā siddho jhāeha loyasiharattho.

and intuition (*kevalasamyaktva jñāna darśana*), and the settlement in the higher plane of cosmic space (ūrdhvaṃ *gacchatyālokāntāt*) are the distinctive features of *Siddha*.[72] In the introductory verse of *Samayasāra*, Ācārya Kundakunda elaborates the nature of *Siddhas* as the permanent (*acalaṁ*), immutable (*amala*), and incomparable (*anupama*) existence.[73] After the extinction of all types of karmas, the self has not succumbed to any further change and hence, is characterised by unchanging permanency. The complete absence of impurity leads to immutable existence. Having transcended all the sensual experiences, *Siddhahood* is not comparable with any concrete objects of the universe.

Ācārya Kundakunda, in *Samaysāra*, collectively names the object of adoration as *Jita-moha*, i.e., conqueror of delusions. *Jita-moha* denotes both *Arhat* and *Siddha* who is endowed with the characteristics of the subjugation of senses, eradication of the delusions and the realisation of the self intrinsically as of the nature of knowledge.[74] Ācārya Umāsvāmi, in *Tattvārthasūtra* collectively name the state of omniscient existence as *Snātakā*, which means 'the successful and the unbound ascetic'. According to Jain religious tradition, the repeated meditative and conscious chanting of the nature of the omniscient being (*Arhat* and *Siddha*) enhances the auspiciousness and purity in the worshipper.

5.8 Conclusion

This chapter provides a detailed interpretation and examination of the epistemological and soteriological foundations of omniscience (*kevalajñāna*). In Jainism, *kevalajñāna* is characterized as the direct and simultaneous cognition of the

72 Cf. TS: 10. 3-6.

73 Cf. SS: 1.

74 Cf. SS: 31-33.

Self, occurring without the mediation of sense organs or the mind. It encompasses the perception of all substances and their modes, including extrasensory experiences. This direct and simultaneous cognition ensures the immediacy and clarity that define true perception, marking *kevalajñāna* as the epitome of *pratyakṣa pramāṇa*, or direct knowledge. *Kevalajñāna* represents the ultimate realization in the Jaina epistemic framework, embodying the peak of cognitive achievement and the state of liberation. The psychology of *kevalajñāna*, along with the specific stages of spiritual development (*guṇasthānas*) required to attain it, affirms the existence of the omniscient Self. Moreover, the veneration of omniscient beings (*Arhats* and *Siddhās*) in religious practices and prayers (*namokāramantra*) underscores the acceptance and significance of this state. The forthcoming chapter will validate the progression of cognitive development and its culmination in *kevalajñāna*, further elucidating its role within the Jaina philosophical and soteriological context.

CHAPTER 6

Arguments for the Existence of Yogi-Pratyakṣa

Repudiating opponents' staunch criticisms and safeguarding one's dogmatic position, Jaina scholars frame out and furnish rational arguments to prove the existence of *yogi-pratyakṣa*. This chapter highlights these rational arguments. To be concentrative, the research collects the arguments those given by Jaina logicians, such as Ācārya Kundakunda, Ācārya Samantabhadra, Hemacandrasūri and Vadidevasūri. These scholars have provided robust logical frameworks to substantiate the existence of *yogi-pratyakṣa*, a form of direct perceptual experience accessible to advanced practitioners. The chapter is divided into two main sections. The first section presents and analyzes the positive arguments put forth by Jaina logicians to affirm the reality of *yogi-pratyakṣa*. The second section addresses and refutes counterarguments, demonstrating the absence of credible evidence against the existence of *yogi-pratyakṣa*. By systematically examining these arguments, the chapter aims to establish the logical validity of *yogi-pratyakṣa* and elucidate its epistemological and soteriological significance within Jaina philosophy.

6.1 The Postive Proofs for the Existence of Yogi-Pratyakṣa

Imbibed the musings from *Nyāya-Vaiśeṣika* and *Yoga* systems, Jaina would engage in the formation of arguments to prove the existence of *yogi-pratyakṣa*. Obviously, these attempts are deeply rooted in the epistemological and metaphysical presuppositions of Jaina doctrines.

The Jaina tradition presents three key arguments in support of the existence of *yogi-pratyakṣa*:

1. **The Argument from Progression**: This posits that the gradual advancement of a yogi's inherent nature of Self leads to direct perceptual experience.
2. **The Argument from Potentiality**: This suggests that the potential for such direct perception exists within the framework of yogic discipline.
3. **The Argument from Purification**: This asserts that through purification practices, a yogi achieves a state of perception that transcends ordinary sensory experience.

Ācārya Kundakunda laid the groundwork for these arguments, while later scholars such as Ācārya Samantabhadra and Hemacandrasūri further logically refined and structured them.

6.1.1 The Argument from Progression

The argument from progression is one of the most august arguments to prove the higher cognitive faculties. Among the advocates of extrasensory perception, post fifth-century *Nyāya-Vaiśeṣika*,[1]

1 Jayantha Bhaṭṭa in *Nyāyamañjarī* asserts the gradual perfection and culmination of perception. He states that there are various degrees of perception in and among the individual soul. Wherever there are differences in the conception of the objects placed in proximity and

Yoga,[2] and Jaina have formulated their argument against the backdrop of each philosophy. Distinct from both systems (*Nyāya-Vaiśeṣika* and *Yoga*), the inclusion of *yogi-pratyakṣa* in epistemology earmarks Jainas exposition of the argument significant. The argument from progression amounts to the following: 'one can reach the consummation and perfection of cognition because there is a progression of cognition. Since there is a progression of cognition, then there is a gradual unfoldings of cognition. These gradual unfolding are the different stages of cognition, which culminates in omniscience.' Hemacandrasūri, in *Pramāṇamīmāṃsā*,

---

distance, there are variations in the degrees of the perception, such as the limitation of the human perception of perceiving objects in the darkness and the perceving the same object by cats. Therefore, the various degrees of perception necessitate the gradual progression of perception, which consummated in omniscience. There is another mode of argument based on quality, consciousness. Every quality has gradation in an expression, such as the whiteness. The consciousness and its resultant cognition is the quality. Hence, there is gradation in perception, which culminated in the perfect perception. Perfection is the state without any further gradation. The paramount of the gradation is well evident in Yogins who is conversant to objects those are subtle, concealed, distant, past and future. (Cf. *Nyāyamañjarī*: Vol. 1, p. 157. 1-7.).

2 Patañjali in *Yogasūtra Īśvara* is the perfect state of omniscience. He says, "In Him, the seed of omniscience has reached its utmost development which cannot be exceeded." (YS: 1. 25. *tatra niratiśayaṃ sarvajñavijam*). This verse has a sound implication about the progression of cognition and its culmination. The seed of omniscience has a rudimentary state and a completely developed state, and there are grades of development. The developed state cannot have further progression. It is the state of permanency. There is a being who possesses such a state of existence and knowledge. The formal argument is framed in Vyasa's commentary like this: "The seed of omniscience has grades of development and thus is capable of increasing from more to still more. The person in whom it has reached its highest point is a particular being who knows everything." (The commentary to *Yogasūtra*: 1. 25. p. 60).

elucidates it like this: "The progressive development, that is to say, the realisation of degrees of excellence, of knowledge, must reach its consummation somewhere, since this is the way of all progression, as seen in the progression of magnitude."[3] The argument can be logically presented as follows:

> Thesis (*pratiñjā*): There is a culmination of knowledge.
>
> Logical reason (*hetu*): Because there is a progression of knowledge.
>
> Example (*udāharaṇa*): Wherever there is progression, there is the culmination, as the progression of magnitude.

The progression and culmination of magnitude, from the smallest to the highest, elucidate the invariable concomitance between the progression and culmination. According to Jaina, owing to the suppression of karmic obscuration and the concurrent illumination of the Self, there is a progression of cognition. Hemacandrasūri further clarifies the argument with the observation of the common experience regarding the judgement in the case of astronomy. He observes that there is the gradual consummation of the scope of our cognition "in the actual verification of astronomical knowledge, which is unaccountable on any other hypothesis."[4]

The progression of cognition and the existence of *yogi-pratyakṣa* can be logically proved based on the two interconnected syllogisms.[5] The faculties of cognition have

---

3 PM: 1.1.16. no. 55.

4 PM: 1.1.16. no. 55.

5 This argument is constructed in the way of *Yogasūtra* commentary. The commentators endeavour to enumerate and examine the omniscient *Īśvara* scotch in the findings of the proof for the existence of omniscient *Īśvara*. He formulated a method of inferring the existence of *Īśvara*. Here, this method of inferring is being taken into the research in order

innumerable forms because the faculties of cognition are the modification of immeasurable consciousness. Wherever an immeasurable thing is split into fractions, then the fractions would be innumerable, as in the case of time. As time is break up into measured hours, there would be innumerable hours so the immeasurable consciousness modifies into the faculties of cognition, and there would be innumerable cognitions. Succinctly, cognition is the modification of consciousness, which is immeasurable and therefore, the faculties of cognition are innumerable by nature. The conclusion of the above syllogism engenders the second inferential knowledge. The immeasurable and innumerable cognition consummates in the magnitude of cognition because the immeasurable cognitions are taken progressively increasing. Wherever the fractions of immeasurable thing are taken consecutively progressing then the consummation would be a colossal thing, which cannot progress further. That is massiveness more than which does not exist. Without exception, all *Jīva* possess the power of cognition but in a modified form. None of the *Jīva* is bereft of the consciousness. This amounts to claiming that *Jīva* is made of pure consciousness or *Jīva* is a pure embodiment of cognition. As there are innumerable *Jīva*, so there are innumerable cognitions. From one sensed *Jīva* to five sensed *Jīva*, from five sensed *Jīva* to *saṁjñi Jīva*, from *saṁjñi Jīva* to the self-restraint and contemplated *yogi*, the faculty of cognition goes on increasing. Thus, it is progressive. The increase of the velocity and penetration of the cognition concurrently relies on the gradual suppression and annihilation of karmic obscurities. It validates the gradual progression of the faculties of cognition. It would appear that the modifications of the immeasurable consciousness going

to prove the progression of cognition and concurrently to prove the existence of *yogi-pratyakṣa*. (Cf. The commentary to *Yogasūtra*: 1. 25. p. 60).

on increasing and finally consummated in perfect cognition that nothing can exceed it. Hence, the extent of cognition will culminate a state more than which there would be none, i.e., the omniscience.

The progression of cognition necessarily implies the unitary state of cognition. It is the innate and eternal nature of the Self. The various types of cognition, which begin with the sense perception and culminate in the omniscience, have affiliation only to this unitary state of cognition. Ācārya Kundakunda, in *Samaysāra*, comments like this: "Knowledge through sense-perception, knowledge from scriptures, knowledge from clairvoyance, knowledge from telepathy, and supreme knowledge of reality-all these refer to one and the same state. That is absolute. The realisation of that absolute is liberation." [6] Ācārya Amṛtacandra elucidates the unitary state of cognition and the gradual manifestation of the Self that permeates in the progression of cognition with the example of the sun and covered clouds:

> When the sun is hidden by clouds its light is not seen and when the clouds gradually disperse, the sunlight gradually reappears in varying degrees till it regains its full luminosity, when all the clouds completely disappear. So, also the self in the form of knowledge, remains hidden, shrouded by the layer of *karmas*. When the karma-cloud gradually gets dispersed, then the self-knowledge begins to shine in varying brilliancy. This variation in knowledge which is due to the variation in the density of the karmic cloud does not in any way imply any differentiation in the nature of underlying Self, that remains the same one,

---

6 SS: 204.

ābhiṇisudohimaṇakevalaṁ ca taṁ hodi ekkameva padṁ
so eso paramaṭṭho jaṁ lahiduṁ nivvudim jādi.

> non-varying and permanent. That remains without any differentiation. It is identical with the supreme knowledge. When that knowledge is obtained, it is Self-realisation.[7]

The general structure of argument ignites the gradual progression of the cognition and its perfection in full luminosity. At the same time, it annuls the thesis, which states any differentiation in the nature of the Self. Ācārya Kundakunda compares the uninterrupted state of the Self with the gold in the furnace of heat. He says: "Just as gold, however, much it is heated, never loses its intrinsic nature, so also the right knowing Self, however, much it is burnt by associated karmas, does not his intrinsic nature of pure knowledge."[8] Again, it is the state without further gradation. Attaining this state is the consummation of cognition, which is supernatural.

Kumārila criticises the argument from the progression like this:

> Even then, in so far as there cannot be any going beyond the own domain of sense organs, the culmination experienced with regard to some would concern the only visual perception of things which are distant, subtle etc.; but this could not be the operation of the sense of hearing with regard to visual aspects. If the omniscient person can conceive of everything by virtue of any cognitive criterion, then thins cognitive criterion could cognise all tastes etc. through the eye.[9]

---

7 The commentary to *Samayasāra*: 204. Pp. 346-347.

8 SS: 184.

jaha kaṇayamagggitaviyam pi kaṇayabhāvaṁ ṇa taṁ pariccayadi
taha kammodayatavido ṇo jahadi ṇāṇī du ṇāṇittaṁ.

9 *Mīmāṃsa-sloka-varttika*: 2.112; 114, quoted in Piotr Balcerowicz, "Extrasensory Perception (*yogi-pratyakṣa*) in Jainism and its

Jaina would repudiate that the progression of perception widens the possibility of cognition without the senses. The sense perception is the rudimentary form of perception, and there are higher levels of perception. *Yogi-pratyakṣa* is not the intensified or magnified sense perception and not the perfection of sense competency. The role of senses in the case of *yogi-pratyakṣa* is absolutely nothing. It is the Self, being a knower by nature and essentially constituted of knowledge, cognises the complex reality and comprehends it immediately and simultaneously in its entirety. Therefore, the Self is the instrument of cognition. Ācārya Kundakunda frames this argument like this: "The ascetics have the scripture, the doctrine of Lord Jina, as their eyes, the worldly souls have the senses as their eyes, the celestial beings have clairvoyance as their eyes, and the liberated souls have omnipresent eyes that see everything."[10] On another occasion, Ācārya Kundakunda says, "For him who is involving into the perfect knowledge, knows all substance ad modifications directly and simultaneously as he does not rely on the sensory knowledge that knows them by means of stages such as apprehension (*avagraha*)."[11] The perfection of *yogi-pratyakṣa* is endorsed as "the supreme of all cognitions, just as the face is the supreme part of the body."[12] Hemacandrasūri reiterates the supremacy of *yogi-pratyakṣa* in the progression of cognition like this: "It is characterised as the pure in scriptures, since it is independent of the services of sense-organs, is cognisant of all objects, and thus stands apart, having nothing common with other modes of cognition."[13] It can be explained in the words of Amṛtacandra Sūri, as follows:

Refutations", p. 6.

10 PS: 3.34.

āgama-cakkhū sāhū iṃdiya-cakkhūṇi savva-bhūdāṇi
devā ya ohi-cakkhū siddhā puṇa savvado-cakkhū.

11 PS: 1.31.

12 PM: 1.1.15. no. 48.

13 PM: 1.1.15. no. 48.

> Since he (omniscient) himself, at the moment of the annihilation of all obscurations (āvāraṇas), accepted the function of a cause (*kāraṇa*), the innate nature of knowledge which has no beginning, no end, no cause (*hetu*) and has nothing in common with anything else, evolves, becoming the psychic exertion of arising absolute knowledge, which immediately follows the annihilation of āvāraṇas. Therefore, the modifications of all the substances are perceptible for him, since they conjointly become a basis for his consciousness inasmuch as all substances, times, places, and forms of being are appropriated by him simultaneously.[14]

Therefore, there is nothing imperceptible to the individual soul who attains perfect knowledge because of the simultaneous and direct perception by the self-illuminated Self. The progression of cognition has gone through the various degrees of cognitions and finally consummates in omniscience. According to Hemacandrasūri, they are the various instances of pure cognition. 'Owing to the variation of the degrees of the cessation of karmic veils, the transcendental intuition admits *avadhi* and *manaḥparyaya* as the two consecutive stages of progression of *yogi-pratyakṣa* that thriving to *kevalajñāna*.'[15] The apex state of progression (*kevalajñāna*) is that without any further gradation. These various degrees of cognitions with their culmination are the states and perfection of *yogi-pratyakṣa*, respectively. Thus, *avadhi* and *manaḥparyaya* are 'the intermediate stage to the perfection of knowledge.'[16]

---

14 Amṛtachandra Sūri commentary to *Pravaccanasāra*: 1. 21, p. 13.

15 PM: 1.1.18. no. 64.

16 Piotr Balcerowicz, "Extrasensory Perception (*yogi-pratyakṣa*) in Jainism, Proofs of its Existence and Its Soteriological Implications", p. 61.

This is possible because the annihilation of all obscurations entails the manifestation of the innate nature of the Self for a psychic exertion of procuring knowledge. According to Jainas, the practice and mediation necessarily lead to the complete annihilation of the karmic veils and manifestation of the innate nature of the Self. The self-illuminative innate nature of the Self, at once, manifests cognitive agent and cognitive objects. Ācārya Samantabhadra adheres to the practice of gradual progression in cognitive process with a view of the cognitive actuality like this: "The knowledge of realities and *pramāna* at once illuminates every object. The derived knowledge is gradually purified by *naya* of *Syādvāda*."[17] From this point of view, Piotr Balcerowicz infers another variant of the argument of progression, and it is termed 'the argument from progression by necessity.' Further, he enumerates what it means 'by necessity': "It emphasizes that the gradual process towards absolute perfection through various stages is in a way necessarily determined."[18] It vividly states that the incessant practice of *Syādvāda* and unflagging meditation inevitably leads the embodied soul to the various instances of *yogi-pratyakṣa* and finally to its perfect state of existence.

6.1.2 Argument from Potentiality

Jaina scholars develop the argument from potentiality as proof for the existence of *yogi-pratyakṣa*. The potential nature of the subject and object of cognition validates the existence of *yogi-pratyakṣa*. From the side of the subject, every soul inherently is perfect and pure cognition. From the side of

---

17 AM: 101.

tattvajñanaṁ pramāṇaṁ te yugapat sarvabhāsanam
kramabhāvi cha yaj-jñānaṁ syādvāda-naya-saṁskṛtam.

18 Piotr Balcerowicz, "Extrasensory Perception (*yogi-pratyakṣa*) in Jainism, Proofs of its Existence and Its Soteriological Implications", p. 67.

the object, all things are inherently knowable. The argument from the view of the subject sets like this: the individual soul would reach the perfection of cognition because there is the potentiality of perfect cognition in the individual soul, and the pure consciousness is natural to the Soul. Since there is the potentiality of pure and perfect cognition, then the Soul predictably attains the perfection of cognition. This perfection of cognition is beyond the capacity of sense organs and the mind. Thus, it is *yogi-pratyakṣa*. The argument from the view of the object frames like this: someone is there to know objects of knowledge because all things are knowable in nature. Since all things are knowable in nature, then the supra-sensible objects also cognizable to someone. Thus, there is the perceiver of the supra-sensible objects, and so, there is the perception of the supra-sensible objects. Imprints of the argument from potentiality have already seen in the Jainas principle of causation. Ācārya Kundakunda, in *Samaysāra*, briefly explains the principle of causation like this: "The manifested effect conditions the nature of the manifesting agent and similarly the manifesting agent determines the nature of effects. This is the principle of causation that is observed to operate in the world of reality, and no other principle is evident."[19]

The supernatural experiences of sages, anecdotes, personal ephemeral experiences, and recent researches on parapsychology incline one to accept the existence of some sorts of the cryptic source of perception independent of sensory function. For Jainas, the cause of this sort of extrasensory perception is the sole activity of the Self. According to scriptures, some spiritual sages have inherited the state of perfect perception. The Self in spiritual sages and the Self in common people are not qualitatively different. Ācārya Kundakunda says, "Whatever is

---

19 SS: 311.

kammaṁ paḍucca kattā katāraṁ taha paḍucca kammāṇi
uppajjṁtiya ṇiamā siddhī du ṇa dīsae aṇṇā.

produced from a substance has the same attributes as those of the substance. Know that, certainly they cannot be different, just as bangles etc. made of gold cannot be other than gold."[20] Since consciousness is the natural property of the Self, it has to be occurred as the distinctive feature in all the units of the Self. Therefore, whatever is cognised by oneself is capable of being cognised by others also. It means whatever is cognised or perceived by a *yogi*-self is capable of being cognised by the other units of the Self. Ensued from this conclusion, Jaina strongly propels that one cannot simply detain the extrasensory perception cases of sages or the ordinary people are exceptional and the anomaly or abnormal. Instead, it reckons the potentiality of each and every self. The commentator of Āpta-Mīmāṁsā further establishes the potentiality of the Self like this:

> If there be infinity of ideas, each of which is known to only individual at a time, the consciousness of each and every soul is potentially able to know the whole infinity of them. Hence, each and every soul is potentially omniscient, that is to say, the consciousness of every living being is endowed with the capacity to know all things, unlimited by time or space. There is nothing to be surprised at in this conclusion, since knowledge merely means a state of consciousness, which being an affection or modification of the substance of its being, is felt by the soul. This amounts to saying that the soul is made of pure intelligence; in different language the *jīva* is a pure embodiment of knowledge.[21]

---

20 SS: 308.

daviyaṁ jaṁ uppajjai guṇehiṁ taṁ tahiṁ jāṇasu aṇaṇṇaṁ
jaha kaḍayādīhiṁ du pajjaehiṁ kaṇayaṁ aṇaṇṇamiha.

21 The commentary to Āpta-Mīmāṁsā: 1.4. p. 39.

This argument of potentiality claims that pure cognition is tantamount to liberation or Self-realisation. Potential cognition is the modification of consciousness, which is identical to the Self. Therefore, cognition in actuality is the state of pure consciousness, which is identical to self-realisation. To sum up, the Self is a pure embodiment of knowledge.

Having analysed the potentiality from the side knowable objects, Hemacandrasūri and Ācārya Samantabhadra coherently articulate the logical argument. The existence of a thing is cognizable for someone because the existence of a thing is identical to the knowability of the same. It squarely asserts that all things are potentially knowable. At the same time, it does not claim that everything is conversant to a particular individual soul in a particular time and space. But there is no unknown existence. Whatever is existent is knowable by someone. Thus, all things are potentially knowable. Ācārya Samantabhadra crafts the argument from the common experience of the knowledge of distant and minute objects bereft of direct sense perception. The knowledge of the existence of distant objects, such as heavenly bodies like the moon and stars at daytime, non-material objects, such as Dharma, and the knowledge of minute objects, such as atoms, are not the object of sense perception for every self in all the contexts. However, they are known as the inferential knowledge, and thus, these are capable of being 'known by some persons.'[22] Piotr Balcerowicz constructs a thesis of argument founded on the implicit meaning of Ācārya Samantabhadra arguments: "everything which is inferable is potentially perceptible to someone."[23] 'Unopposed to logic and scripture and devoid of blemishes,' *yogi* claims the perception

22 AM: 1.5.

23 Piotr Balcerowicz, "Extrasensory Perception (*yogi-pratyakṣa*) in Jainism, Proofs of its Existence and Its Soteriological Implications," p. 75.

of supernatural objects.[24] In fact, there are "objects, which are subtle, intercepted by barriers and remote, are perceived by some person, since they are knowable, as is the case with a jar."[25] Ācārya Kundakunda clearly states that 'the omniscient knows and sees the objects including supernatural as the sense organ eye knows and perceives material objects.'[26] Therefore, the existence of supernatural objects is inferable because it is known, by *yogis*. To conclude, the knowability of objects and concurrent demand for a knower defend the existence of *yogi* and *yogi-pratyakṣa*.

6.1.3 Argument from the Purification

Recapturing three metaphysical credentials of Jaina philosophy is relevant to understand the argument from purification: the consciousness is the innate and eternal nature of the soul, the karmic matter obfuscates the innate nature of the Self, which results in the different modification of the consciousness, the modification of consciousness is effected in the form of cognition, which moulds a relation of identity and difference between cognition and cognisor. In this regard, the Self is 'the cognitive subject', 'the cognitive agent' and 'the cognitive instrument'.[27]

Piotr Balcerowicz encapsulates the argument like this: "one can purify oneself completely because there is a method. Since one's nature is consciousness, then once one is absolutely pure, one is endowed with absolute knowledge."[28] The Self

24 Cf. AM: 1.6.

25 PM: 1.16. no. 55.

26 PS: 1.29.

27 Piotr Balcerowicz, "Extrasensory Perception (*yogi-pratyakṣa*) in Jainism, Proofs of its Existence and Its Soteriological Implications," p. 74.

28 Piotr Balcerowicz, "Extrasensory Perception (*yogi-pratyakṣa*) in Jainism, Proofs of its Existence and Its Soteriological Implications", p. 74.

is pure in nature. The purity is being curtailed by external imperfections. On account of the karmic obscurity, the Self is in the state of impurity, as the luminous sun is obscured by the veil of dust or fog or cloud. Like the extirpation of the opacity over the sun allows the sun to shine forth by its own nature, the suppression of karmic veils amounts to the manifestation of the self-luminous Self. Thus, there is the realization of the illumination of the pure nature of the Self because there is a method of meditation that removing obscurities over the Self, as the blowing of wind removes the clouds over the sun.[29] Hemacandrasūri quashes the incompatibility between the beginningless origin of karmic veils and the removal of them at a particular point through the analogy of dross found in gold and the process of calcination. He says, "The dross found in ore of gold is as old as the gold, but sill it is found to be removed by the action of an alkaline substance, or by calcination in a sealed vessel. Exactly like this case, the removal of knowledge obscuring karmas, though without beginning, can become a possibility by repeated practice of the triple jewel, which is its antidote."[30] Karma corrupts internal qualities of the Self and externally procures attachment, delusion, activity and ignorance etc. This purification purges external and internal impurities, and brings out the pure Self, as the gold is purified from the external mud and internal alloy. Therefore, Ācārya Samantabhadra declares: "As from causes belonging to itself the destruction of external and internal impurities takes place, so in some soul owing to a particular excellence, destruction of faults and impediments happens."[31] Hence, the purity of the

29 Cf. PM: 1.1.15.no. 50.

30 PM: 1.1 15.no. 51.

31 AM: 1.4.

doṣāvaraṇayorhānir niḥśeṣāśtytiśāyanāt
kvachid yathā svahetubhyo bahirantar malakṣayaḥ.

Self is the self-illumination or manifestation by its own nature and not external imposition or addition by the work of an external instrument. The destruction of karmic impediments and the self-illumination of the Self are working in tandem in the process of purification of the Self.

The purity of the Self is purity in its existence, which is pure consciousness. Ācārya Kundukanda states the nature of the Self unleashed from karma like this: "The Self who by nature all-knowing and all-perceiving when soiled by his own karmas, is dragged on towards *saṁsāra*, the cycle of births and deaths, and becomes incapable of all things completely."[32] On another occasion, he claims, "The Self that has become pristine through pure cognition, and has washed away, by own effort, the dirt of karmas, comprehends fully all objects of knowledge."[33] It reckons that the total purification of the Self is identical with the total purified cognition. Necessarily, it implies that the gradual purification is tantamount to the gradual progression of cognition. According to Hemacandrasūri, the different stages of *yogi-pratyakṣa* are gauged on account of the purity of the Self.[34] Thus, *avadhi*, *manaḥaparyaya* and all other instances of *yogi-pratyakṣa* are considered as the intermediate stages of pure *yogi-pratyakṣa*. The notion of intermediate stages squarely proposes that they are not the final in the constitution. The contentment of these instances of *yogi-pratyakṣa* precludes an individual soul from entering the final consummation because the deluded and infatuated knowledge carries impurity. Ācārya Samantabhadra

---

32 SS: 160.

so savvaṇāṇadarisī kammarayeṇa ṇieṇa occhaṇṇo
saṁsārasamāvaṇṇo ṇa vijāṇadi savvado savvaṁ.

33 PS: 1. 15.

uvvogavisuddho jo vigadāvaraṇatarāyamoharo
bhūdo sayamevādā jādi paraṁ ṇeyabhūdāṇṁ.

34 Cf. PM: 1.1.18-19.

says, "Bondage (*bandha*) follows from ignorance (*ajñāna*) if there be infatuation (*moha*), but not from ignorance where infatuation has disappeared. Therefore, liberation (*mokṣa*) may take place even from a little knowledge but not where infatuation exists."[35] Hence, it is said that "when *moha* (infatuation) disappears, liberation can take place even if *ajñāna* in some matters exists. If there be infatuation, there must be bondage."[36] Each stage of progression of the Self obtains an excellent efficacy of purity and consciousness free from infatuations. It indicates that the knowledge which is devoid of *moha* only attain liberation.

Here, Vādidevasūri has given commendable remark on the gradual progression of cognition that ensued from gradual destruction of impurities: "Their order (progression of cognition) is such, because they are perceived (to come up) in such an order and because their origination is due to gradual destruction and abatement of one's own karma."[37] Founded on the psychology of *yogi-pratyakṣa*, this argument functions in two ways; there is 'a gradation of purification of cognitions' and correspondingly, there is 'a gradation of the abatement of impurities.' Both formations finally scotch in one conclusion that the purity of the Self is the perfect cognition, which is the ramification of the suppression and annihilation of karmic impurities. Therefore, Siddhasena Divākara rightly observes: "That which is characterized as free from all obscurations and shines as the absolute alone is called transcendental perception (*yogi-pratyakṣa*); it uninterruptedly illumines the nature

35 AM: 10. 98.

ajñānānmohato bandho nājñānād vītamohataḥ
jñānastokācchcha mokṣaḥ syādmohān mohitonyathā.

36 The Commentary to Āpta-Mīmāṁsā, p. 159.

37 PNT: 2.14

kramopy amīṣām ayam eva tathaiva saṁvedanāt
evat-kramāvirbhūta-nija-karma kṣayopaśama janyatvāc ca.

of all objects."[38] To recapitulate, the argument from purity conflates with two explicit arguments: the purity of the Self is achievable because there is a method of purification and the purity of the Self is equal to the pure cognition because there is the extinction of karmic impurities. Extricated from all impurities, the pure Self perceives everything without any limitations.

6.2 Lack of Contradicting Proofs

Critics challenge the notion of *yogi-pratyakṣa* by highlighting the lack of evidence from established sources of knowledge—namely perception, inference, and verbal testimony. They argue that there are no clear cognitive criteria to substantiate the existence of *yogi-pratyakṣa*. In response, scholars such as Ācārya Samantabhadra, Hemacandrasūri, and Vādidevasūri robustly defend the validity of *yogi-pratyakṣa*. They do so by emphasizing the absence of counter-evidence to refute its existence. For these scholars, the conventional means of knowledge—perception, inference, and verbal testimony—are deemed inadequate for disproving *yogi-pratyakṣa*. The absence of contradictory evidence, they argue, actually reinforces the Jaina position. These scholars contend that the phenomena described by *yogi-pratyakṣa* consistently align with both scriptural teachings and logical reasoning. This section will outline and analyze their arguments in detail.

6.2.1 Absence of Proof from the Perception

Vādidevasūri asserts that perception cannot contradict (*bādhaka*) the possibility of *yogi-pratyakṣa*.[39] According to Jaina, there are two types of perception: transcendental

38 NV: 27.

sakalāvaraṇamuktātma kevalaṁ yat prakāśate
pratyakṣaṁ sakalārthātma satataprathibhāsanam.

39 Cf. The Commentary to PNT: 2. 23. pp. 135-137.

perception and transactional perception. The transcendental perception (partial or complete), by its constitution itself, cannot be held to be opposed to the possibility of omniscience. The transactional perception has bifurcated into external and internal perception. Internal perception, such as *Prātibha*, ratifies the possibility of omniscience. The external perception has two alternatives; own perception and others perception. A detractor may say that all individual cannot perceive the supersensible objects by own perception, and therefore, those perceptions are invalid. Jaina also never proposes that *yogi-pratyakṣa* is present in all persons and at all places and time. On account of the opacity of karma, there are variations in perception. But the non-perception of such a person, at a particular moment, is not conclusive proof or ultimate reference for the perception of all time and space. On the other hand, if the own perception is the perception of all time and space, and then the possibility of *yogi-pratyakṣa* is validated by that perception. As Hemacandrasūri says, "It could not be effective without direct intuition of the whole race of mankind spread over all the divisions of space and time, and the admission of such possibility would only establish the position we seek to prove."[40] The non-present modes of the substance are beyond the capacity of sense perception.[41] Rejection of *yogi-pratyakṣa* can be based on others perception and testimony. If it is so, then the question will come; why can't one accept the possibility of *yogi-pratyakṣa* based on others perception and testimony? Above them, *yogi-pratyakṣa* and its perfection, i.e. *kevalajñāna* cannot be gauged with the diktats of sense perception because *kevalajñāna* is a clear and distinct perception without the assistance of senses. It is well evident that cognition as *pramāṇa* is not knowable by sensuous perception, and therefore, it is inefficient to determine the various degrees of *yogi-pratyakṣa*.

40 PM: 1.1.17. no. 60.

41 Cf. PS: 1.40.

On another way, in terms of *Mimāṁsa* school of thought, the non-existence of something cannot be known by direct perception because the non-perception becomes a *pramāṇa* only when it cognises the non-existence of particular object bereft of all perceptible contents. Non-perception also cannot challenge the possibility of *yogi-pratyakṣa*. Jaina retorts by saying that the absence of perception of the object in sleep does not repeal the non-existence of that particular object in reality. Therefore, the absence of perception is not a condition for the non-existence of the object.

6.2.2 Absence of Proof from the Inference

The inference also cannot contradict the possibility of *yogi-pratyakṣa*. For such an inference, there would require a subject (*yogi-pratyakṣa*) and knowledge of the subject. The knowledge of the subject presupposes the organ of knowledge to cognise the subject. Instead of annulling the possibility of *yogi-pratyakṣa*, it validates such perception. Quashing of the organ of knowledge, and subsequently, the existence of subject is the negation of the abode of *hetu*, which embroils to the fallacy of the unproved minor term. Presuming the subject as the individual person (possessor of *yogi-pratyakṣa*), then *Sadhya* can either be non-existence of such a person or be the non-existence of such a person sans extrasensory perceptual cognition. The first view (non-existence) is a precarious and nasty position because the historic existence of such persons who inherits and performs extrasensory perception is well evident truth. Considering omniscience as the subject, Hemacandra puts the second view in the following syllogism.[42]

---

42 Cf. PM: 1.1.17. no 61.

Hemacandra frames out two syllogisms based on two different *hetu*. They are; speakership and manhood. The speakership-based syllogism is enumerated and examined in the text. The humanness also explained in the same manner:

Thesis (*pratiñjā*): The person under dispute is not omniscient.

Logical reason (*hetu*): Because he speaks.

Example (*udāharaṇa*): Whoever speaks is not omniscient like the man in the street.

The speakership is the reason for the conclusion of non-omniscience in a perfect yogi. The property of speaking has presented in three equivocal senses. Jaina interrogates that in what sense the speakership becomes the reason. In the first sense, the property of speaking appears in the sense of *pramāṇa* or valid knowledge. According to Jaina, the omniscient or the perfect yogi speaks what is known by 'reason and scripture' and 'devoid of faults', and therefore, the words of an omniscient are always in accordance with *pramāṇa* or non-contradictory to *pramāṇa*.[43] Thus, the speakership, in the first sense, would rather prove that the speaker is omniscient. Then, the conclusion would not satisfy the intent of inference. The second sense presents the property of speaking as the reprimand of *pramāṇa*. Hemacandra states that the argument "would be a case of proving an admitted truth." He continues to say, "It is admitted that a person who speaks what is contrary

---

Thesis (*pratiñjā*): The person under dispute is not omniscient

Logical reason (*hetu*): Because he is a human being

Example (*udāharaṇa*): Whoever speaks is not omniscient like the man in the street.

The manhood also has three equivocal senses. If it is used as the uncorrupted state of manhood, then it would prove the opposite of the intended conclusion. If it means being a person corrupted by defects, it would be a case of admitted truth that such a polluted person can never be escalated to the status of omniscience. If it means merely being a person, the hetu is a matter of doubt because it may prove either omniscience or its absence. Therefore, it does not infer that the person is not omniscient or bereft of extrasensory perception.

43 Cf. AM: 1.6; PNT: 2.25.

to the verdict of all organ of knowledge is not omniscient."[44] The third sense exposes the property of merely being a speaker. This application provides a doubtful *hetu* because "it is also found to be not opposed to the effect of omniscience.[45] Hence, *hetu* becomes *anaikāntika*. Succinctly, in all these senses, the property of speaking does not prove non-omniscience. For all these reasons, inference lacks contradictory proofs to revoke the possibility of extrasensory perception (*yogi-pratyakṣa*).

6.2.3 Absence of Proof from the Verbal Testimony

The scriptural authority also does not rebuke the possibility of *yogi-pratyakṣa*. The staunch opponent (*Mīmāṃsa* system) of *yogi-pratyakṣa* adheres to the superiority of the scripture (*Veda*) in the judgement of knowledge. For them, the scripture (*Veda*) is eternal (*anādi*), uncreated (*apoureṣeya*) and primordial cause of everything (ādikāraṇa). Admitting *yogi-pratyakṣa* and its apex *kevalajñāna* is a menace of the superiority of the scripture, and therefore, they eschew the existence and validity of all-knowing knowledge. But the absence of direct citations and references in the scriptures, which quashes the existence of *yogi-pratyakṣa* explicitly, saps the criticism. Furthermore, the Vedic knowledge constructively proves the existence of *yogi-pratyakṣa*. The teachings of Veda contain the knowledge of everything, including subtle objects, irrespective of time and space. The Vedic injunctions yield their fruit (*phala*) only when a qualified subject cognise them. Hemacandra reckons the argument like this: "In the very act of such assertion (cognition of inconceivable objects), it presupposes a duly qualified subject who is certainly capable of cognising the truth, which holds good for three division of time."[46] Hence, the Vedic injunctions presuppose a competent

44 PM: 1.1.17. no 61.

45 Cf. PNT: p. 142.

46 PM: 1.1. 16. no. 56.

addressee who is capable of cognising and realising them. The competent addressee is a corollary to the acceptance of supernatural perception. To conclude, the adherence to Vedic injunction and its knowledge necessarily admits that the extrasensory perception is possible for some competent person. On the other hand, some believe in the creatorship behind the scripture of their systems. For them, the acceptance of the omniscience is the necessary prerequisite for the logical and spiritual validity of their infallible creatorship. If the author of scripture is omniscient, then the denial of the existence of omniscience becomes self-contradictory. If the author is non-omniscient, then the validity of statements in scripture is in question. Hence, in any way, the scriptural authority cannot bring contradictory proofs against the existence of *yogi-pratyakṣa*.

6.3 Conclusion

The compilation of arguments aimed at proving the existence of *yogi-pratyakṣa* is initially discussed within Jaina philosophical texts in the context of omniscience. While acknowledging the influence of broader Indian philosophical systems, these arguments are distinctly Jaina in their approach and framework, firmly rooted in Jaina dogma. A critical examination reveals that these arguments, though rigorous, exhibit a dogmatic style and presentation characteristic of Jaina philosophy. The lack of empirical cognitive criteria to disprove *yogi-pratyakṣa* serves as a counter-argument to criticisms challenging its validity. These proofs substantiate the notion of perception occurring independently of the senses and mind, highlighting various degrees of *yogi-pratyakṣa* and the pure perception of the Self. This validation underscores the cognitive validity and soteriological significance of these perceptions, aligning them with the Jaina view that the cognitive actuality is tantamount to liberation. While these arguments convincingly demonstrate that the concept and existence of *yogi-pratyakṣa* are part of a progressive journey toward perfection, they are not without their flaws. Both their strengths and weaknesses are closely tied to Jaina ontological and epistemological assumptions. Thus, while the arguments are effective within their own philosophical context, they may not universally address all critiques or objections.

General Conclusion

An enquiry into the hermeneutical understanding of *yogi-pratyakṣa* (extrasensory perception) in the Jain philosophy was an investigation into the interpretive understanding of the nature and function of *yogi-pratyakṣa* in the contemporary context. Precisely, the research aims at understanding salient features of *yogi-pratyakṣa* in the Jain philosophy and interpreting them in the context in terms of certain hermeneutical principles. By employing hermeneutical analysis, this study reveals the epistemological and soteriological dimensions of *yogi-pratyakṣa*, shedding light on its foundational implications for knowledge and liberation in Jain philosophy. The general conclusion of the research synthesizes and summarizes these findings, offering a comprehensive overview of the study's insights.

Jaina *Āgamic* literature initally more focused on the practical aspect of life, and therefore, showed less interest in philosophical discourse. However, with the emergence of independent works, notably those by Ācārya Umāsvāmi and Ācārya Kundakunda, the Jaina tradition began to hold a significant place within the broader Indian philosophical landscape. Later, Ācārya Samantabhadra and Siddhasena Divākara have enrobed Jaina doctrines with logical deliberations. Resonated to the medieval development of Indian epistemology, Jaina logicians, such as Hemachandrasūri and Vādidevasūri, have contributed much to the development of Jaina epistemology. Interpretations of these Jaina texts (independent works and Tārkic literature) definitely yield a right understanding of the Jaina concept of *yogi-pratyakṣa*. These interpretive frameworks not only enhance our understanding of *yogi-pratyakṣa* but also address contemporary questions within its context. Thus, hermeneutic analysis serves as a crucial tool for interpreting Jaina texts in light of their broader philosophical and practical implications. This research focuses on elucidating the key features of *yogi-pratyakṣa* within Jain philosphy and explores its epistemological and soteriological foundations and implications. The findings of the research are summarized as follows.

The Nature of Yogi-Pratyakṣa

Yogi-pratyakṣa is, according to Jaina, the direct perception of the self-luminous, self-conscious and self-evolving Self without the assistance of sense organs and mind. In other words, it is the cognition of the Self, independent of any other means of knowledge. Calibrating the nature of *yogi-pratyakṣa*, Jaina impeccably states that sense organs or contact of sense organs and mind cannot be the defining instrument of *yogi-pratyakṣa*. Application of medicine, ointments and intoxicates may stimulate sense organs to acquire certain extraordinary powers, but they are not *yogi-pratyakṣa*. Similarly, although meditative techniques can influence the operation of the senses to apprehend suprasensible objects, and mental reconstructions or memories might stimulate certain mental faculties, these are still constrained by the inherent limitations of sense organs and the unconscious nature of the mind. All these are also deprived of the scope of *yogi-pratyakṣa* because the sense organs, including mind, are the inherently limited and unconscious instrument, according to Jaina doctrine. Jaina would say that even if one possesses certain extraordinary powers or perception through the mental mediation, they plummet in the lower degrees of cognition. Again, Jainas would agree that the spiritual and ethical practices can facilitate the attainment of *yogi-pratyakṣa*, but they are neither the defining attribute nor the immediate cause of the *yogi-pratyakṣa*. Hence, Jaina would reckon the destruction cum annihilation of *karma* and self-luminosity of the Self as the defining attributes for *yogi-pratyakṣa*.

A limpid penetration into the Jaina metaphysics envisages the doctrinal backup of *yogi-pratyakṣa*. The self-luminous, self-conscious and self-evolving Self, the multi-faceted objects, and the obscuring influence of *karma* are the inevitable metaphysical postulates to understand the Jaina concept of *yogi-pratyakṣa*. The Self, an eternal and conscious substance, is characterized by pure cognition (*upayoga*). Karma, while capable of obscuring the Self's pure nature, does not completely obscure it. As karmic influences are progressively suppressed and eradicated, the Self becomes increasingly illuminated, allowing for a clearer perception of objects and an enhancement of cognitive processes. Ultimately, this leads to a state where the Self is fully illuminated and free from karmic veils. In this perfected state, the Self becomes both the subject and instrument of cognition, achieving a direct, clear, and distinct perception without the aid of external agents. This state is known as *yogi-pratyakṣa*. Thus, the essence of *yogi-pratyakṣa* lies in the complete extinction of karmic obscurities and the full manifestation of the Self's inherent nature. The outcome of *yogi-pratyakṣa* is a precise and accurate understanding of the nature of objects.

The gradual suppression of karmic veils simultaneously reveals the self-illuminating nature of the Self. The different gradations of *yogi-pratyakṣa* represent the progressive unfolding of pure cognition (*cetanasya svarūpāvibharvā*), which is the inherent quality of the Self. Each stage of *yogi-pratyakṣa* thus possesses its own cognitive validity. Ultimately, the perfection of *yogi-pratyakṣa* encompasses and transcends these lower degrees, illustrating a comprehensive framework that recognizes both the various stages of *yogi-pratyakṣa* and its most perfected state. In this framework, the lower degrees of *yogi-pratyakṣa* are categorized into two types: *Avadhi* (clairvoyance) and *Manaḥparyaya* (telepathy). The highest state of *yogi-pratyakṣa* is singular: *Kevalajñāna* (omniscience). In Jainism, the concept of *yogi-pratyakṣa* encompasses *Avadhi*, *Manaḥparyaya*, and *Kevalajñāna*, representing a continuum from lower degrees of extrasensory perception to the ultimate state of perfect knowledge.

Avadhi perceives definite, formed material objects that are not accessible through ordinary sense-object contact. In modern psychology, this ability aligns with clairvoyant cognition. *Avadhi* can be innate (*bhāvapratyaya*) for some individuals or acquired through practice and spiritual development (*guṇapratyaya*). With a high degree of spiritual and moral excellence, one exerts to covet the second type of *avadhijñāna*. *Manaḥparyāyajñāna* is the direct cognition of the modes of mind. Modern psychology renders different names for it, such as telepathy, mind-reading, thought reading and mentalism etc. *Manaḥparyāyajñāna* is not a sequential stage following *avadhijñāna* but rather a distinct form of cognition. The purity (*viśuddhi*) and infallibility (*apratipātābhyāṃ*) demarcate between the transitory state (*ṛjumati*) and the eternal state (*vipulamati*) of *manaḥparyāya*. Therefore, *vipulamati* state remains until one attains omniscience. Only the self-disciplined human beings have the competency to inherit telepathic knowledge (*manaḥparyāyajñāna*). 'The difference between *avadhi* and *manaḥparyāya* consists in the difference of purity (*viśuddhi*), scope (*kṣetra*), subject (*svāmin*) and object (*viṣaya*).'[1]

The pinnacle of *yogi-pratyakṣa* is the state of omniscience (*kevalajñāna*). This state is characterized by a clear and distinct

1 Cf. TS: 1. 26; PM: 1.1.19.

perception of the nature of objects, the complete absence of karmic obscurities, and the full illumination of the Self's intrinsic nature. *Kevalajñāna* differs from *Īśvarajñāna* in that it represents the cognition of the Self achieved through the complete eradication of karma and the illumination of the Self. Kevala*jñāna* signifies "perfect knowledge that exists alone." From the perspective of the knower (*jñānayaka*), it reflects the sole existence and manifestation of the knower's nature. From the perspective of knowledge (*jñāna*), it represents the sole valid *pramāṇa* after eliminating the limiting adjuncts (*kārmic-āvaraṇa*) of all other *pramāṇas*. From the perspective of the knowable (*jñeya*), it provides the perfect determination of the nature of objects by comprehensively apprehending their myriad modes and qualities (*sarvadravyaparyāyeṣu*). Thus, *kevalajñāna* is defined as "the direct and simultaneous cognition of all substances and their modes by the self-illuminative, self-conscious, and self-evolving Self."

For Jainism, *yogi-pratyakṣa* is a cognitive activity. *Yogi-pratyakṣa* suspends any sort of operative, immediate and instrumental functions of senses and mind in its cognitive process. It is clear and distinct the perception of the Self. At the same time, Jaina acclimatizes the progressive manifestation of the Self on account of the suppression and annihilation of karmic veils. This process ensures the cognitive validity accross various stages of *yogi-pratyakṣa*. In the consummation of the progression of *yogi-pratyakṣa*, the self-evolving Self finds its perfect state of existence, which is a pure and perfect perception of the Self and objects. The culmination of this progression is the state of pure consciousness, which in Jainism is synonymous with liberation. Thus, the perfection of *yogi-pratyakṣa* represents the ultimate realization of pure consciousness and ultimate liberation.

The Epistemological and Psychological Implications

A close affinity between psychology and epistemology in the Jain philosophy systematize Jaina cognitive psychology. For Jaina cognitive psychology, the identity and difference between the subject (*pramata*) and instrument of cognition (*pramāṇa*) is the nucleus of *yogi-pratyakṣa*. The self-luminous and self-conscious Self is the subject of cognition, and the modification of the self-evolving Self is the instrument of cognition. Thus, cognition is the right determination of objects by the self-luminous and self-conscious Self through its inherent faculty of consciousness (*upayoga*). The consciousness drive (*upayoga*) of the Self is the operational source in the cognitive process. Therefore, Jaina logicians would say that the cognition is *pramāṇa* because the cognition is the efficient cause (*karaṇa*) and specific condition for the right determination of an object.

A *pramāṇa* is 'that capable of illuminating itself (*sva*) and manifesting other objects (*parā*) without any obstruction (*bādha*).'[2] It avails the possibility and the logical and cognitive validity of *pramāṇa* beyond the scope of sensual cognition. For Jaina, the sense organs (*indriya*) and mind (*manas*), the proximity of sense organ (*sannikarṣa*), and the assemblage of different elements (*sāmagrī*) are unconscious material (karmic) products. Whatever is inherently unconscious cannot manifest or determine the conscious object (*jīva*). In the case of unconscious objects (*ajīva*), the innumerable aspect of an object certainly falls beyond the cognition of the physical sense organ and mind, and thus, they cannot definitely determine the nature of the object too. Since they are deprived of self-illumination (*sva-vyavasāyī*) and object manifestation (*para-vyavasāyī*), they can never invariably produce valid knowledge. Succinctly, any means of physical grasping is incapable of the

2 Cf. NV: 1; PNT: 1.2; NV: 7.

cognition of the conscious subject and innumerable aspect of objects. Hence, they are not *pramāṇa*. In this regard, Jaina would claim that cognition is *pramāṇa*. Pramāṇa-hood (*hetu*) of cognition is proved, compatible, and clear. It contains no matter (*vipakṣa*) that invalidates the existence of valid knowledge. It absolutely removes the ignorance (*ajñānivaṛthi*) and perfectly determines the nature of an object (*artha prakāśa*), which engenders to accept agreeable objects, to reject the disagreeable objects and to make indifference towards negligible objects, and which precludes from doubt, error and inattention. Thus, cognition manifests the object. Since cognition is inherently self-illuminative, it does not require any other agent or cognition to manifest itself. It leads to a critical and decisive epistemological conclusion that the subject of cognition (*pramātr*), the means of cognition (*pramāṇa*), and the resultant of cognition (*pramiti*) are the object of cognition (*prameya*) because cognition manifests itself and objects.

The self-evolving Self modifies into the different forms of cognition (*jñāna-pramāṇa*). It is due to the various degrees of the karmic conditions (āvaraṇa) over the Self. Depended on conditions of cognition (*pramāṇāvaraṇa*), the Self conceives objects directly (*pratyakṣa*) and indirectly (*parokṣa*). Hence, Jaina tradition accepts two *pramāṇa*; immediate (*pratyakṣa*) and mediate (*parokṣa*). *Pratyakṣa* is the independent knowledge; whereas, *parokṣa* is dependent knowledge. *Avadhi* (clairvoyance), *Manahaparyāya* (telepathy) and *Kevalajñāna* (omniscience) come under *pratyakṣa*, which are perceived by the Self directly without the assistance of sense organs and mind. These are extraordinary or extrasensory means of knowledge. *Mati* and *Śruta* are *parokṣa* of which the Self is dependent on the sense organ and mind for the manifestation of objects. In this regard, according to Jainism, *pratyakṣa* knowledge is extrasensory knowledge (*yogi-pratyakṣa*).

The essence of perfect *yogi-pratyakṣa* lies in its immediacy, a defining characteristic of *pratyakṣa*.[3] Among Jaina scholars, immediacy is interpreted in two primary ways: as the direct perception of the Self (according to *āgama* interpretation) and as cognition that is independent of any other means of knowledge (according to *tarka* interpretation). Both interpretations emphasize the possibility of perception without reliance on the senses. Both interpretations leave space for perception without the mediation of sense organs. Jaina scholars unanimously agree on the 'immediacy and lucidity (*viśadaḥ/spaṣṭatvam*)' as the defining attribute of perceptual cognition.[4] 'It indicates independence from the service of another organ and the clear and distinct apprehension of its content.' Perceptual knowledge is self-revealing and object-revealing, which is determinate or conceptual and is essentially clear, direct and distinct. The clarity always implies the extinction of obstruction, i.e., the karmic matter. The directness denotes the agent-hood or subject-hood of the Self, and the distinctness indicates the right determination of the nature of the object. A clear, direct and distinct cognition becomes the epistemological postulate of *yogi-pratyakṣa*.

Significantly, it portrays the psychology of *yogi-pratyakṣa*, which amounts to the cognitive process of *yogi-pratyakṣa*. It contributes much to parapsychology researches. Jaina cognitive psychology constructs on the two psychic processes; the progressive illumination of the Self and the gradual suppression of karma. They are not successive stages, but they appear simultaneously and benefit mutually in the progression. In the cognitive process, the Self is illuminated as the subject of cognition. The illumination of the Self in the psychology of *yogi-pratyakṣa* highlights the definite and

3 Cf. TS: 1.12.

4 Cf. PM: 1.1.13. NKC: 1. 3; PKM: 2. 3; PNT: 2. 2-3.

decisive role of the Self for the genesis of *yogi-pratyakṣa*. It is the gradual manifestation of the conscious nature of the Self (*cetanasya svarūpāvibāvo*). In other words, it is not seizing, releasing, and not evolving into anything else, but it is a self-evolution, owing to its own characteristic nature of pure consciousness. Since there is an identical relation between the subject and instrument of cognition, the opacity of the Self has a corresponding influence on the instrument. It implies the removal of karmic obscurities over the Self concurrently extinct the limiting adjunct (*karma*) over the instrument. Thus, the psychic states (*bhava*) of the Self due to the partial or complete suppression and annihilation of karmic veils (*ksāyopaśamika*) have an epistemological relevance in the Jain philosophy. It means that the origination of each verity of knowledge, whether empirical or supernatural, is due to the gradual extrication from the influence of *karma*. The progressive removal of karmic veils necessitates consecutive gradation in cognition. It substantiates various instances of cognition in the progression. It admits lower degrees of *yogi-pratyakṣa* as the consecutive stages of the progression of cognition that moves towards perfect and pure cognition. At the total manifestation or full illumination of the Self, the progression of the cognition reaches its zenith. It is the state of perfect perception (*kevalajñāna*) where the Self alone (*kevala*) remains as the operative agent and function. Therefore, Jaina epistemology confers cognitive and logical validity for the lower degrees of *yogi-pratyakṣa* and establishes the perfection of *yogi-pratyakṣa* as a logical concomitant.

Yogi-pratyakṣa is direct and distinct perception. A cognitive activity has two indissoluble aspects; indeterminate (*darśana*) and determinate (*jñāna*). No cognition occurs without both aspects. Their occurrence and function determine the psychology of cognition. Jaina logicians interpret *darśana* as the intuition of the Self and *jñāna* as the manifestation of cognition of the object. At the state of perfect *yogi-pratyakṣa*, both aspects occur simultaneously due to the annihilation of karmic imprints. *Sāṁvyvahārika pratyakṣa* (sensory perception) depicts these aspects into four stages; *avagraha*, īhā, *avāya*, and *dhāraṇā*. Except for the state of perfection (*kevalajñāna*), all other means of knowledge are sustained by the successive occurrence of both aspects. In the absence of gradation in cognition, the *kevalajñāni* perceives objects directly and simultaneously, in respect of their substance (*dravya*), place (*kṣetra*), time (*kāla*), and being (*bhāva*). Consequently, it substantiates the pure perception, which once illuminates every object.[5]Thus, the manifestation of the self-conscious Self arguably holds the direct and simultaneous cognition of objects.

As the self-illuminative lamp manifests the adjacent objects, so the self-illuminative Self uninterruptedly illumines the nature of all objects. 'The subject matter of direct perception is all the substances with all their modifications.'[6] The nature of the object of knowledge is constituted of the substance (*dravya*), qualities (*guṇa*), and modes (*paryāya*). Owing to the permanency cum transitory nature (*sat*), there are modifications, which extend over three times and infinite space. It is irrevocable truth that sensory cognition is deprived of these innumerable aspects (*anekānta*) of an object. Thus, the limited apprehension of sensory cognition cannot have an absolute determination of the nature of the object. It is merely a probability, which expects other modes of predications (*syādvāda*). Hence, according to Jaina, there are seven forms of the judgement of the object of knowledge (*sapta-bhaṅga-naya*). The limited cognition is gradually uplifted by the acceptance of the limitation of the judgement (*naya*). The

5 Cf. AM: 101. *tatvajñānaṁ pramānaṁ te yugapat sarvabhāsanam.*

6 Cf. TS: 1.29.

comprehension of the multi-facets object presupposes the higher degrees of cognition, which surpassed the limitations of the sense organs and the mind. As a logical concomitant, there should be someone to comprehend these objects, and there should be some means to apprehend these objects. Hence, there is the existence of the extrasensory perception as a means to cognize the multi-facets object. Incrementally, the presence of positive proofs and the absence of counter proofs for the existence of *yogi-pratyakṣa* through valid means of knowledge impair criticism. In this regard, *yogi-pratyakṣa* is always compatible with logical reasoning.

The Soteriological Implications

Jaina cognitive psychology endorses the conspicuous correlation between *yogi-pratyakṣa* and the state of liberation. Pure consciousness is the inherent nature of the Self. It is natural to the Self. It reckons that a Soul is potentially conscious, and there is the possibility of perfect and pure cognition in every embodied soul. The cognitive process is the gradual unveiling of pure consciousness. In this regard, pure cognition is identical to the realisation of the pure nature of the Self. The auspicious modification (*śubhapariṇāma*) of the Self exists in the manifestation of the pure consciousness (*śuddhaupayoga*), which conceives in the pure and perfect cognition. Therefore, in Jainism, the cognitive actuality is tantamount to the liberation (*mokṣa*). Owing to the gradual destruction and removal of karma, gradual purification of cognitions progressively has to consummate in the purity of soul, i.e., the perfect perception. It is the state free from ignorance and delusion. The self-illumination of the Self after the annihilation of karma implies the progression of cognition. There is a progression of cognition, and therefore, there is a culmination of cognition. Wherever there is progression, there is the culmination, as the progression of magnitude. In case of *yogi-pratyakṣa*, *Avadhi* and *Manaḥparyāya* are the stages of progression, which culminates in the *kevalajñāna*. It uninterruptedly illuminates the nature of all objects. The lower degrees of *yogi-pratyakṣa* behave as an intermediary state in the path to liberation, and the higher degree of *yogi-pratyakṣa* remains as its logical concomitants. Therefore, liberation is a corollary to *yogi-pratyakṣa*.

The availability and applicability of the method for complete purification validate the possibility of the existence of the pure Self. The fourteen stages (*guṇasthānas*) for the spiritual development of the Self design the trajectory of the Self towards liberation. Jain method of liberation is definitely oriented towards the complete illumination of the Self. *Guṇasthānas* also divulges a clear depiction of the progressive stages of *yogi-pratyakṣa*. With the wake of the fourth stage (*samyak-dṛṣṭi*) onwards, the Self embarks with glimpses of the extrasensory perception. The ephemeral existence of this extrasensory perception is attainable even for the one who is bereft of the practice of spiritual and moral conduct. Up to the tenth stage, the supernatural powers are attuned and conversed by spiritual and moral practices. The tenth stage (*sūkṣma-sāmparāya*) earmarks with the suppression of karmic obscurities except for the subtle (*sūkṣma*) greed. When the eleventh stage (*upaśānta-kaṣāya*) suppresses all kinds of passions, the twelfth stage (*kṣīṇa-moha*) annihilates imprints of passions, which leads to the subsequent stage of perfect intuition and perfect knowledge. The thirteenth is the stage of 'the omniscient soul with physical activity (*sayoga-kevalī*)', detached from all infatuations and passions. Here, the soul no longer searches for reputation and recognition. Thus, physical activity has no more succumbed to any karmic influences. The elimination of both destructive and non-destructive karma suspends physical activities (*ayoga-kevalī*). It is the fourteenth and last stage of liberation. In Jainism, the *Arhat* (or *Arihant*) and the Siddha embody the two distinct forms of the perfect state of *yogi-pratyakṣa*. The *Arhat* represents *sayoga-kevalī*, the state of omniscience achieved with the aid of psychic and spiritual activities, while the *Siddha* represents *ayoga-kevalī*, the state of perfect enlightenment attained after the complete cessation of all karmic influences and spiritual activities.

Jaina scholars earmark the words and lives of the real practitioners of *yogi-pratyakṣa* are unopposed to logic and scriptures.[7] They should be in agreement with the *yukti* (reasoning) and *śāstra* (scripture). A perfect *yogi*, in the temporal world (*sayoga-kevalī*), is stainless, spotless, free from infatuations, benevolent to the people, and not being veered by gain, fame, and worship etc. It is the state of perfect bliss and self-contentment. The Self itself is of the nature of unmatched happiness, and then sensual pleasures have no role to play. Extricated from the bewildering external causes, a possessor of *yogi-pratyakṣa* shins forth with the innate nature of knowledge, faith, energy, and bliss and worthy of adoration. A perfect *yogi* performs actions as a self-illuminated Self without karmic influences and ignorance. It always amounts to the perfect state of existence, i.e., the liberation.

In Jainism, immediate extrasensory perceptions and experiences are considered fundamental to *yogi-pratyakṣa*. The progression of *yogi-pratyakṣa* involves several stages:

1. **Rudimentary Stage**: The rudimentary experience of sudden and instant extrasensory perception, without the support of spiritual and moral practices.
2. **Preliminary Stage**: The preliminary stage of *yogi-pratyakṣa*, achieved with the suppression of karmic influences and the incorporation of spiritual and moral practices.

7 Cf. AM: 1.6.

3. **Intermediate Stage**: The phase following the suppression and eradication of infatuations and passions, where *yogi-pratyakṣa* becomes more refined.
4. **Advanced Stage**: The perfect state of *yogi-pratyakṣa*, characterized by cognitive actuality and the highest form of perception.

Supernormal experiences and extrasensory perceptions that are accompanied by infatuations and passions represent imperfect states of *yogi-pratyakṣa*. Contentment with these lower degrees can lead to complacency, hindering progress to the higher levels of *yogi-pratyakṣa*. The soteriological goal of spiritual advancement requires the complete renunciation of infatuations and passions. Consequently, the lower degrees of *yogi-pratyakṣa* serve as rudimentary, preliminary, and intermediary stages on the path to liberation, while the higher degrees represent the ultimate attainment.

To sum up, Jaina epistemology squarely defines, enumerates, and examines the concept of *yogi-pratyakṣa*. For Jaina logicians, *yogi-pratyakṣa* has cognitive and soteriological implications. It has paved the way for the contextual interpretation of Jain texts and addresses various contextual questions with potential answers. Thus, an enquiry into the hermeneutical understanding of *yogi-pratyakṣa* in Jain philosophy was an investigation into the understanding and interpretation of the nature and function of *yogi-pratyakṣa* in the contemporary context. The research challenges detrimental trends in the scientific realm that regard extrasensory perception as abnormal or anomalous, asserting the epistemological and logical foundations of *yogi-pratyakṣa*. It also critiques the politicization of spiritual matters, where extrasensory perception is often viewed through the lens of material and temporal power, and instead emphasizes the soteriological significance of *yogi-pratyakṣa*. By systematically unveiling the epistemological and soteriological foundations of *yogi-pratyakṣa*, the study critiques the misleading approaches of pseudo-scientists in Western parapsychology and pseudo-spiritual gurus in New Age movements. It addresses the distortions of extrasensory phenomena and contributes valuable insights to the development of Indian cognitive psychology and the establishment of authentic spirituality.

Bibliography

Source Texts

Ācārya Kundukunda. *Pravacanasāra*. Translated by Vijay K. Jain. Dehradun: Vikalp Printers, 2018.

Ācārya Kundakunda. *Samayasāra*. Translated and edited by A. Chakravarti. New Delhi: Bharatiya Jnanpith, 2008[5].

Ācārya Pūjyapada. *Sarvārtha Siddhi*. Translated by S. A. Jaina. Calcutta: Vira Sasana Sangha, 1960.

Ācārya Samantabhadra. Āpta-Mīmāṃsā. Translated and edited by Saratchandra Ghoshal. New Delhi: Bharatiya Jnanpith, 2010[2].

Ācārya Umāsvāti. *Tattvārtha Sūtra*. In *Tattvārtha Sūtra: That Which Is, with combined commentaries of Umāsvāti, Pūjyapāda, and Siddhasenagani*. Translated and edited by Nathmal Tatia. New York: Harper Collins Publishers, 1994.

Ācārya Umāsvāti. *Tattvārtha Sūtra*. In *Pt. Sukjlaji commentary* on *Tattvārtha Sūtra*. Translated by K. K Dixit. Ahemadabad: L. D Institute of Indology, 2000[2].

Akalaṅka. *Tattvārthavārttika* (*Rājavārtika*): *the Commentary* on *Tattvārtha Sūtra*. Kashi: Bharatiya Jnana Pitha, 1953.

Annaṁbhaṭṭa. *Tarkasaṁgraha-Dīpikā* on *Tarkasaṁgraha*. Translated and elucidated by Gopinath Bhattacharya. Kolkatta: Sri Kamal Mitra for Progressive Publishers, 2009 reprint.

Bhāsarvajña. *Nyāya-bhūṣaṇa*. In *Śrīmad-ācārya-Bhāsarvajña-praṇītasya Nyāya-sārasya svôpajñaṃ vbyākbyānaṃ Nyāya-bhūṣaṇam*. Ṣaḍ-darśana-grantha-mālā, no. 1. Edited by Yogīndrānanda. Vārāṇasi: Ṣad-darśana Prakāśana Pratiṣṭhānam, 1968.

Dharamakirti. *Nyyāybindu*. Banares: Chowkhamba Sanskrit Series, 1954.

Dharmaraja Adhvarindra. *Vedānta Paribhāsha*. Translated and annotated by Swami Madhavananda. Kolkata: Advaita Ashram, 2011.

Hemacandrasūri. *Pramāṇamīmāṁsā*. Translated with critical notes by Satkari Mookerjee in collaboration with Nathmal Tatia. Varanasi: Tara Publication, 1970.

Isvara Krisna. *Sāṁkhya Kārikā*. Translated by Swami Virupaksananda. Chennai: Sri. Ramkrishna Math, 2008.

Kaṇāda, Muni Jambuvijaya (Hrsg.). *Vaiśeṣikasūtra*. In *Vaiśeṣikasūtra of Kaṇāda with the Commentary of Candrānanda*. Translated and Introduction by Anantalal Thakur, Gaekwad's Oriental Series. Baroda: Oriental Institute, 1961.

Gaṅgeśa. *Tattvacintāmaṇi*. Translated and explained by V. P. Bhatta. Michigan: Eastern Book Linkers, 2005.

Goutama. *Nyāya Sūtra*. In *Nyāya Sūtra* of *Goutama with Bhāṣya* of *Vātsyāna*. Translated and edited by Ganga Nath Jha, Vol 1. Delhi: Motilal Banarsidass, 1984.

Jamini. *Mīmāṃsa Sūtra*. Translated and edited by M. L Sandal. Delhi: Motilal Banarsidass, 1985.

Jayanta Bhaṭṭa. *Nyāyamañjarī*. In *Nyāyamañjarī of Jayanta Bhaṭṭa with the Commentary of Granthi-bhaṅga by Cakradhara*. Edited by Gaurinath Sastri,

M. M. Śivakumāraśāstri-Granthamālā, no 5. Vārāṇasī: Sampūrṇānand Saṃskrta Viśvavidyālaya, 1984.

Patāñjali. *Yoga Sūtra*. In *Yoga Philosophy of Patāñjali with Bhasvati*. Translated and edited by Swami Haraharananda Aranya. Calcutta: University of Calcutta, 2012.

Prabhacandra. *Premeyakamalamārtaṇḍa: the Commentary on Manikyanaṇdi's Pariksāmukha*. Bombay: Nirnaya Nagar Press, 1941.

Praśastapāda. *Padārthadharmasaṅgraha*. Translated and edited by Mahāmahopādhyāya Gaṅgādhara Śāstri Tailaṅga. Banares: E. J Lazarus & com., 1916.

Sadānanda. *Vedānta-sāra*. Translated by Swami Nikhilananda. Kolkata: Advaita Ashram, 2010.

Śaṅkarācārya. *Aparokṣanubhūti*. Translated and edited by Swami Vimuktananda. Almora: Advaita Ashrama, 1938.

Śaṅkarācārya. Ātmabodha. Translated and commented by Swami Chinmayananda. Mumbai: Central Chinmaya Mission Trust, 2012[3].

Śaṅkarācārya. *Tattvabodha*. Translated and commented by Swami Chinmayananda. Mumbai: Central Chinmaya Mission Trust, 2016.

Siddhantideva, Muni Nemichandra. *Dravya Sangraha*. Translated and edited by Saval Chandra Ghoshal. Bombay: Shri Chandraprabha Digambhara Jain Mandir Trust, 1986.

Siddhasensa Divākara, *Nyāyavatāra*. Edited with introduction and notes Satya Ranjan Banarjee. Calcutta: Sanskrit Book Depot (P) Ltd, 1981.

Srīdhara. *Nyāyakandali*. Translated and edited by Mahāmahopādhyāya Gaṅgādhara Śāstri Tailaṅga. Banares: E. J Lazarus & com., 1916.

Vācaspati Miśra. *Sāṁkhya-Tattva-Kaumadi: Commentary on Sāṁkhya Kārikā*. Translated by Mahamahopadhyaya Ganganath Jha. Delhi: Chaukhamba Sanskrit Prathishthan, 2004.

Vādidevasūri. *Pramāṇa-Naya-Tattvālokalaṃkāra*. Rendered into English with a commentary by Hari Satya Bhattacharya. Bombay: Jain Sahitya Vikas Mandal, 1967.

Vādirāja. *Nyāyaviniścayavivaraṇa (the Commentary on Akalanka's Nyāyaviniścaya)*. Kashi: Bharatiya Jnana Pitha, 1949.

Visvanātha-Nyāya-Pancānana. *Bhāṣa Pariccheda*. Translated and edited by Swami Madhavananda. Uttarakhand: Advaita Ashrama, 1940, 6th impression.

Vidyanandi. *Tattvārtha* Ślokavārtika: the Commentary on *Tattvārtha Sūtra*. Bombay: Nirnaya Nagar Press, 1918.

Books

Baron, Robert A. *Psychology*. New Jersey, USA: Englewood Cliffs, 1996.

Bhatt, Govardhan P. *The Basic Ways of Knowing: An In-depth Study of Kumarila's Contribution to Indian Epistemology*. Delhi: Motilal Banarsidass, 1989.

Bhattacharya, Hari Satya. *Reals in the Jaina Metaphysics*. Bombay: The Seth Sant Das Khestsy Trust, 1966.

Bhattacharya, Hari Mohan. *Jaina Logic and Epistemology*. Calcutta: K. P Bagchi & Company, 1994.

Bothra, Pushpa. The Jaina Theory of Perception. New Delhi: Motilal Banarsidass, 1996.

Chari, S.M. Srinivasa. *Fundamentals of Viśiṣtadvaita Vedānta*. New Delhi: Motilal Banarsidass, 1998, reprint.

Chatterjee, Satish Chandra. *The Nyāya Theory of Knowledge*. New Delhi: Rupa Publications, 2015.

Crotty M. *The Foundations of Social Science Research*. St. Leonards, NSW: Allen & Unwin, 1998.

Das, J. P. *Consciousness Quest: Where East Meets West on Mind, Meditation, and Neural Correlates*. New Delhi: Sage Publications, 2014.

Datta, D.M. The Six Ways of Knowing. New Delhi: Motilal Banarsidass, 2017.

Dorairaj, Joseph. *Philosophical Hermeneutics*. Chennai: Satyanilayam, 2011.

Durveka Miśra. *Dharmottara-pradīpa*. In *Paṇḍita Durveka Miśra*'s *Dharmottara-pradīpa [Being a sub commentary on Dharmottara's Nyāya-bindu-ṭīkā, a commentary on Dharmakīrti's Nyāya-bindu]*. Edited by Dalsukhbhai Malvania. Patna: Kashi Prasad Jayaswal Research Institute, 1971.

Frauwallner, Erich. *History of Indian Philosophy*, Vol I. Delhi: Motilal Banarasidass, 2008 reprint.

Frauwallner, Erich. *History of Indian Philosophy*, Vol II. Delhi: Motilal Banarsidass, 2008 reprint.

Gadamer, Hans-Georg. *Truth and Method*. Translated by Joyel Weinsheimer and Donald G. Marshall. London, New York: Continum, 2004^2.

Hoy. *The Critical Circle: Literature, History, and Philosophical Hermeneutics*. Los Angels: U of California Press, 1978.

Jain, N. L. *Jaina Karmology: English Translation with Notes on Chapter Eight of Tattvārtha-Rāja-vāartika of Akalanka*. Varanasi: P. V Research Institute, 1991.

Jung, C G. *Psychology and Occult*. Routledge, New York: Ark Paperbacks, 1977.

Kalghatgi, T. G. *Some Problems in Jain Psychology*. Dharwar: Karnataka University, 1961.

Mehta, Mohan Lal . *Jaina Philosophy*. Varanasi: P. V Research Institute, 1971.

Mehta, Mohan Lal . *Jaina Psychology*. Varanasi: P. V Research Institute, 2002.

Miśra, Durveka. *Dharmottara-pradīpa*. In *Paṇḍita Durveka Miśra*'s *Dharmottara-pradīpa* [*Being a subcommentary on Dharmottara's Nyāya-bindu-ṭīkā, a commentary on Dharmakīrti's Nyāya-bindu*], ed., Dalsukhbhai Malvania. Patna: Research Institute, 1971.

Rao, K. Ramakrishna, *Experimental Psychology*. Springfield, Illinois: Charles C. Thomas, 1966.

Rhine, J.B. *Extra-Sensory Perception after Sixty Years*. New York: Henry Holt, 1940.

Rhine, J. B. *The Reach of Mind*. New York: William Sloane Associates, 1947.

Rhine, J. B. *New Frontiers of the Mind*. New York: Farrar Rhinehart, 1937.

Ricoeur, Paul. *Interpretation Theory: Discourse and the Surplus of the Meaning*. Texas: The Texas Christian UP, 1976.

Satprakashananda. *Methods of Knowledge*. Kolkatta: Advaita Ashrama, 2013, 7th reprint.

Schubring, Walther. *The Doctrine of the Jainas*. Translated by Wolfgang Beurlen. Delhi: Motilal Banarasidass, 1962.

Shastri, Indra Chandra. *Jain Epistemology*. Varanasi: P. V Research Institute, 1990.

Shastri, Devendra Muni. *A Source Book in Jain Philosophy*. Translated by T. G. Kalkhatgi. Udaipur: Sri Tarak Jain Granthalaya, 1980.

Sikdar, J.C. *Jaina Theory of Reality*. Varanasi: P.V Research Institute,1991.

Sikdar, J.C *Concept of Matter in Jain Philosophy*. Varanasi: P.V Research Institute, 1987.

Singh, Ram Jee. *The Jaina Concept of Omniscience*. Ahemadabad: L.D Institute of Indology, 1974.

Sinha, Jadunath, *Indian Psychology: Perception*. London: Kegan Paul, Trench, Trubner & Co. Ltd, 1934.

Svabodha, Robert E. *Aghora: At the Left Hand of God*. New Delhi: Rupa Publications, 1986.

Spangler, David. *Emergence: the Rebirth of the Sacred*. New York: Delta/Marylord Lawrence, 1984.

Tatia, Nathmal. *Studies in Jain Philosophy*. Varanasi: P. V Research Institute, 1951.

Thottakara, Augustin. *Self and Consciousness; Indian Interpretation*: Banglore: Dharmaram Publication, 1998.

Articles

Balcerowicz, Piotr. "Extrasensory Perception (*yogi-pratyaksa*) in Jainism, Proofs of Its Existence and Its Soteriological Implications." In *Yoga in Jainism*. Routledge Advances in Jaina Studies, ed., Christopher Key Chapple. Oxon–New York: Routledge, 2016. pp 48–108.

Balcerowicz, Piotr. "Extrasensory Perception (*yogi-pratyaksa*) in Jainism and Its Refutations." In *Yoga in Jainism*. Routledge Advances in Jaina Studies, ed., Christopher Key Chapple. Oxon–New York: Routledge, 2016. pp 109–124.

Bem, D. J., & Honorton, C. "Does psi exist? Replicable Evidence for an Anomalous Process of Information Transfer." *Psychological Bulletin*, 115 (1994), pp. 4-18.

Gadamer, Hans-Georg. "On the Natural Inclination toward Philosophy", *Reason in the Age of Science,* trans. F. G Lawrence. Cambridge, M.S, & London: The MIT Press, 1982.

Jash, Anupam. "Historical development of Jaina Epistemology and Logic." *Jain Journal*, 49 (2014- 2015), pp. 59-66.

Riceour, Paul. "The Task of Hermeneutics." Translated by, Pellauer, *Philosophy Today*. 17. 2 (1973).

Paul, Jibin. "The Concept of Isolation in Indian Thought System." in *Philosophy Today*, Vol, 1, No. 1. (2020).

Wachterhauser, Brice R. "History and Langauge in Understanding." In *Hermeneutics and Modern Philosophy*, ed., Brice R. Wachterhauser. Albany: SUNY, 1986.

Internet Source

Addeo, Felice. "Hermeneutic as a Research Method: How to do research using Hermeneutic approach."Available from https://www.slideshare.net/FeliceAddeo/hermeneutic-as-aresearchmethoddraft; accessed on 11 December 2018.

https://www.academia.edu/3735850/Hermeneutic_as_a_Research_Method; accessed on 11 December 2018.

Kinsella, Elizabeth Anne. "Hermeneutics and Critical Hermeneutics: Exploring Possibilities Within the Art of Interpretation." *Forum: Qualitative Social Research*, (7) 2006, pp. 1-16. Available from

https://www.qualitative-research.net/index.php/fqs/article/view/145/320; accessed on 29 November 2018.

Beichler, James E. "Physical Theories of Psi: An Investigative Study." pp. 1-41. Available from. https://www.academia.edu/8200362/Physical_Theories_of_Psi_An_Investigative_Study; accessed on 30 December 2018.

Higgs, Joy and Margo Paterson. "Using Hermeneutics as a Qualitative Research Approach in Professional Practice", *The Qualitative Report*, 10 (2005), pp. 339-357. Available from https://www.researchgate.net/publication/228640854_Using_Hermeneutics_as_a_Qualitative_Research_Approach_in_Professional_Practice; accessed on 25 November 2018.

Finnegan, Jack. "The New Age Movement: A New Religion." *The Furrow* 43, no. 6 (1992), pp. 351-59. Available from: http://www.jstor.org/stable/27662219; accessed on 03 January 2019.

JAINA: Federation of Jain Associations in North America, "The philosophy of Karma and Jain Tattvas."Available from https://www.jaina.org/page/KarmaTattvas; accessed on 11April 2019.

New Age Lecture Notes, Available from: www.ucs.mun.ca/~jporter/New Age Lecture Notes.pdf; accessed on 24 November 2018.

Parker, A. "Ganzfeld." *Psi Encyclopedia*. London: The Society for Psychical Research, (2017). Available from https://psi-encyclopedia.spr.ac.uk/articles/ganzfeld; accessed on 15 January 2019.

Rao, K R. "Indian psychology, Parapsychology and Spiritual Psychology". *International Journal of Yoga - Philosophy Psychology Parapsychology* [serial online] 1 (2013), pp. 4-14. Available from http://www.ijoyppp.org/text.asp?2013/1/1/4/123286; accessed on 25 June 2019.

Steyn, Chrissie. "The New Age Movement in South Africa." *Journal for the Study of Religion* 7, no. 2 (1994): pp. 83-106. Available from http://www.jstor.org/stable/24764191; accessed on 10 January 2019.

About the Author

Jibin Paul is a dedicated scholar with a PhD in Philosophy and Religion from Banaras Hindu University, Varanasi. His academic journey has been marked by significant contributions to the field, including the publication of articles and the presentation of research papers at various conferences. Dr. Paul has a passion for teaching and has imparted his knowledge of philosophy across several institutions. Currently, he serves as a resident teacher at Marymatha Institute of Philosophy in Thrissur.